Teaching Information Literacy Concepts:
Activities and Frameworks from the Field

Active Learning Series No. 6

Trudi E. Jacobson

Timothy H. Gatti

Contributing Editors

Library Instruction Publications

Table of Contents

Section 3—Hierarchy of Learning, Publication Flow, and Formats . 127

Section 4—OPACs, Databases, and Indexes: Content and Searching Techniques 157

Preface

"Information literate" students are increasingly recognized on university, college, and high school campuses as essential. Part of the impetus comes from employers, who want a workforce that knows how to find information to meet new situations and needs. More and more academic administrators understand that one or two course-related instruction sessions are not enough for students to learn the sophisticated information seeking skills that they need.

Not surprisingly, there has recently been a surge in the number of higher education institutions that are offering for-credit information literacy courses. Some institutions, such as SUNY College of Environmental Science and Forestry in Syracuse, N.Y., have taught such a course for two decades or more. Others may have just added a course in the past few years. Here at the University at Albany, SUNY, Albany, N.Y., we have resurrected a course that had not been taught for over a decade.

Some of these courses are primarily basic classes that teach important information concepts and searching skills. Others are more specialized and sophisticated. Regardless, putting together such a course and developing the material for the class sessions can be daunting and extremely time consuming. However, by borrowing ideas, lessons, and assignments that have already been developed and tested, it becomes much easier.

This book shares hands-on activities, lesson plans, assignments, and course frameworks that are being used by over 40 librarians throughout the United States. Many are designed for introductory information literacy classes, while others have been developed for use in more specialized classes. There are also some chapters that address course frameworks and assessment. The book is divided by broad categories:

> Course Frameworks and Assessment;
> Library and Research Skills and Strategies;
> Hierarchy of Learning, Publication Flow, and Formats;
> OPACs, Databases, and Indexes;
> Internet: Content and Evaluation; and
> Social, Ethical, and Legal Issues Related to Information Literacy.

Each chapter includes information on how the material in the chapter is presented, its objectives, its components; and how to evaluate the instruction or assignment. Most chapters include supplementary materials related to the hands-on activities used with the class. A few of the larger supplementary materials are available only on a web site— http://library.albany.edu/usered/concepts/—and are so noted in the pertinent chapters.

While these hands-on activities are designed to be used in the context of information literacy courses, many of them would work well in "single-shot" library instruction sessions. Many of the contributors have provided a section titled "Variations" in which they describe how the activity can be adjusted into a single instruction session.

The editors are grateful to the 42 contributors from all types of libraries who have provided a variety of very creative and motivating chapters. Without them, the book is simply an idea with no substance.

Please feel free to use the lessons and hands-on activities in any way you wish as well as to contact the individual authors via e-mail for further clarification and/or comments. The publisher places no restrictions as far as using the lesson plans on LANs in your institution. We hope you will enjoy using these effective and creative ideas in your classes.

Trudi E. Jacobson
Timothy H. Gatti
University at Albany, Albany, N.Y.

August 1, 2001

Meet the Contributing Authors

Sara Baron (sara.baron@umb.edu) is the Director of the Instructional Technology Center and Coordinator of Library Instruction at the University of Massachusetts Boston. Her Master's degrees are in Speech Communication and Library Science.

Susan E. Beck (susabeck@lib.nmsu.edu) received her MS in Library & Information Science from the University of Illinois at Urbana-Champaign and her MA in Linguistics from Ohio University. Her undergraduate degree is from The Evergreen State College where she focused on Italian language and literature and art history. She developed a love for teaching as Peace Corps volunteer in Morocco where she taught English as a Foreign Language to often very rowdy high school students. Her research interests include problem solving as a learning device, learning assessment, and development of teaching materials to promote critical thinking.

Colleen Bell (cbell@darkwing.uoregon.edu) is Library Instruction Coordinator at the University of Oregon. She received her MLIS from the University of Western Ontario in 1991, and is active in the Oregon Library Association and ACRL Instruction Section. Her interests in the area of instruction are in teaching information literacy concepts outside of the library research context, and in using the web for instruction. She also has an intense interest in web design and in librarianship as a profession, and is co-editor of the webzine, *NewBreed Librarian* (http://www.newbreedlibrarian.org/). She is especially interested to hear from you about how you used the ideas she presented in this book.

Deborah Bernnard (bernnard@csc.albany.edu) is the User Education Librarian for the Dewey Graduate Library. She holds a BA in Politics from Fairfield University and an MLS from the University at Albany. Her responsibilities include providing reference services as well as scheduling and teaching workshops to help students more efficiently accomplish their research. She is also an instructor for UNL 205, Information Literacy, a one-credit undergraduate course. Her most recent publication is "Teaching Full-Text Databases on the Web: New Concepts for New Technology." *Reference and User Services Quarterly* 39(1) Fall 1999. She is also co-author of the new web tutorial: *Criminal Justice: A Self-Paced Tutorial*.

Gregory Bobish (bobish@albany.edu) is a User Education/Reference Librarian at the University Libraries, University at Albany, SUNY, where he teaches an Information Literacy class intended to meet general education requirements. He has an MLS and an MA in Russian from the University at Albany and a BA in Russian/French/Spanish from the University of Delaware.

Amy Boykin (awboykin@cnu.edu) is an Assistant Reference Librarian at Christopher Newport University and an Assistant Professor in the Library Science Department. She has a BA in English from Christopher Newport and an MLIS from the University of North Carolina at Greensboro. She has been at Christopher Newport since 1995 and has taught several for-credit "Intro to the Internet" courses and many bibliographic instruction sessions for students, Lifelong Learners, and faculty. Amy's interests include information literacy and student attitudes, active and collaborative learning/teaching techniques, and web site development.

Sue Ann Brainard (brainard@geneseo.edu) is a Reference/Instruction Librarian at SUNY Geneseo. After obtaining her MLS from SUNY Albany in 1984, she spent six years working for the New York Public Library as a young adult librarian, then six years at Finger Lakes Community College. At Geneseo, Sue Ann has co-taught a one-credit Information Literacy seminar for two years. She has recently been appointed the library's Assessment Coordinator, and is busy working with the Local Arrangements Committee preparing for the CIT 2001 Conference, to be held at Geneseo.

Janet Dagenais Brown (jbrown@twsuvm.uc.twsu.edu) is Education Librarian at Wichita State University's Ablah Library. She is one of several team teachers of the library's one-credit course, Introduction to Library Research. Janet holds an MLS from Emporia State University and has been a Reference Librarian for 24 years. Janet previously served as Science Librarian at Kansas State University.

Gerald T. Burke (gtb03@csc.albany.edu) is the Humanities Bibliographer at the University at Albany. Previously he worked at Hudson Valley Community College as a technical assistant in academic computing. In addition, he teaches composition as an adjunct instructor at HVCC. He holds an MLS and an MA in English from SUNY Albany.

Catherine Collins (catherine_collins@tamu-commerce.edu or at tfortx@yahoo.com) is the Business Reference Librarian at the Gee Library at Texas A & M University - Commerce. She holds an MLS from the University at Buffalo, SUNY, an MPA from the University of North Texas, and a BA from the University of Texas at Austin.

Christopher Cox (ccox@wpi.edu) is currently Reference/Instruction Librarian at Worcester Polytechnic Institute. He earned a BA in English from Susquehanna University, and has Master's degrees in English and Library Science from the University of Connecticut and the University at Albany, respectively. Chris is also the moderator for NELIG-L, the mailing list for the New England Library Instruction Group of New England ACRL.

Bartow Culp (bculp@purdue.edu) has been the Chemistry Librarian at Purdue University since 1994. He obtained his MLS from Indiana University and a Ph.D. in Organic Chemistry from the University of Delaware. He is an active member of the Special Libraries Association and the American Chemical Society's Chemical Information Division. In the summer he battles beetles on his bean plants.

Connie Dalrymple (dalrympl@twsuvm.uc.twsu.edu) is Life and Health Sciences Librarian at Wichita State University's Ablah Library. Her duties also include sharing in the teaching of the library's one-credit course, Introduction to Library Research. Connie holds an MA in Biology as well as an MLS from the University at Buffalo and has worked in academic, special, and public libraries.

Kimberly Davies (davies@geneseo.edu) is a Reference/Instruction Librarian, who also coordinates the Government Documents collection at SUNY College at Geneseo. She received her MLS from the University at Buffalo in 1997 and a BA in French and International Affairs from the University of New Hampshire in 1995. Currently, she is preparing a conference session that will evaluate web syllabi for semester-long credit courses in information literacy. She will present this session at the Stop Surfing-Start Teaching 2001 National Conference in Myrtle Beach, South Carolina.

Celita DeArmond (cdearmond@utsa.edu) is a Reference Librarian and Bibliographer, University of Texas at San Antonio. Celita holds a Bachelor of Music degree in Music History and Literature from Baylor University and a Master of Science degree in Library and Information Science from the University of North Texas. She is currently a member of ACRL/IS and recently attended the Institute for Information Literacy Immersion 2000 program. Her instructional experience includes working with UTSA faculty to develop course-integrated instruction.

Janet DiPaolo (janet.dipaolo@umb.edu) is a reference librarian at the University of Massachusetts Boston. She received her Masters in Library Science degree from San Jose State University.

Kimberley Donnelly (kmdonnel@ycp.edu) is an assistant professor and reference librarian at York College of Pennsylvania (YCP) in York. Prior to joining YCP, she served as reference librarian at Wilkes University in Wilkes-Barre, Pennsylvania. Kimberley holds a BS degree in Communication and an MSLS from Clarion University of Pennsylvania. She teaches two sections of Information Literacy 101 each semester at YCP and is co-author of the Information Literacy eText that can be accessed at http://www.ycp.edu/library/ifl/. She often presents and publishes on the topics of information literacy and the changing roles of librarians.

Angela Dunnington (adunnington@utsa.edu) is a Reference Librarian and Bibliographer, University of Texas at San Antonio. Angela holds a Bachelor of General Studies degree from Southeastern Louisiana University and a Master of Library and Information Science from Louisiana State University. She is currently active on various American Library Association Division and Round Table committees including the ACRL/IS and LIRT. Her instructional experience includes working with at-risk/provisional, non-traditional, and learning community college students.

Elizabeth A. Elkins (eaelkins@esf.edu), now Director of College Libraries at the SUNY College of Environmental Science and Forestry, Syracuse, NY has been teaching information literacy to students since the mid-seventies. She and a former colleague developed one of the first credit courses and wrote a text (now out of print and out of date!) *Library Searching: Resources and Strategies*. While the basic objectives of the course have remained constant through the years, the specific sources taught and teaching methods utilized have changed dramatically.

Rebecca Feind (feindrs@jmu.edu) is a Reference Librarian at James Madison University. She received her MLS at the University of Missouri-Columbia.

Timothy H. Gatti (tgatti@csc.albany.edu.) is the Head of Cataloging Services Department at the University at Albany. He is currently the only Technical Services and Systems Division librarian who teaches the University at Albany's credit-bearing information literacy course. He received both his BA in History and MA in Library and Information Science from the University of Iowa.

Carol Anne Germain (cg219@albany.edu.) is the Networked Resources Education Librarian at the University at Albany. This position includes reference, bibliographic instruction, and the development of web-based instruction. In the Fall 2000 semester, the University at Albany Libraries implemented a credit-bearing information literacy course. Ms. Germain and colleagues were instrumental in the development of this course. She is currently teaching several sections each academic year. Ms. Germain received her MLS from the University at Albany in 1997. Her most recent article, "URLs: Uniform Resources Locators or Unreliable Resource Locators?" appeared in the July 2000 issue of *College & Research Libraries*.

Jeffrey Harr (harrj@aurora.sunyocc.edu) is an Instruction and Technical Services Librarian at Onondaga Community College. His special area of research is the impact of computers on society. He holds an MA in History from SUNY Cortland and an MLS from the University at Albany.

Gregory Heald (gtheald@unoc.edu) is an Instruction Librarian and Assistant Professor of Library Science at the University of Northern Colorado. He earned an AB from St. John's College–Annapolis and received an MLIS from the University of Rhode Island.

Holly Heller-Ross (Holly.Hellerross@plattsburgh.edu) is Coordinator, Instruction Services Unit at Plattsburgh State University of New York. She gratefully acknowledges the support and encouragement of her husband Jerry Ross and son Ravi Ross, librarian Michelle Toth for reading drafts for clarity, and the many Plattsburgh State students who helped to improve this assignment. Holy holds the MLS.

Janice R. Hylen (jhylen@lib.nmsu.edu) spent 17 years as a high school English teacher, 10 1/2 years as a high school librarian, and now is the Education Librarian/Assistant Instruction Coordinator at New Mexico State University. She has a BS in Education from the University of Dayton, MST in English from the University of New Hampshire, and her MLIS from the University of Rhode Island.

Trudi E. Jacobson (tj662@csc.albany.edu) is the Coordinator of User Education Programs at the University at Albany, SUNY, and an adjunct faculty member at the School of Information Science and Policy at the same institution. She coordinates and teaches the undergraduate Information Literacy course, UNL 200 that reaches approximately 1,000 freshmen and sophomores each year. Her professional interests include the use of critical thinking and active learning activities in the classroom. She is the co-editor of *Teaching the New Library to Today's Users* (Neal-Schuman, 2000) and editor of *Critical Thinking and the Web: Teaching Users to Evaluate Internet Resources* (Library Instruction Publications, 2000), and has published articles in *The Journal of General Education, College & Research Libraries, Journal of Academic Librarianship, Research Strategies, College Teaching*, as well as a number of other journals.

Angelynn King (liaking@uor.edu) is Bibliographic Instruction & Collection Development Librarian at the University of Redlands in Redlands, CA where she serves as liaison to the natural sciences and women's studies departments. Her research interests are in feminist and nontraditional pedagogies, information literacy, information equity, and instructional technology. She holds a BA in Linguistics from the University of Virginia and an MS in Library & information science from the Catholic University of America.

Janice M. Krueger (jkrueger@uop.edu) is currently the Instruction and Outreach Librarian for the University of the Pacific in Stockton, CA. She obtained her Masters of Science in Information Studies from Drexel University in June, 1988, and has worked in public, law, and academic libraries throughout California. She has an undergraduate degree in Education from Duquesne University in Pittsburgh, PA and has taught at various grade levels in Pennsylvania, Ohio, and California.

Michael Lorenzen (lorenze1@msu.edu) is the Library Instruction Coordinator at Michigan State University. He has a BA from Bowling Green State University, MLS from Kent State University, and MEd. from Ohio University. He has published articles in a variety of journals including *The Reference*

Librarian, Journal of Library Administration, and *College & Research Libraries News*. His web address is http://www.lib.msu.edu/lorenze1.

Sue Maberry (maberry@otisart.edu) is the Director of the Library at Otis College of Art & Design in Los Angeles. She has been teaching a required 1-unit Information Literacy course to freshman art students for the past 7 years. She has a degree in art and an MLS.

Stephan J. Macaluso (ref@newpaltz.edu) team-teaches research classes in music and nursing at SUNY New Paltz. He currently administers the Electronic Information Center, SUNY's branch library, in Middletown, NY. He is actively involved in delivering library services to distance learners.

Alexius Smith Macklin (alexius@purdue.edu) is the User Instruction Librarian at Purdue University. She received her Master of Science in Library and Information Science in December 1997 from the University of Pittsburgh. Since joining the profession, she has developed and provided bibliographic instruction for students, faculty, and staff on electronic and print resources. She has team taught undergraduate students online since spring 1999. Her current research interests include learning and teaching in networked environments, teaching critical thinking skills with problem based learning, curriculum development and implementation of information literacy standards across disciplines, and ways of improving access to online information.

Kate Manuel (kmanuel@csuhayward.edu) is Physical Sciences Librarian in the Instructional and Interpretive Services department of University Library, California State University, Hayward. She teaches Fundamentals of Information Literacy and Discipline Based Information Research, both graded, credit classes. She has a MS in Library and Information Science from Catholic University and an MA in Classical Studies from Duke University.

Patrick McCarthy (pjmccar@unco.edu) is Manager of Instructional Services and Assistant Professor of Library Science at the University of Northern Colorado. He has a Bachelor of Arts from the University of Wisconsin Whitewater and a Masters of Library and Information Science from the University of Wisconsin Milwaukee.

Anne C. Moore (annemoor@bellsouth.net) most recently served as Branch Librarian at the Alamogordo campus of New Mexico State University and as Electronic Resources Librarian at the Zuhl Library of New Mexico State University, Las Cruces. She also worked as Prince William Campus Librarian at George Mason University in Virginia. She is currently completing her dissertation on information literacy for a doctorate in the Educational Management and Development department of the College of Education at New Mexico State University.

Coleen Parmer (parmer@bgnet.bgsu.edu) has been working with documents for 25 years and is Head of Jerome Library's Government Documents Department at Bowling Green State University. She is active in Ohio GODORT and has given presentations at state and national conferences. She has written several articles and taught the Government Documents course for the Kent State University School of Library and Information Science. She teaches sessions about government information in a variety of courses each semester.

Mary Sellen (msells@csc.albany.edu) is Assistant Director for User Services at the University at Albany, SUNY. She has worked with her colleagues in developing and expanding the User Education Department at Albany and has taught in the Information Literacy program. In a previous position she developed a multi-media Freshman Seminar experience at Chapman University, Orange, CA.

Carol A. Singer (singerc@bgnet.bgsu.edu) received a BA in French and Russian from BGSU in 1975 and an MLS from Indiana University in 1979. She has worked as a government documents librarian at college and university libraries in Nebraska and Ohio and as a reference librarian at U.S. government libraries in Washington, DC. She is currently a Reference Librarian at Bowling Green State University. She is active in Ohio GODORT and has given presentations at state and national conferences. She has written several articles and taught the general reference course for the Kent State University School of Library and Information Science. She gives presentations on library and Internet research to a variety of classes.

Martha Stephenson (stephenm@mail.uww.edu) is the Bibliographic Instruction Coordinator in the Collection Development and Information Access Department of the University of Wisconsin - Whitewater's Andersen Library. She received the Master's Degree in Scandinavian Studies and the Master's of Library Science Degree from the University of Wisconsin–Madison. She is interested in identifying and accommodating special needs and minority students during bibliographic instruction sessions.

Ru Story-Huffman (rshuff@cc.cumber.edu) is Public Services Librarian at Cumberland College in Williamsburg, KY. She has worked in special, public and academic libraries, and as an adjunct instructor of children's literature. In addition to presenting workshops on a variety of topics, she is the author of *Nursery Rhyme Time*, *Newbery on the Net* and *Caldecott on the Net*, all published by Highsmith Press. She has contributed to a number of educational journals and books, and writes the "Virtual Wisdom" technology column for the Big6 eNewsletter. Ru has a MLS from Emporia State University, Emporia, KS.

Gregory Szczyrbak (gszczyrb@eagle.ycp.edu) is an Assistant Professor and Reference Librarian at York College of Pennsylvania where teaches a two-credit, required core curriculum information literacy course. He earned an MSLIS from Drexel University.

Nancy B. Turner (nturner@lib.nmsu.edu) is the Electronic Resources Coordinator at New Mexico State University Library. She has a BA in Anthropology (University of Pennsylvania), an MA in the Social Sciences (University of Chicago) and an MSLS (Clark Atlanta University). Her recent work has included developing the Library's online catalog interface, usability testing, library web site design, and teaching an upper-level undergraduate course on information literacy.

Jane M. Verostek (jmveros@esf.edu) is an Assistant Librarian at the Franklin Moon Library at the SUNY College of Environmental Science and Forestry. In the past, Jane has held positions at the Syracuse University Law Library, local public libraries, ERIC, and Gaylord Brothers. Her main focus is teaching a 1-credit information literacy course and reference work but also finds time to provide computer support and training for library staff and work on cataloging projects. Jane holds an MLS from Syracuse University and a BS in Environmental Science from SUNY ESF.

Section 1—Course Frameworks and Assessment

Meta-Learning Research Project

Library Ambassadors

Using Poster Sessions in a Chemical Information Literacy Course

Research Notebooks: A Framework for an Information Literacy Course

Annotated Bibliography Project

Research Presentation

Using a Concept Map to Assess Student Learning

Culmination Project for an Information Literacy Course (or series of workshops) for Art Students

Authentic Assessment in Information Literacy Classes: A Holistic Framework of Student Evaluation

Critical Thinking in an Information World

Meta-Learning Research Project

SUSAN E. BECK

Head, Humanities & Social Sciences Services Department
NEW MEXICO STATE UNIVERSITY
susabeck@lib.nmsu.edu

Circumstances of the Instruction

Students typically learn the research process by doing it; however the quality of their learning this process can be a hit or miss affair. Furthermore students' retention of good research practices is often spotty. This unevenness in learning the research process makes it difficult for them to extend and expand their knowledge about how to do research from one project to the next. Why is this so? Most likely it occurs because few professors actually teach the research process. They assume students know the process. They assume that this type of instruction has taken place at the high school level and it isn't their responsibility. By the same token, many faculty members do not realize that they themselves learned the research process over a much longer period of time—from high school through doctoral studies. Thus, what students often lack in their undergraduate studies is the big picture of the research process. They are missing the understanding of the repetitive, incremental practices of research—

- that of formulating a query,
- retrieving information,
- digesting and analyzing that information,
- reformulating a new query, and
- continuing the cycle until the researcher has a new or different view of the topic in order to create new understanding and new meaning.

This meta-learning research activity is the final project for New Mexico State University students enrolled in an upper level undergraduate general education course titled Information Literacy. Multiple course sections are offered each semester and each section is limited to 24 students.

Essentially, the project described here is the culmination of an entire semester's research; it is the capstone experience for the course. This is a semester-long project, therefore all class sessions and assignments that relate in some way to the research process (i.e., searching for, retrieving, evaluating, and documenting sources) assist the students with their final projects.

Objectives of the Instruction

Students will:
- define and communicate their information need,
- select and employ the most appropriate search strategies and search tools to gain access to the needed information,
- analyze and evaluate information sources retrieved.
- apply their knowledge of citation style to sources retrieved, and
- analyze and evaluate their research process.

Components of the Instruction

Introduction

The project is introduced during the first class session so students are well aware of the project's scope and its importance from the very start of the semester. This also helps induce students to begin working on the project early, otherwise they will not be successful. Students have three assignments directly related to their research project that are due throughout the semester: topic choice, a first draft, and a second draft of their research project. Examples of these assignments are noted at the end of this chapter and are provided on the accompanying disk. Because students are required to turn in drafts during the semester, they cannot leave all the research and the writing until the last week of the classes. The drafts provide the instructor with a method to gauge student progress, to detect problem areas, and serve as guidance to students about their project.

The project has two main parts: a 20-item annotated bibliography and a research essay. The bibliography is a typical product of any research assignment. The research essay, however, is very different from what most students have encountered in the past. This essay requires that students **write about** their research process and not their research topic.

In some ways, students are telling their research story. They are expected to explain their topic's parameters, why it interests them and what they already know about it but they are not to write a typical research paper. The underlying assumption for this type of assignment is that if one is more aware of how one goes about doing a task or solving a problem, one is better equipped to expand one's ability to do more complex but similar tasks and solve more complicated, related problems.

The concept of writing an essay that analyzes and evaluates one's research process can be very difficult for some students to grasp. They will be tempted to submit a typical research paper in place of the essay. At the outset students frequently do not see the validity for such a project. Instructors can provide examples of good to excellent essays students have submitted in the past as a way of reinforcing the project's value. Another way of demonstrating the project's value is to ask students to describe their current research process and ask them where they have problems.

Students are given explicit instruction on what their final project should look like and what it should say and do. They receive a Final Project handout detailing due dates, points, scope, and purpose of the assignment. They are also given explicit instructions about the format and the contents. Students receive guidance about how to organize their project to the extent that the section headings are already provided to them. For the essay, they are given prompt questions to answer and specific areas that must be addressed.

Assignment 1: Topic Choice

After the first several weeks of class, students are given an assignment where they need to commit to a topic. This is a good time for the instructor to discuss what makes a good topic. It is also a good idea to give examples of good and not-so-good topics. In this assignment, students are required to submit an essay describing their topic, their interest in it, any prior knowledge of their topic, and what they hope to learn. Parts of this preliminary essay can later be folded into the introduction for the final research essay.

Assignment 2: 1st Draft

By the fifth or sixth week of class, students should have completed enough work on their project to have found at least 8 sources. The first draft assignment requires that they hand in citations for 8 sources on the project. They are given a citation form to use for documenting these 8 sources. Other than requiring students to list the citation, the form also asks them to note where they found the source (catalog? database? web?), how they found it (i.e., search strategy used, keywords, or subject headings used), and why they selected that particular source. Students are also required to submit photocopies of the first page of each of the 8 sources.

Assignment 3: 2nd Draft

For the second draft, students need to submit at least 16 sources for their annotated bibliography. The requirements are the same as for the first draft. They need to use the citation form and submit photocopies of the first page of each source they have included. Students are also required to write a draft of at least one section of the research essay. They have the choice of drafting the introduction, the description or the evaluation. By submitting a rough draft of one section of the essay, students will receive direction on areas needing more work.

Final Project

Starting several weeks prior to the final project submission deadline, the instructor should start asking students how they are doing with their projects, whether they have any questions, and what problems they are having. Providing this type of forum for discussion should help to clear up common points of confusion as well as ease any anxieties. At this same time, the instructor distributes the final grade profile. This is essentially a grading sheet that the instructor uses to evaluate final projects. Point values are provided for each area. By closely studying the grade profile, students have a good indication of what points they need to concentrate on in both their essay and their bibliography.

Final projects are to be submitted at least two weeks prior to the end of the semester. This is done so that students will have time to re-submit their projects if some areas need more work or are confusing or are missing entirely. For the final, students must submit the essay, the annotated bibliography, both drafts, their initial topic selection essay, and photocopies for all 20 sources.

Evaluation

The proof is in the pudding, so to speak. If students have grasped the research process they should demonstrate it within their essay. They should be able to analyze their activities, their choices, and the problems they encountered through the writing component.

Supplementary Materials

The materials in this section have been placed on the accompanying disk so they can easily be copied and/or modified to fit the needs of individual libraries and instructors.

- Final Project handout
    [This is provided to students the first day of the semester. The document provides an overall description of the project and includes the specific elements they need to address in both the annotated bibliography and the research essay.]
- Final Project Topic: Description & Rationale
- Final Project: 1st Draft
- Citations of Items to Be Used in the Annotated Bibliography
- Final Project: 2nd Draft
- Final Project Grade Profile

Library Ambassadors

SUE ANN BRAINARD

Reference/Instruction Librarian
SUNY GENESEO
brainard@geneseo.edu

KIMBERLY DAVIES

Reference/Instruction Librarian
SUNY GENESEO
davies@geneseo.edu

Circumstances of the Instruction

A semester-long course on information literacy would benefit most college freshmen. Unfortunately, institutional philosophy, staffing shortages, and logistics often prohibit enrolling hundreds or thousands of freshmen in such a course. Another problem preventing freshmen from learning research skills is that they are reluctant, for many reasons, to approach the reference desk to ask a librarian for help. Those students prefer to seek help from their peers who may or may not have had training in research skills. A Library Ambassador program can successfully combat these two situations on an academic campus.

A one-credit information literacy course should be offered every semester. Selected graduates of the course will then become Library Ambassadors. These "ambassadors" serve as tutors of research skills in their residence halls and in the departments of their majors. The program can be formal or informal, depending on the situation at the institution. The ambassadors' names can be advertised in the residence hall office and in the office at the department of their major, as someone willing to provide peer tutoring to students doing library research.

Another option involves the organized peer-tutoring program many institutions already have. These programs pay students, who have done well in a course, to tutor others who are struggling in those same courses. At these institutions, certain Library Ambassadors can simply join the ranks of other peer tutors and they would be paid in the same way as the others. The Ambassador program can also be a much more informal program, with the student simply keeping an eye out for friends and classmates who are unsure about research. The information literacy course and the Ambassador program can be especially useful to libraries that hire students to cover non-peak reference desk hours; new hires can be recruited from among the Ambassadors. Whatever form the Ambassador program takes, the information literacy course becomes a training program, preparing the student not only for his or her own college research needs, but preparing him or her to help peers struggling with research.

Objectives of the Instruction

- Students will be able to define basic terminology such as research, information literacy, information technology, information overload, information rich/poor, and access.

- Students will recognize the differences between popular, scholarly, refereed, and trade publications.
- Students will locate library materials in the circulating collection, reference collection, periodical collection, government document collection, and other special collections in the library.
- Students will seek help from the reference librarian, the interlibrary loan office, the circulation desk, and the computer technical help desk as appropriate.
- Students will be able to choose the most suitable database for a task and will know how to perform a keyword search, a subject heading search, proximity, adjacency, truncation, and field limiting when necessary.
- Students will understand that an effective way to find information on the web is by first predicting what government agency or organization is most likely to have the information, and then accessing the web pages.
- Students will teach concepts and information resources to other students.

Components of the Instruction

Preparation

Prior to the beginning of the semester, the instructor should garner support for the Library Ambassador program by discussing it with the residence life office, the academic departments, and the peer tutor office if one exists. It should be explained to them that this is an informal, volunteer program in which the ambassadors serve as peer tutors for students who are struggling with research. The role of the residence life office and the academic department would be to refer struggling students to one of the assigned ambassadors. If the residence life office and departments are willing to participate, the instructor of the information literacy course should contact them at the end of every semester with the names of students who have successfully completed the course and are willing to help their peers.

As an alternative to this arrangement, if the departments or residence life office are not interested in participating, the instructor may be able to simply impress upon the students themselves to be aware of their friends and classmates' research problems and to offer informal, friendly advice.

While designing methods and assignments to teach information literacy skills, the instructor should keep in mind that these students will soon be giving advice to other students about these techniques and resources. The instructor should design several group projects, so he or she has the opportunity to observe how the students work together.

Presentation

The course should be taught as any other information literacy course, with the exception that the instructor should let students teach each other whenever possible. At the beginning of a lesson, the instructor should discover if one of the students has experience with the material to be covered (a research database, for example), and ask that student to teach it to his or her peers in the classroom. The instructor should interrupt with gentle reminders, guidance, and positive feedback. This should help create a comfortable learning environment and show students how to become non-threatening, non-judgmental teachers. The instructor, then, will serve as a model that the students will emulate when giving advice in the future.

Throughout the course, the instructor should focus on the role of librarians in the undergraduate research process, stressing that librarians have expertise that no student, even after completing an information literacy course, can be expected to have. To do this, the instructor should take care to present some very tough research topics and scenarios. This is risky, since it may frustrate the students in the course. Ultimately, though, it is a good way to prove to students that for some research projects it is necessary to consult a librarian, and that even a good student researcher frequently needs a librarian's help. This is essential to prevent the future ambassador from promoting him or her self as a librarian on campus.

At the end of the course, the students who have received good grades and have shown excellent promise as future Library Ambassadors should be asked if they would be willing to participate in the Library Ambassador program. (However, they should be told that their interest or lack of interest in the Library Ambassador program would not affect their grade for the course.) The students who are interested should be given the details about how the program works at the institution, such as how they will be contacted about a student who needs tutoring, and how to keep track of the number of times they help other students.

Evaluation

A survey should be designed and given to Library Ambassadors at the end of every semester. It should include questions about how much help they gave to struggling students that semester, what the circumstances were, how many times they referred a student to a librarian, and whether they thought the student ended up seeking help at the library. There should also be a question asking if the ambassadors feel that they were adequately trained, and if they needed more training on a particular research concept or resource.

If they exist, other library surveys may be used to gather information from the general student population as to whether they know about the ambassador program and if they were ever referred to one by an instructor or a residence life staff member.

Supplementary Material

The material in this section has been placed on the accompanying disk so it can easily be copied and/or modified to fit the needs of individual libraries and instructors.

- Library Ambassadors Survey

Notes:

24

Using Poster Sessions in a Chemical Information Literacy Course

BARTOW CULP

Chemistry Librarian/ Assistant Professor of Library Science
PURDUE UNIVERSITY
bculp@purdue.edu

Circumstances of the Instruction

An instructor is forever reconciling the opposing forces of content inclusion with class time availability. If he or she is lucky enough to have a full semester course, it is rarely more than a one credit/one class a week offering. That is barely enough time to teach the sources and skills necessary to fulfill minimal course objectives.

While this chapter describes the use of poster sessions in the context of an undergraduate course in chemical information, the general concepts and guidelines are applicable to a wide range of information literacy courses.

The chemical information course at Purdue University is required for most of the undergraduates majoring in chemistry. Most enrollees are 2nd and 3rd year students, but there are usually some seniors and even graduate students in the class. The course meets for one hour weekly for a full semester. The class size is usually 20–25 students. Grading is based on weekly homework assignments (35%), midterm (20%) and final (25%) exams, and a final project (20%).

Initially the final project in the course was an individually written research project. The original purpose of this project was for the student to choose a research topic and to carry out the information-gathering portion of that research using the skills and resources learned in the course.

Despite preliminary conversations with each student about the suitability of his or her topic and written guidelines that gave an exemplary topic outline and listed the objectives and expectations, the results of this assignment were frequently disappointing. The necessary placement of the project at the end of the semester put it in competition with other, more "important" (at least in terms of grade points) deadlines for most students. The results were usually uninspiring and consisted of rushed and boring rehashes of the class notes that only occasionally met the assignment objectives. Student comments on the class evaluations, although generally positive about the class, were specifically critical of this assignment. It was replaced with a collaborative poster session in the 1996 spring semester. This was an immediate success and has been part of the class curriculum ever since.

Poster sessions have long been an important means of communication at scientific and technical meetings. They are an ideal forum for graduate and undergraduate students to present research in progress, and play an integral part of local, regional, and national conferences of the American Chemical Society (ACS). Even in the age of virtual conferences, this casual and interactive way to communicate research retains a high popularity and shows no signs of disappearing. The unique environment of a chemical information course in which emphasis is more on learning applied skills than on theoretical concepts, lends itself well to the poster session as a way to demonstrate a summative mastery of these skills.

Objectives of the Instruction

This chapter describes the use of a student poster session at the end of the semester to achieve several instructional aims:

- It maximizes the use of valuable class time.
- Students apply many of the information literacy skills learned during the course when they assemble their posters.
- The project requires students to collaborate within groups to achieve desired outcomes.
- The actual poster sessions give students the opportunity to have their work evaluated by their teachers and peers.

In addition, there can be other advantages to the inclusion of poster sessions in an information literacy course. They frequently cover topics and concepts not otherwise covered in the course and they can provide good publicity for the library's information resources.

Components of the Instruction

Preparation

The timeline of steps leading up to the poster session is as follows:

1. 1st week of class: Brief explanation of poster project within general discussion of course syllabus.
2. 3rd– 4th week: Formation of groups—collaborative homework assignments from this point.
3. 6th week: Poster topic is due, accompanied by a brief abstract.
4. 10th–11th week: Each group discusses detailed poster design and content with instructor; "story board" of poster due.
5. 13th week: Poster session is held during regular class period.
6. 14th week: Class feedback and grade discussion.

Project Management

The ability to work effectively in a group is a measure of success in the "real" (i.e., post-college) world; similarly, the exercise of putting together a poster presentation, whether real or virtual, is a valuable one for students, since they will frequently be called upon to do so as professionals. However, the majority of students at this level have not worked together on a group project, and practically none of them has collaborated in a poster presentation. Therefore, the project needs to be managed carefully for it properly to achieve the desired learning outcomes.

To facilitate this, the instructor must carefully control the following elements:

- Group formation and maintenance
- Topic selection and development
- Presentation guidelines

Group Formation and Maintenance

Critical to the success of the poster session are the early formation of groups and the setting of the overall goal and intermediate objectives for the project. Establishing the "best" group size and membership is a subtle task, and is generally dependent on the frequency and size of the projects to be accomplished. For this type of project, a group size of four works best; it is large enough to spread the work around equitably, and can function even if one member drops out (either officially or *de facto*). Conversely, it is small enough so that the group members can find time to meet regularly, and the inadequate performance of the group slacker (there is always one) is immediately noticeable. For a class size not divisible by 4, groups of 5 are formed as needed.

After the groups are formed, most of the weekly homework assignments are designed to be collaborative. These assignments allow the groups to shake out prior to the more serious effort of the poster preparation. "Jumping" among groups is also allowed within the first few weeks of their creation. However, by the time the poster topic is due in the 6th week, all group memberships are frozen.

Poster Topic Selection

In order to maintain a coherent theme for all the groups' posters, the instructor establishes a general theme in advance. Examples of this theme have been "Electronic databases in chemistry," "Comparing print and online chemical information resources," and "Things you didn't know were in the library." A particularly popular topic was to have each of the groups design web pages that described different aspects of the library's services.

Presentation Guidelines

There are several sources of guidelines for effective poster presentations. The guidelines used for this course are those provided by the ACS as part of its *Handbook for Speakers*—http://www.acs.org:80/meetings/handbook.html#poster—and the supplements to this site found on the ACS Chemical Information Division Web site—http://www.lib.uchicago.edu/cinf/guidelines_for_posters.html. A further "Do and Don't" list was also created for this activity (see Supplementary Materials). While these guidelines refer to technical posters, most of them are applicable to other such presentations.

Show Time!

The session is usually held in a well-traveled hallway outside the library. Poster boards, easels, pushpins and tape are provided for the groups, who must have their posters in place by the be-ginning of class time. Handbills advertising the event are distributed around the building several days ahead and members of the faculty are urged to attend. Gratifyingly, many do, joining the passing students in questioning the group members about their poster topics and imparting legitimacy to the session. Digital pictures are taken of the session for future posting on the class web site. After the hour-long session is over, the posters stay up for the remainder of the day.

Evaluation

The poster projects are graded according to three criteria: topic selection, project execution, and poster presentation. For the last criterion, the class is involved in the grading. During the class period in which the poster session is conducted, each group uses an evaluation form (see Supplementary Materials) to judge the other groups' posters. The purpose here is to have the students look critically at each other's presentations. In addition, the members of each group must complete a group self-evaluation form (see Supplementary Materials). This is to allow some normalization of grading in cases of unequal contributions by group members. During the class period that follows the poster session, the composite evaluation of each poster is reviewed and small prizes (usually Purdue coffee mugs) are awarded to the group with the "champion" poster based on its presentation score.

Conclusions

The inclusion of a poster session in the structure of an information literacy class can accomplish many teaching objectives that are central to the overall goal of increasing the information competency of students. If properly managed, it can also provide students with valuable experience in-group dynamics and in making presentations. Furthermore, it can enhance the visibility of the library by showcasing different aspects of its services in a lively yet informative fashion.

Supplementary Materials

The materials in this section have been placed on the accompanying disk so they can easily be copied and/or modified to fit the needs of individual libraries and instructors.

- Poster Presentation Guidelines
- Poster Session Evaluation Form
- Poster Session Team Self-Evaluation Form

Research Notebooks: A Framework for an Information Literacy Course

KIMBERLEY M. DONNELLY

Assistant Professor and Reference Librarian
YORK COLLEGE OF PENNSYLVANIA
kmdonnel@ycp.edu

Circumstances of the Instruction

One of the predominant criticisms of credit-bearing information literacy courses is that they teach research process in a vacuum.[i] Advocates of course-integrated, collaborative information literacy initiatives argue that students will not transfer the concepts and skills from a survey course to their discipline-based coursework.

The challenge to those of us who teach introductory information literacy courses is to respond by developing some kind of overarching course framework that invites interesting research questions—questions that students care about and questions they feel are worth pursuing. The framework must encourage creative thought, exploration, and interest, yet somehow encompass, integrate and reinforce connections to real world, real life information needs. The task for an instructor is to help students create a model information-seeking project on a topic of personal importance and to communicate the pivotal point that students can return to that project as a guide to searching other topics and questions.

The framework I use in my two-credit core course and describe here has several names in the literature: research portfolios or notebooks, information-seeking journals or logs.[ii] In fact, this technique is mentioned in the ACRL *Information Literacy Competency Standards for Higher Education.* The outcomes for Standard Two, Performance Indicator 2 include:

    a. develops a research plan appropriate to the investigative method and
    b. identifies keywords, synonyms and related terms for the information needed.

---

[i] For an in-depth discussion of the pros and cons of credit-bearing information literacy courses, see the *BI-L Mailing List Archive*—http://bubl.ac.uk/mail/bild/—from April 29, 1999 through June 4, 1999.

[ii] Two articles by Daniel Callison are of note. "The Potential for Portfolio Development," *School Library Media Annual* 11 (1993): 30–39 and "Key Words in Instruction: Portfolio," *School Library Media Activities Monthly* 14.2 (1997): 42–45. Also see Trudi Jacobson and Beth Mark, "Teaching in the Information Age: Active Learning Techniques to Empower Students," *The Reference Librarian* 51/52 (1995): 105–120.

In addition, the outcomes for Standard Four, Performance Indicator 2 include:

a. maintains a journal or log of activities related to the information seeking, evaluating, and communicating process and
b. reflects on past successes, failures, and alternative strategies.[iii]

I use the name "research notebooks" for the semester-long projects students do in my class. Each class has a maximum of 24 students and includes freshmen through seniors.

Here is the process in a nutshell. Students keep logs of topic question development, possible keywords and subject headings, and personal reflections about their research. They write plans for all searches, follow the plans as homework, keep a log of their work, and make printouts and/or photocopies of results as appropriate. They apply selection criteria when adding citations to their notebooks and evaluation criteria after they obtain the actual sources. Students are encouraged to re-evaluate their questions during personal reflections and continually fine-tune or flat-out change them when appropriate. If they feel they have answered their original question, they are invited to investigate a new aspect of the topic, or move on to another question. The notebooks are assembled throughout the semester and include the best information sources available. Because a part of the value of the notebooks is that they document students' growth, revisions are invited regularly.

Objectives of the Instruction

Essentially, all the course goals and objectives can be integrated into this project.[iv] Students prove mastery by doing real research.

What do students have at the end of the semester?
- Search plans for each type of material covered—*in their own words.*
- All the research for a topic question—*which they might use for a paper or presentation in another class.*
- An example of a thorough research process—*which they can use as a template for other topic questions.*
- A collection of handouts—*I require them to print selected web pages, handouts and e-mail messages about the major concepts we cover, like evaluation.*
- A record of their development as a searcher—*from their reflections and logs they can see the proof that they have become better information seekers.*

[iii] See ACRL Task Force on Information Literacy Competency Standards, "Information Literacy Competency Standards for Higher Education," *C&RL News* (March 2000): 207–215. Also available at http://www.ala.org/acrl/ilcomstan.html.

[iv] See our course goals at http://www.ycp.edu/library/ifl/etext/ethome.html.

Components of the Instruction

Supplies: Students need a binder, notebook paper, and divider tabs.

The research notebook described below is compiled in conjunction with course content, such as Boolean operators, source evaluation, and information ethics. Work on the research notebook intensifies and pauses in response to the flow of course content. The lesson plans included in this book can be used to deliver the content for which the binder demonstrates mastery.

Instructor preparation for each plan/log/results series:
1. Identify the course goals and skills to be targeted by the activity.
2. Prepare a basic plan for students to follow that requires them to practice the skills. This plan may be distributed to students during class as a handout, presented to students on a whiteboard or transparency, or simply delivered orally. Students should customize the basic plan to fit their topic questions.
3. Write a lesson plan or script for teaching book searching. Use a combination of discussion, lecture, demonstration, and hands-on practice as appropriate.

Sample Book Search Goals:
Students should be able to:
- formulate search strategies, execute searches, and interpret results;
- use the library's online catalog; and
- use the area consortium union catalog and other online catalogs.

Sample Book Search Plan:
This example assumes previous coverage of Boolean logic.
- Write your current topic question on a sheet of paper.
- Write two or three keyword searches you will use. Include Boolean operators and truncation where appropriate.
- Search Step 1—Search library catalog for books and materials available here.
- Search Step 2—Search union catalog for books and materials in the local area.
- Search Step 3—Search at least one other catalog or an online bookstore for books and materials worldwide.
- Goal—Try to identify at least one book that looks like it might answer your question.
- Include a log of each search and a printout of the best source you identify.
- Justify the printout by handwriting on it how it meets our selection criteria: relevance, currency, audience and purpose.

Sample Book Search Lesson Plan:
- Segment A: Why use books?
    - Begin with a brief discussion of strengths and weaknesses of books.
    - Ask students to share their experiences—what do they already know?
- Segment B: How to find books?
    - Introduce the concept of a library catalog.
    - Introduce step one of the search plan and tell why it is important.

- Demonstrate step one.
- Give students a few minutes to try step one.
- Introduce step two of the search plan and tell why it is important and different.
- Demonstrate.
- Give practice time.
- Introduce step three of the search plan and tell why it is important and different. Show students the various options available for this search and ask them to write their selection(s) on their plans.
- Demonstrate.
- Give practice time.
- Announce that anybody who didn't finish all three steps should finish the plan/log as homework.

Possible components of the research notebook

The notebook should include a record of topic development, logs or research processes and personal reflection, and copies of actual information sources. The notebook might contain the following tabs:

1. Topic—question, audience, purpose; all revisions to topic question; keyword list; periodic personal reflections about topic question
2. Handouts—from instructor or Web which reinforce main concepts like Boolean operators
3. Reference source—plan, process log, and printout/copy
4. Books—plan, process log, and printout/copy
5. Book reviews—plan, process log, and printout/copy
6. Periodical articles—plan, process log, printout/copy, and formal evaluation of one of the articles found
7. Newspaper articles—plan, process log, and printout/copy
8. Newsgroup & electronic discussion group postings—plan, process log and printout
9. Web pages/sites—plan, process log, printout, and formal evaluation of one of the web pages
10. Conclusion—reflection on completed research process

For each search a minimum and maximum amount of time, perhaps 20–30 minutes, might be announced. Periodic free writing can be used to help students reflect on the topic question and whether the information gathered to date answers the question. In addition, free writing can encourage students to revise and refine the topic question. Occasional group discussions can be used to invite students to share their searches with one another. Discussions can bring to light common problem areas and help students see how the same techniques can be applied to widely differing topic questions. If possible, the instructor might also compile a research notebook. Discussions might begin with the instructor sharing his/her successes and struggles and then inviting others to share the stories of their searches. The instructor's notebook can be passed around as a model of the process.

Evaluation

The easiest way to evaluate the students' notebooks is to collect them frequently and give feedback about how searches could be improved. I collect the entire binder every two to three weeks because I want to grade the new materials in the context of the evolving research question and previously selected sources. Other instructors may find it more practical to just collect new materials. Developing a grading key is helpful. Make a list of all the requirements of a particular search. These requirements should all tie directly back to the original goals and objectives. Check the students' binders for each item on the list. Ask yourself, can this student perform the tasks required to meet the goals?

For example, a grading key for the search plan described above might give points for:
- The student submitted a plan, log, and printout.
- The student's log shows that he/she conducted searches for all three steps.
- The searches on the log indicate the student applied search techniques adequately.
- The student wrote the selection criteria on the printout.
- The source the student selected seems appropriate to the topic question.

In order to manage the workload, an instructor might choose to have students compile the research notebook in pairs or small groups, rather than individually. Alternatively, electronic portfolios could be used. Ask students to submit plans, logs, and citations on a disk or via email attachment.

The I-Search Paper is another variation on this theme. In an I-Search Paper, "A person conducts a search to find out something he needs to know for his own life and writes the story of his adventure."[v] An I-Search Paper is a narrative of a process. While the research notebook contains narrative logs, no comprehensive story is written. Additionally, I-Search Papers place heavy emphasis on people as sources. Students are encouraged to ask and interview experts before conducting exhaustive literature searches.

---

[v] Ken Macrorie, preface to *The I-Search Paper*, rev. ed. (Portsmouth, NH: Boynton/Cook Publishers, 1988).

Notes:

Annotated Bibliography Project

GREGORY HEALD

Assistant Professor of Library Science
UNIVERSITY OF NORTHERN COLORADO
gtheald@unco.edu

PATRICK MCCARTHY

Assistant Professor of Library Science
UNIVERSITY OF NORTHERN COLORADO
pjmccar@unco.edu

Circumstances of the Instruction

The Annotated Bibliography is the major project in an elective information literacy class, LIB 150: Introduction to Undergraduate Research, offered by the University of Northern Colorado Libraries. Students collect at least 25 resources on a focused research topic approved by both Library and English Department Faculty. The citations are collected from a proscribed number of publication formats using various search techniques. Improving the quality of student information literacy skills, rather than the simple mechanics of research and documentation, is the primary purpose of both the course and Annotated Bibliography Assignment. This assignment is the culmination of LIB 150's lectures and weekly assignments.

The Annotated Bibliography Project is intended for first year university students and the majority of the students are freshmen. However, upperclassmen and an occasional graduate student will enroll in the course for elective credit. While sections of the course are capped at 25 students, the assignment itself is essentially scalable to the limits of the instructor's workload.

Since this assignment is designed to link with ENG 123: College Research Paper, students have the first eight weeks of a 16-week semester to complete the bibliography. Thus the "Annotated Bibliography" for LIB 150 becomes their ENG 123 papers' "working bibliography" which is due eight weeks later at the end of the 16-week term.

Objectives of the Instruction

- Students will gain experience identifying, locating, retrieving, and evaluating a variety of information resources.
- Students will synthesize information literacy with a concrete information need.
- Students will develop confidence in their research abilities.
- Students will master a reproducible model for the research process.
- Students will have reinforced the connection between information literacy skills and the quality of the student's work across the curriculum.
- Students will demonstrate comprehension of course content.

Components of the Instruction

Preparation

- Copy a sufficient supply of the Annotated Bibliography Assignment Worksheet and the Bibliography Worksheets (see Supplementary Materials).
- Place sample Annotated Bibliography Projects on reserve, if available.

In-Class Presentation

Provide a detailed explanation of the assignment during the second week of the semester by examining the assignment point by point. Then review the components of a successful Annotated Bibliography in class by handing around a sample project. Allow 30 minutes for the presentation and questions. Schedule a conference with each student for the fifth week of the semester to ensure adequate progress.

Grading

Evaluating Annotated Bibliography Projects is challenging in several ways. Foremost there is the question of what weight to place on various components of the whole project. As an information literacy course, the majority of the grade is based on comprehensiveness of the search. See the Supplementary Materials for the Annotated Bibliography Grading Rubric. A second and perhaps more difficult challenge is the time needed to grade each project, which ranges between 30 and 60 minutes each.

Evaluation

In addition to anecdotal conclusions drawn from the quality of students' Annotated Bibliographies, we receive both quantitative and qualitative student evaluations. Both assessment instruments ask about the difficulty and appropriateness of the assignment.

Supplementary Materials

The materials in this section have been placed on the accompanying disk so they can easily be copied and/or modified to fit the needs of individual libraries and instructors.

- Annotated Bibliography Assignment
- Annotated Bibliography Grading Rubric
- Government Publication Worksheet
- Magazine Article Worksheet
- Monograph Worksheet
- Newspaper Article Worksheet
- Reference Book Article Worksheet
- Scholarly Periodical Article Worksheet

Research Presentation

HOLLY HELLER-ROSS

Coordinator, Instruction Services Unit
PLATTSBURGH STATE UNIVERSITY OF NEW YORK
Holly.Hellerross@plattsburgh.edu

Circumstances of the Instruction

This group research presentation assignment has been used for several years in Plattsburgh State University's LIB101: Introduction to Library Research. This one-credit course has been a general education requirement since 1979. Between 20 and 22 sections of the course are taught during the first eight weeks of each semester, with a class size of 30 in recent years. The course is taught in a computer classroom where both the instructor display station and the student desktops have live Internet connections. Students in the allied health sections of traditional on-campus courses and in newer distance learning Internet courses have all successfully completed this group project.

The assignment has both in-class and out-of-class components and requires most of two 50-minute class sessions to complete as designed. The class meets once each week, so students have time between classes to complete their homework assignments. Modifications could be made to enable students to complete the work in one session, and while student groups of three work well with a class size of 30, pairs or groups of four would work equally well. This assignment is worth 15%, a significant component of the total course grade. The assignment is given before the individual final research projects are assigned and serves as a preparatory bridge to that final project. It could also be used as a comprehensive final project by itself. In session 1, student groups work together in class to define a topic and write potential topic research questions, and then individuals work out-of-class to select and use background resources, book and journal access tools, or Internet access tools. The groups must pull their results together and offer a presentation in session 2, with live Internet links using a word processing or presentation software program, a student Internet page, or by posting to a class Internet page. Session 2 is exciting and fun, according to comments students have made about the assignment.

Objectives of the Instruction

This activity supports student learning by addressing some of the 2000 Association of College & Research Libraries *Information Literacy Competency Standards for Higher Education*. The performance indicators are only paraphrased here, librarians should refer to the original document for clarification.
- **Standard One, Performance Indicator 1** (defining and articulating an information need)
- **Standard One, Performance Indicator 2** (identifying types and formats of potential information sources)
- **Standard Two, Performance Indicator 1** (selecting appropriate methods and information retrieval systems)
- **Standard Two, Performance Indicator 2** (constructing and implementing effective search strategies)

- **Standard Two, Performance Indicator 3** (retrieving information online or in person)
- **Standard Three, Performance Indicator 2** (articulating and applying evaluation criteria)
- **Standard Four, Performance Indicator 3** (communicating the product or performance effectively to others)

The activity is designed to help students apply these discrete skills in a comprehensive way, leading to a greater understanding of their purpose. Additional comprehensive objectives are listed below:
- The group research presentation assignment helps students pull together previously learned research planning and searching skills.
- The work reinforces and requires application of the concepts of resource selection and critical evaluation of information.
- The assignment provides opportunity for student group presentations of information using Internet technology.
- The presentation evaluation section allows students to further explore research and critical evaluation by reviewing each class presentation and offering their classmates feedback.

Components of the Instruction

Session 1 Preparation

The instructor needs to prepare students by introducing basic research concepts and strategies. This assignment will work best if students have had previous instruction in selecting and focusing a topic and are somewhat familiar with the reference resources and research tools. Students will need instruction or review in the important concepts of critical evaluation of information resources. If they have not used a word processing program to create Internet (HTML) documents or posted materials to a web page before, the instructor should discuss that as well. The instructor can make the assignment clear by providing a Research Presentation Assignment Handout, a Research Presentation Format Handout, and a Research Presentation Example Handout (see Supplementary Materials). These materials need to be finished and ready for distribution before the assignment is introduced.

Session 1 Presentation

The instructor can use the presentation example as both a teaching and review tool. After introducing the assignment and explaining the objectives, students are asked to self-select or are assigned into research groups. The presentation example is distributed on paper and displayed to the class using the instructor's display station and Internet connection. The instructor guides students through the assignment step-by-step, carefully reviewing the concepts and providing opportunity for discussion. The instructor makes the example's underlying research decisions as explicit as possible and attempts to elicit student alternatives. The instructor then models how students will critically evaluate the group presentations by using the evaluation form to evaluate the research example. This important step ensures that students know the criteria by which their work will be evaluated, and usually motivates them to give the assignment their best efforts. This instruction takes between 20 and 30 minutes. The groups then begin their work using the class handouts for the remaining time. By the end of the session, the groups should have settled on a research topic, a research question, broader and narrower topics, selected types of information, and should have divided up their individual research tasks. Students then work independently on their research tasks, meet or e-mail attachments to one group member, and assemble their presentations before the next class meetings.

Session 2 Preparation

For session 2, the instructor needs to set up a schedule for the class presentations, or assist students to set up their presentations on computers around the classroom as in a conference exhibit or poster session. If the conference exhibit model is selected, two group members circulate to review other presentations, while one group member remains with their presentation. The instructor calls for students to change to a new presentation every 10 minutes and at that time a different group member takes charge of each presentation station. Depending on the size of the class, not every student will have the opportunity to review every presentation.

Session 2 Presentation

The instructor reviews the session schedule and then distributes one Research Presentation Evaluation Handout (see Supplementary Materials) to each group. Group members sign their names on the top of the handout. If each group will be presenting their research on the instructor's display station, the instructor can re-distribute the signed handouts to anther student group for evaluation comments.

If the conference exhibit model is selected, the signed handout stays at their presentation station and is filled out by their classmates as they visit each different presentation. If needed, the instructor assists students in setting up their presentations on computers around the classroom. Two group members circulate to review other presentations, while one remains with the presentation. The instructor also circulates around the room to offer encouragement and facilitate critical thinking in the student evaluations. As stated earlier, the instructor calls for students to change to a new presentation every 10 minutes and at that time a different group member takes charge of each presentation station. If there are more than five groups in a 50-minute session, not every student will have the opportunity to review every presentation.

Evaluation

Students evaluate their classmates' work as part of session 2. The instructor provides additional feedback and grades the assignment on the quality of both the research and the presentation. The instructor uses the same evaluative questions as the students do when grading the presentations. As with any group project, the instructor needs to stay alert for any problems within the groups regarding distribution of work and student efforts on the presentation and adjust grades as appropriate.

Supplementary Materials

The materials in this section have been placed on the accompanying disk so they can easily be copied and/or modified to fit the needs of individual libraries and instructors.

- Research Presentation Assignment Handout
- Research Presentation Format Handout
- Research Presentation Example Handout
- Research Presentation Evaluation Handout

Notes:

Using a Concept Map to Assess Student Learning

TRUDI E. JACOBSON
Coordinator of User Education Programs
UNIVERSITY AT ALBANY, SUNY
tj662@csc.albany.edu

Circumstances of the Instruction

Information literacy courses often present students with a large number of topics and concepts, and there is not always time to relate each topic directly to the others. Instructors might be concerned that students are unable to make connections between the disparate topics they are learning. Asking students to draw a concept map part way through a course will help instructors understand how students are making connections between topics, or if they are making connections. It will allow instructors to make the relationships clearer while there is still time available in the course.

This activity can be used as a segment within a class devoted to other information literacy topics. It will take about 15–30 minutes, including introducing students to concept maps and how to draw them. It can be used with any size group. Ask the students to draw their own concept maps or ask small groups of 2 or 3 students to develop a joint concept map. It might seem odd to group students to work together on this project, since each one will have his/her own concept of how the course topics fit together. However, when students discuss the topics among themselves, they may begin to see connections that they did not make before and come to a better understanding of how a particular topic fits in with others. Having students work together will garner a somewhat different result from asking each student to draw a concept map on his/her own.

Objectives of the Instruction

- Students will be reminded of all major topics covered in class to date.
- Students will reflect on and draw connections between these topics.

Components of the Instruction

Preparation

Make a list of all significant topics covered in your course to date. Students will most likely find the list easiest to use if the topics are presented in the same order in which they were covered in class.

Prepare a concept map to use as an example so they will understand what you are asking them to draw. Sample concept maps can be found in the articles in the reference list at the end of this lesson plan. The sample concept map might be on a topic related to the course but should not show the same material that you are asking your students to map.

Decide if you would like students to draw their own concept maps to assess individual learning, or joint concept maps, where student discussion may lead to new knowledge but may not reflect any one student's understanding. Also decide if you would like several students/groups of students to present their concept maps briefly to the rest of the class. Adding brief presentations will take this activity to the high end of the time range.

Presentation/Hands-on Activity

Display the sample concept map included in this lesson plan to the class on a document camera or overhead projector. If neither of these tools is available, make a copy for each student (if students have their own copies, they may concentrate too much upon making direct connections with the sample, rather than developing their own). Explain what a concept map is and that you will be asking students to draw a concept map based on course material. Encourage students to ask questions about the construction of the sample concept map. If you would like students to explicitly label relationships (i.e., the lines between topics), make that clear to them. Reassure them that there is not one right way to draw this concept map so that they will not feel that this is a test.

Give each student or group of students a list of the course topics. Ask them to use all of the topics in their concept map, linking topics in a way that makes sense to them, and to label relationships between the concepts. Tell them how much time they have, and give notice when five minutes and one minute are left. Circulate among the students to answer any questions that they have. If you have decided to have presentations when the students are finished, ask two or three students or groups to briefly present their concept maps. This can lead to a very fruitful discussion among the entire class. Collect the concept maps for review.

Evaluation

The concept maps act as a form of assessment of student learning and of your teaching. Understanding how students see the relationships between class topics will allow you to provide additional instruction to correct misconceptions, and might suggest that your instruction be altered next time to directly address areas where students had difficulties.

Alternative Uses for Concept Maps

- Concept maps might be used at the very beginning of an information literacy course to assess students' understanding of course topics before they start to learn course content. If concept maps are used at this early stage, you might alter what you teach in class to address specific concerns based upon the contents of the concept map.
- Concept maps could also be used at the end of a course to assess students' learning. If used at this point, modifications might be made the next time you teach the course.
- Concept maps can also be used for just intricate course topic, rather than all topics learned to date.

Sources:

Angelo, Thomas A., and K. Patricia Cross. *Classroom Assessment Techniques: A Handbook for College Teachers.* 2nd ed. San Francisco: Jossey-Bass, 1993. See chapter 16, Concept Maps (pp. 197–202).

Osif, Bonnie. *Teaching Research Skills: Innovative Strategies for Library Use Instruction. Concept Mapping for Undergraduates.* 1996. 18 December 2000
http://www.iti.nwu.edu/slatran/bonnie.html

Romance, Nancy R., and Michael R. Vitale. "Concept Mapping as a Tool for Learning." *College Teaching* 47.2 (1999): 74–79.

Sherratt, Christine S., and Martin L. Schlabach. "The Applications of Concept Mapping in Reference and Information Services." *RQ* 30.1 (1990): 60–69.

Supplementary Materials

The Concept Map is included on the following page and is not on the accompanying disk.

- Sample Concept Map: Library Collection

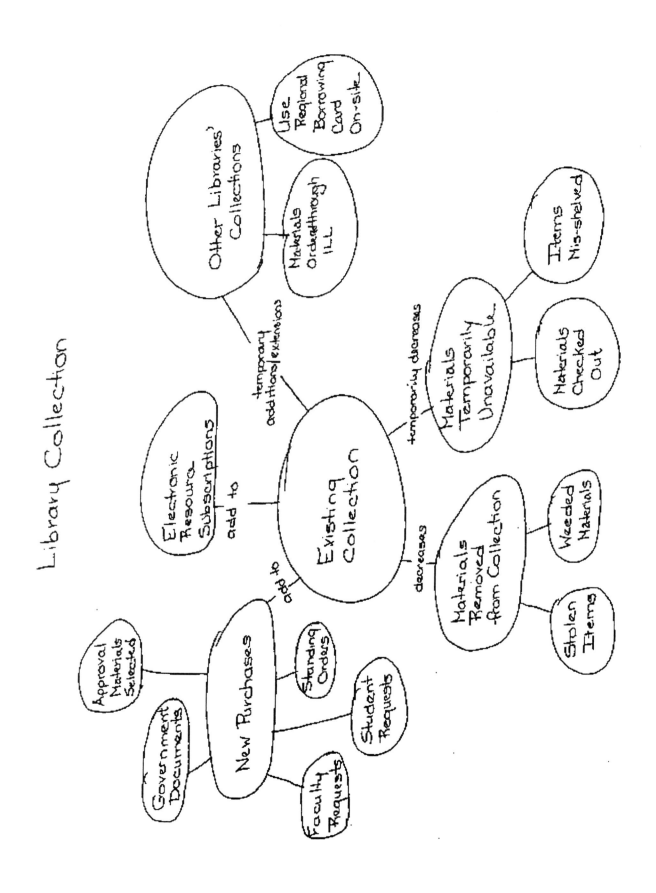

Library Collection

Culmination Project for an Information Literacy Course (or Series of Workshops) for Art Students

SUE MABERRY

Director
OTIS COLLEGE OF ART & DESIGN LIBRARY
maberry@otisart.edu

Circumstances of the Instruction

Art students are sometimes resistant to learning how to do research in a library. However, they love to browse books, look at images, and view the work of artists. When teaching Information Literacy workshops to freshman-level students, I often assign them research on a contemporary artist. Surprisingly, most beginning art students are quite unfamiliar with all but the most famous contemporary artists. I pre-select the artists to ensure that each student will be successful. Choosing artists who address issues in some way related to the role of information in society is a good subtle method of raising their consciousness. (See Supplementary Materials for a partial list of artists.)

The assignment provided here is a culmination project to be completed after a period of about 6 to 8 hours of instruction. Students need to know how to use basic research tools like the OPAC, indexes, search engines, etc. The project could, however, be integrated into instruction over time and parts of the project could be completed as each tool is presented. The value is really having the students pull it all together and create a visual resource for themselves showing the results of searching for the same subject in a variety of basic tools.

Objectives of the Instruction

- To allow students to demonstrate their ability to use basic reference tools, specifically the OPAC, indexes, and online databases
- To ensure that students can find their way around the library
- To expose students to the work of an artist who addresses the (broadly defined) role of information in society, particularly as related to media and popular culture

Components of the Instruction

Preparation

- Create a list of possible artists (see Supplementary Materials) and make sure that enough information about each can easily be found in the sources students will use. The most difficulty will probably be in the biographical sources.
- Prepare the Assignment Handouts in advance (see Supplementary Materials). The instructor should write in the name of a different artist for each student.

Assignment

Tell students that although the final project will be due at the end of the course, they should plan on doing a little bit each week as a way to practice using the various research tools that are being presented. The research part should be easy. Tell them to evaluate the sources carefully and choose the most reliable one available. Refer them to the source—http://www.otisart.edu/wh/library/evaltut.htm—that lists some questions they must answer about their web sites.

Let them know that the artists and their work may be challenging and require some reading and critical thinking. Stress that all the artists on the list deal with popular culture and comment upon it in some way. Encourage them to focus on what information the artist is trying to convey through their work.

Students could additionally be asked to present information about their artist to the class. If a projection unit is available, they can show one or two images of the artists' work by going to a good web site. If this option is chosen, expect lively discussions.

Evaluation

Projects should be graded and comments given related to the quality of the sources the students have used. The student evaluation of what was learned is built into the project—they are asked to summarize what they learned.

Supplementary Materials

The materials in this section have been placed on the accompanying disk so they can easily be copied and/or modified to fit the needs of individual libraries and instructors.

- Assignment Handout: "Project: Researching An Artist"
- List of Possible Artists

Authentic Assessment in Information Literacy Classes: A Holistic Framework of Student Evaluation

Stephan J. Macaluso

Electronic Information Librarian
SUNY NEW PALTZ
ref@newpaltz.edu

Introduction

Authentic assessment is the evaluation of student learning through real-life, "authentic" tasks. Authentic tasks may include projects, journals, process writing, demonstrations, or any number of interactive exercises. These activities challenge the student to apply knowledge in complex and creative ways (Fischer, 5). Some tasks provide insight into information-gathering behaviors, e.g., process writing and research logs. Others simulate the way work is accomplished in the business environment, e.g., team-based projects and demonstrations. Authentic evaluation techniques, like rubrics, enable us to see new facets of student progress. Summative compilations of student work, like portfolios, convey a vivid picture of what the student has accomplished during the semester. Because they evaluate student-learning processes, they integrate well into semester-length information literacy courses.

A music department faculty member and I created a 14-week information literacy experience for undergraduates who would write a senior thesis in music history. Our primary goal was to immerse the students in the research process and to expose them to the modes of inquiry, writing, and research that were common to the arts. We wanted to create an ongoing dialogue with the students and mentor their research in a way that their applied music instructors nurtured their repertoire. Finally, we wanted to develop a means to evaluate the students' learning outcomes in a way that was comparable to their applied music classes. These would provide opportunities for the students to express themselves and critique each other in a collegial environment. We used a variety of authentic assessment strategies to meet these goals. Authentic assessment strategies also transformed the classroom experience. Interviews and instructor surveys provided us with frequent, valuable feedback, while peer critiques and collaborative projects energized the course.

Authentic Assessment and Information Literacy

Authentic tasks and evaluation strategies measure student progress and growth. Several authors have linked holistic assessment with critical thinking or information literacy. Donham and Stein (1999, 227) have written that students become lifelong learners when they can assess their own successes and shortcomings in applying information to problem solving and decision-making. Fischer (26) has suggested that assignments measure the student's ability to understand a task, make decisions, apply problem-solving strategies, verify solutions, make connection, and give examples. Authentic tasks should challenge the student's ability to recall, explain, analyze, challenge [others], communicate, synthesize, and invent new uses for information (Stripling 1993, 47). These suggest a close correlation with the "Big Six" information literacy skills discussed by Eisenberg and Berkowitz (1990)—defining a task, formulating search strategies, and then locating, using, synthesizing, and evaluating information.

Information literacy courses prepare students to use information in real-world situations. It is not surprising that authentic assessment strategies fit well with the ACRL Information Literacy Competency Standards for Higher Education (2000). Below are some examples of ACRL standards and performance indicators, with the authentic tasks that can be implemented to meet them:

- Students should devise a realistic research plan and timeline; they should organize and manage information (Standard 1, Performance Indicator 3 and Standard 2, Indicator 5). *Process logs* and other journaling techniques can help achieve this goal.
- Students should be able to summarize and synthesize information (Standard 3, Indicators 1 and 3). *Authentic writing* like abstracting, annotated bibliographies, and reaction essays can indicate student mastery of this area.
- Students should be able to repackage and communicate information, and use information in class discussions (Standard 4, Indicators 1 and 3 and Standard 3, Indicator 6). *Projects*, *demonstrations*, *panel discussions*, and *peer review* opportunities can help meet this objective in a real-world manner.

Challenges to Authentic Assessment in Information Literacy Programs

Authentic assessment can require a large investment of preparation and class time. Authentic tasks and grading policies should be clearly articulated to students. Instructors should also be aware of issues of objectivity and reliability in grading.

It is time-consuming but essential that students buy into alternative assessment. The instructor should articulate expectations clearly, share "model" assignments with the class, and make sure students understand evaluation tools, e.g., rubrics. The instructor must be available outside class for interviews and consultations. Individual student attention becomes more challenging as class size increases. Finally, students must be given time for in-class reflection. Journaling can take considerable class time (Mark and Jacobson, 1995; Thomas, 130) but it provides the instructor with beneficial feedback. Additionally, peer instruction and critique allow students to learn from each other and enables the instructor to offer more individual attention to students.

Many authentic tasks, like journals and peer critiques, are not formally graded. This may be a new experience for students. Students are used to having an "average" and may not know how to interpret critiqued but ungraded assignments. Authentic evaluation strategies can be combined with graded pen-and-paper tests to create a multifaceted grading framework that makes the student comfortable.

Authentic Tasks

Student Projects

Authentic projects encourage students to locate, synthesize, and repackage information. Projects like demonstrations and poster sessions compel students to answer questions posed by their peers and instructors. This engages them in higher order thinking.

Students in our music research class compiled a "webliography" of sources on a composer. They later demonstrated their search techniques and reasons why the sources were useful to an invited audience of faculty and fellow students. Students reported that this was a worthwhile learning experience that helped codify what they had learned in class.

Other authentic projects include

- Creating a model web site and explaining why it meets criteria discussed in class
- Poster presentations, e.g., "How to Create an Abstract" or "What is Keyword Searching?"
- Debates and panel discussions in which sources must be quoted
- "Become the Teacher," e.g., demonstrate how to cite an Internet source

Instructors should consider projects that enable students to describe their research processes visually. In our class, students used a computer-drawing program to create a multicolor map of keywords and concepts within an article. This later helped them create an article abstract. Other well-known "visuals" include Venn diagrams and research process flowcharts.

Authentic and Process Writing

Authentic writing assignments relate directly to a course of study or are formats that are found frequently in the college experience. Authentic writing tends to be short so drafts can be reviewed frequently. Some examples of authentic writing include reaction essays, annotated bibliographies, and article reviews. Students in the music research class created article abstracts, concert notes, and a concert review. They handed in drafts on a weekly basis; some were peer-critiqued in class while the instructor reviewed others via e-mail.

A subset of authentic writing is process writing. Process writing involves giving attention to the individual components of the writing process. Stripling (1993, 51) argues that the evaluator can better understand student information gathering and synthesis by evaluating the constituent parts of a paper—the thesis statement, research plan, outline, annotated bibliography, abstracts and reviews—rather than assigning the term paper they would create.

A research prospectus is an excellent cumulative exercise (Nilson, 175). Prospecti are generally short (2–3 pages) and are a common mode of scholarly communication–it should therefore be easy to produce samples and critique numerous drafts. A prospectus can indicate a student's mastery of information gathering, synthesis, writing and citation style, and their ability to plan a course of endeavor. A research prospectus can also be used later in the student's program. The music department and I have discussed the possibility of a "best research prospectus" competition among music majors.

Authentic Methods of Grading and Evaluation

There are many ways to evaluate student learning. Frequent, multidimensional assessment of student progress provides insight into the students' learning styles, as well as the instructor's ability to convey the course content. Kirk (2000, 12) and Donham and Stein (1999, 222) have surmised that tools like student portfolios, observation, self-evaluations, conferences, and questionnaires can evaluate both the student and the information literacy program as a whole. Students in the music research class were evaluated using a number of assessment tools.

Rubrics and Checklists

Evaluating authentic projects can be a challenge as many factors can influence the overall grade. Authentic assessment can easily appear subjective (O'Neil 1992, 18). In order to be more objective, the instructor can evaluate the project using a rubric. Rubrics use carefully constructed criteria to quantify student work. Well-constructed rubrics provide easy-to-read scoring criteria from which to determine a numerical grade. When the rubric is shared and discussed in class before the assignment is given, it can encourage questions and spell out exactly what is expected. Students can use the rubric as a guide while performing an assignment.

Often, rubrics can be generated from criteria agreed upon in class. Rubrics designed with student input motivate them and helps the instructor frame the criteria in "student language" (Donham and Stein, 1999, 216). For example, a class might develop a list of qualities common to informative web sites after in-class demonstrations and discussion. A rubric can be based upon those qualities, and the students could use it as a framework while building their own sites.

Constructing a Rubric

Space does not permit us to explore the many variations on rubric creation. Most are created like this:

1. Create categories that demonstrate the key elements by which to judge the project. Categories for an informative web page might be: Use of Color and Graphics, Neatness, Text Accuracy, and Links.
2. Assign criteria for each category, starting from the point of excellence, then
3. Assign scores, in descending order of excellence, for each criterion.
4. An often-used option is to assign a label for each degree of excellence. For example, students who earn a score of 4 in any given category may be called "Capable," while 3 through 1 could be "Developing," "Beginning," and "Novice."

A rubric for the Use of Color and Graphics category of a student-created web site might be:

Score   **Degree of excellence**   **Criteria**

4. Capable. Background and text colors are complementary and easy to read. Graphics are small and pertinent to the page. On average, the page takes less than 10 seconds to load.

3. Developing. Background colors and text colors are good. Page is easily readable. Graphics are small and pertinent. On average, the page takes between 10 and 20 seconds to load.

2. Beginning. Background and text colors make reading somewhat difficult. Graphics may be a little too large, but are pertinent. On average, the page takes between 20 and 30 seconds to load.

1. Novice. Colors are not complementary and reading is difficult. Graphics are too large or are gratuitous. On average, the page takes longer than 30 seconds to load.

Many might argue that each category above attempts to measure too much at once; there is no gray area for those with large, gratuitous graphics but no other issues. Certainly, the categories and criteria can be subdivided as needs arise, as long as the criteria do not become so specific as to inhibit grading. The more categories and the more specific the criteria, the more difficult the rubric will be to use. About 4–5 categories and about 4–5 evaluation criteria should be used for any given assignment.

Students in the music research class looked at numerous web sites and devised a similar list of criteria for use in assembling their composer webliographies. These criteria—e.g., the intended audience, the tone or "slant" of an article, the author's qualifications—were later assembled into a checklist-style rubric. The checklist is based on 100 points, and was used as a student guide and grading tool during their web site demonstrations (see Supplementary Materials).

Self-assessment checklists accomplish similar goals, in that they act as guides to what is expected in a given assignment. Students in the music research class used a checklist like this one while creating their abstracts.

Abstracting Checklist

_____I incorporated _____ keywords from the article into my abstract.
_____I have spell checked my abstract. There are no spelling errors.
_____The abstract is _____ words long. It conforms to the maximum number of 75.
_____My abstract includes a phrase that summarizes the "background" section of the article.
_____My abstract includes a phrase that speaks to the author's methodology.
_____My abstract includes a phrase that summarizes the author's conclusions.

Peer Review

Peer review enables students to get feedback from colleagues who are undertaking similar projects. Students can be counted on to give each other an honest assessment of their work (Stripling 1993, 43). Peer evaluation encourages students to ask questions, as student evaluators apply their own understanding of a topic to the work of one of their peers (Glover 1994, 185).

Peer critique should take place in class, and students being evaluated should have ample opportunity to clarify points and defend their research. Ideally, students should present several drafts of an assignment to their peers—this is admittedly a challenge with larger classes.

Students can evaluate each other's work with a checklist, or by writing comments on photocopied drafts. These would be returned to the student being evaluated after class. The evaluated student should make notes and later reflect upon the experience: what can be improved and what peers especially liked about their work. One way to codify student reflection is through a response form (see Supplementary Materials).

Our music students were acquainted with peer review through their lessons and ensemble classes. Drafts of abstracts, bibliographies, and concert notes were distributed via e-mail. Another copy was projected onto a whiteboard in the classroom. Students and the instructor "marked up" the whiteboard copy while the student being evaluated took notes.

Journaling

Journaling compels students to self-assess and outline future steps in their research. Such reflective writings provide the instructor with insightful feedback that can be used during student interviews and classes.

Journals can be informal—anonymous loose sheets with student responses to instructor questions–or can be formally recorded on index cards or in a notebook. Process logs or research logs are examples of formal journals, where students record class notes, research findings, and reflections on their work. Some journals are made up of folded pieces of paper; one column for notes, bibliographic citations, etc., and the other for reflections and annotations.

Journals need not be graded, but instructors should collect and read them often. Students will be more motivated to use their journals if they know that their work will be read. Formal journal entries can be discussed with the student directly, while anonymous ones can be read between class meetings. Students can be motivated and encouraged to write their opinions and reflections if the instructor frequently asks summative and reflective questions for in-class response.

Below are some examples of journaling questions that might be asked in an information literacy or research class. They are applicable to both formal and informal situations. I have divided the list into "discovery" questions, ones that serve to highlight student research challenges, and ones that help students to summarize what they have learned.

Discovery Questions
- The most interesting thing I found as a result of this demo/lesson/assignment is...
- Today I set out looking for... I found... This is how I found it...
- As a result of today's lesson/demo/assignment, I have changed my mind about...
- This is how today's lesson fits into my research plans...
- I think I used (this resource) very well...
- I would like to know more about...

Research Challenge Questions
- One problem I met with today (during this assignment) is... This is how I tried to solve it...
- This is the point where my research hit a dead end...

- The piece of the research puzzle that is still missing is... (ask the student to visualize and describe the "perfect" information resource)
- I feel I need practice with (e.g., this resource)...
- This is not working well for me...

Summative Questions

- This is what I accomplished in the library today...
- The top 10 (5?) things I learned about this database are...
- One concept I feel I'll remember most from this demo/assignment/lesson is...
- The next step in my research is...

The music research class did not have enough time for frequent journaling, but similar questions were asked during instructor evaluations and interviews. (See below)

Interviews

Instructor-student interviews (or "conferences") should be compulsory and should take place frequently. Interviews build dialogue; they can be used to discuss students' research projects, frustrations, and journal entries. Instructors can encourage student dialogue through open-ended questions, like:

- How did you find this information? Describe the process.
- How do you think your research is progressing?
- How are you recording/organizing the materials you find? Describe whatever system you're using.
- What have been the most frustrating parts of this class? (Computer use, database commands, etc.)

If the student is to assemble a portfolio as a final project, such conferences can be "portfolio check-ups," in which potential portfolio elements, presentation styles, and revisions can be addressed. The instructor should encourage the student to show the portfolio to his/her peers, for additional opinions.

Because of our small class size, it was fairly easy to meet with students in person, via phone, and by e-mail. We discussed how student projects were progressing, and how the class related to the students' upcoming senior projects. The interviews brought to light additional class topics; one student was interested in learning to use her Internet browser and PowerPoint more effectively, while another student requested information about interlibrary loan services.

Instructor Evaluations

Instructors often distribute surveys or questionnaires to determine their session's effectiveness. Short (fewer than 20 questions) surveys distributed midway through a semester-length class can offer valuable insight into the students' learning and perceptions of the course.

Like the questions used in journaling or in interviews, survey questions should challenge the students to reflect upon their most memorable moments of the class, the concepts or tools they have struggled with, and their overall opinions of the course. The responses can act as talking points for future classes. Consider how reflective questions like: "Describe one research tool that you have learned in this class," or "What has been the most confusing lesson for you?" can inform the content and pace of the remainder of the semester.

We impressed upon our students that their opinions were valuable and that their surveys would affect the content and delivery of the class, but not their grades. They were given a week to reflect and respond to the evaluation questions. In order to promote their anonymity, they returned their completed evaluations to the library reference desk in sealed envelopes with their names on them. A neutral party—a student assistant—collected the envelopes, recorded names, and then discarded the envelopes. While their responses are not graded, students received credit for returning their instructor survey. (See Supplementary Materials for a sample mid-term survey.)

Portfolios: A Cumulative, Reflective Exercise

When a semester's work is compiled into a portfolio, students have an opportunity to reflect upon their achievements, growth, and shortcomings during the semester. Compiling a portfolio also gives them the opportunity to use multimedia and presentation software in order to show off their work.

Portfolios are common in the professional world as job interview tools and for performance review. Portfolios have enjoyed great attention in art and as a holistic evaluation method in elementary reading and writing programs. At the college level, they are often used as an admissions tool and in teacher training programs. Portfolios have also been used in information literacy classes delivered via distance learning (Fourie and Van Niekirk, 1999, 333-352).

Portfolio elements can be collected into a binder, a file folder, a shoebox, or stored electronically on a disk or web site. There are many possible portfolio formats. They can be made up of completed, graded projects; required and optional elements; or they may contain a variety of process works. Portfolio elements can be arranged in strict chronological order, by achievement level, or by project or topic (Thomas, 1999, 140). Completed portfolios can be evaluated for neatness or completeness using a checklist or rubric. A portfolio may be evaluated by the instructor, or by an external committee. Instructors might also consider having the students submit their portfolios for peer review before the final submission.

When students decide what goes into their portfolios, they gain a sense of ownership over their grades (Farr and Tone 52, 59). Invite students to choose portfolio elements by suggesting some criteria. For example:
- This is my best project/work
- I enjoyed writing/compiling this
- This gave me the most trouble, or took the most revisions
- This is very well written
- This is the point when I discovered...
- This was a real turning point in my research/personal growth

- I want to remember this for later
- This still confuses me

Students in the music research class compiled their bibliographies, concert notes, abstracts, and even a digital video of their web site presentations into a portfolio. For them, portfolios were analogous to musical repertoire. Just as a student's repertoire was an often-performed sample of diverse musical styles, their portfolios were made up of writing and research samples they would use often in their academic careers. And just as a student's repertoire was composed of pieces that would improve with time and practice, their portfolio elements were evolving works in progress.

Handwritten works—journal entries, evaluations, class notes—were kept in file folders and maintained by the students themselves. Electronic copies of drafts, final revisions, saved web sites, e-mails, and digitized movies were compiled on floppy disks. These were showcased at the end of the semester and were graded according to the rubric found on the syllabus (see Supplementary Materials).

In general, portfolios should include a table of contents. This will enable the reviewer to move easily through the portfolio. The portfolio should also include a statement of ownership. Depending upon the course, this may be a letter of introduction, a summary, or a mission statement. These instruct the reviewer as to why elements were included in the portfolio, and give the student an opportunity to respond in writing to their class experiences. The student should also summarize or reflect upon their journal entries and peer comments.

Others portfolio elements may include:
- Search strategies (written, or drawn as flow charts or diagrams)
- Database search printouts. These may include written annotations.
- Printouts of pertinent e-mail communications with the instructor or classmates.
- All drafts of a given project or paper, and pertinent review forms. When drafts of a project accompany the final copy, the instructor and student can both reflect on how their work has improved with each revision, and if the student has taken the advice of peer reviewers. Drafts from some of the projects listed above (e.g., concert notes, abstracts, and bibliographies) should indicate improvement in writing and citation style.
- Works revised since their initial due-date. While "second chance" grading is at the discretion of the instructor, students may appreciate being able to revisit a project for the final portfolio (Fourie and Van Niekirk, 345).
- Pen-and-paper tests, surveys
- "Extra Credit." In addition to revising required work for the portfolio, students may opt to create a second bibliography, critique an additional web site, etc.
- Rubrics and checklists filled out by the student, colleagues or the instructor.
- PowerPoint presentations
- Hypermedia demonstrations, model web sites
- Electronic brochures, posters

Conclusion

Authentic assessment strategies can be incorporated into semester-length information literacy classes. Authentic tasks are "real life" assignments that introduce the student to the research process, and germinate an ongoing dialogue between the instructor and the student. Both the instructor and the student gain from reflective exercises like journals, peer review, and instructor assessments. Instructors gain a new perspective on their teaching as well as student progress while the student reflects upon their achievements as a researcher.

Sources:

Association of College and Research Libraries. *Information Literacy Competency Standards for Higher Education: Standards, Performance Indicators, and Outcomes.* January 18, 2000. http://www.ala.org/acrl/ilstandardlo.html—12 December 2000.

Baron, Mark A, and Floyd Boschee. *Authentic Assessment: The Key to Unlocking Student Success.* Lancaster, PA: Technomic, 1995.

Cizek, Gregory J. "Innovation or Enervation? Performance Assessment in Perspective." *Phi Delta Kappan* 72.9 (May 1991): 695–699.

Donham, Jean and Barbara Barnard Stein. "Assessment: A Tool for Developing Lifelong Learners." *Learning and Libraries in an Information Age: Principles and Practice.* Ed. Barbara K. Stripling. Englewood, CO: Libraries Unlimited, 1999. 206–228

Eisenberg, Michael B., and Robert E. Berkowitz. *Information Problem Solving: The Big Six Skills Approach to Library and Information Skills Instruction.* Norwood, NJ: Ablex, 1990.

Farr, Roger and Bruce Tone. *Portfolio and Performance Assessment: Helping Students Evaluate Their Progress as Readers and Writers.* Fort Worth, TX: Harcourt Brace College Publishers, 1994.

Fiderer, Adele. *35 Rubrics and Checklists to Assess Reading and Writing.* New York: Scholastic Professional Books, 1998.

Fischer, Cheryl and Rita King. *Authentic Assessment: A Guide to Implementation.* Thousand Oaks, CA: Corwin, 1995.

Fourie, Ina and Daleen van Niekirk. "Using Portfolio Assessment in a Module in Research Information Skills." *Education for Information* 17.4 (December 1999): 333–52.

Glover, Robert. "Assessing Information Skills Instruction." *The Reference Librarian* 44 (1994): 173–189.

Heiges, Janice M. "Portfolio for Doctoral Candidacy: A Veritable Alternative." *Situating Portfolios: Four Perspectives.* Ed. Kathleen Blake Yancey and Irwin Weiser. Logan, Utah: Utah State Press, 1997.

Kirk, Thomas G., Jr. Information Literacy, Assessment, and our Students. *LOEX News* 27.2 (Summer 2000): 3, 12.

Kurfiss, Joanne G. *Critical Thinking: Theory, Research, Practice, and Possibilities.* ASHE, 1988.

Leahy, Rick. "The Power of the Student Journal." *College Teaching* 33.3 (1985): 108–112.

Maeroff, Gene I. "Assessing Alternative Assessment." *Phi Delta Kappan* 73.4 (December 1991): 272–281.

Mark, Beth L. and Trudi E. Jacobson. "Teaching Anxious Students Skills for the Electronic Library." *College Teaching* 43.1 (Winter 1995): 28–31.

Mitchell, Ruth. *Testing for Learning: How New Approaches to Evaluation can Improve American Schools.* New York: Free Press, 1992.

Neuman, Delia. "Alternative Assessment: Promises and Pitfalls." *School Library Media Annual 1993.* Ed. Carol Collier Kulthau. 11. Englewood, CO: Libraries Unlimited, 1993. 13–21

Nilson, Linda B. *Teaching at its Best: A Research-based Resource for College Instructors.* Bolton, MA: Anker, 1998.

O'Neil, John. "Putting Performance Assessment to the Test." *Educational Leadership* 49.8 (May 1992): 14–19.

Pittendrigh, Adele S and Patrick C. Jobes. "Teaching Across the Curriculum: Critical Communication in the Sociology Classroom." *Teaching Sociology* 11.3 (April 1984): 281–296.

Stripling, Barbara K. "Practicing Authentic Assessment in the School Library." *School Library Media Annual 1993.* Ed. Carol Collier Kulthau. 11. Englewood, CO: Libraries Unlimited, 1993. 40–57.

Thomas, Nancy Pickering. *Information Literacy and Information Skills Instruction: Applying Research to Practice in the School Media Center.* Englewood, CO: Libraries Unlimited, 1999.

White, Edward M. "Holisticism." *College Composition and Communication* 35.4 (December 1984): 400–409.

_____. *Teaching and Assessing Writing.* San Francisco: Josey-Bass, 1985.

Wickcliff, Gregory. "A Hypertext Authoring Course, Portfolio Assessment, and Diversity." *Situating Portfolios: Four Perspectives* Ed. Kathleen Blake Yancey and Irwin Weiser. Logan, Utah: Utah State Press, 1997.

Worthen, Blaine R. "Critical Issues That Determine the Future of Alternative Assessment." *Phi Delta Kappan* 74.6 (February 1993): 444–454.

Supplementary Materials

The materials in this section have been placed on the accompanying disk so they can easily be copied and/or modified to fit the needs of individual libraries and instructors.

- Syllabus for the Undergraduate Music Research Class
- Rubric Grading Checklist
- Abstract Writing Checklist
- Journaling Questions
- Peer Critique Response Form
- Mid-Term Instructor Assessment
- How to Create a Student Portfolio

Critical Thinking in an Information World

Ru Story-Huffman

Public Services Librarian
Cumberland College
rshuff@cc.cumber.edu

Circumstances of the Instruction

This instruction session has been developed to enhance any information literacy curriculum and will be part of a curriculum proposal for an information literacy component on a college campus. It can be used in a 50-minute session for undergraduate education, but can be tailored to meet the needs of a specific class or time frame. A librarian can conduct the session, or it can be team-taught with another member of the college faculty.

The instruction session is devoted to enhancing information literacy skills by including critical thinking components. Developing reflective judgment skills, engaging inquiry learning and seeking information beyond the classroom are all indicative of critical thinking skills. This exercise is partially web-based to further enhance the skill of resources evaluation. Students will devise strategies for locating and evaluating information through critical thinking skills. When combined with critical thinking, the concept of information literacy takes on an added element and further enhances skills being stressed in the learning outcomes.

Objectives of the Instruction

- Augment information literacy skills
- Develop critical thinking skills necessary for academic excellence
- To go beyond the traditional locating and retrieval of books and journal articles necessary to complete a research assignment
- To use technology as a tool to increase learning
- To enhance research techniques

Components of the Instruction

Preparation

Before beginning this activity, it is necessary to conduct research on the chosen topic. This research will need to include print materials specific to the organization and resources from the Internet. In addition, students will be directed to locate information using a variety of Internet search engines. It is important to remember that each time the assignment is given, you need to be certain the resources are still available and contain the specific information desired. Through questions designed to stimulate critical thinking, students will investigate a subject. They are presented with a hypothetical situation, and asked to locate information, make decisions, and evaluate information. With the question format, students should be academically stimulated and encouraged to evaluate and critically consider information being presented. Information literacy skills are enhanced, as students are directed to locate, research, synthesis and evaluate information.

This assignment can be presented as a lab assignment or outside of class. This assignment can also be presented as a web-based assignment, in which case you would need to mount the assignment on the appropriate server. Also, note the URL to provide students with the location where the assignment can be found.

Presentation

Students participating in the exercise might be enrolled in a campus information literacy class, or the session can be presented as part of a regular class session. Also, if done in a lab situation, it would be advantageous to have a computer and video projector unit so the instructor can have the specific web pages on the screen that students will see on their computers.

Hands-on Activity

If presented in a paper format, students would take their questions to the library or media center to locate and evaluate information. If web-based, students will be directed to follow the web-based assignment during the class session. In addition, an element could be implemented that students complete outside of the classroom situation.

Variations

As stated in the Preparation section, mount the assignment on the web if this is the desired route of instruction. For the purposes of this exercise, the assignments included in this section can also be found at the following URLs:

> *Critical Thinking in an Information World*
> http://www.cumber.edu/library/Li/critical.htm
>
> *Decisions, Decisions*
> http://www.cumber.edu/library/Li/critical2.htm

If the activity is to be completed in paper format, use the handouts that accompany this chapter (see Supplementary Materials).

Evaluation

Successful evaluation of this exercise will be an ongoing process. Critical thinking, as defined by Barry K. Beyer, is the "ability to assess authenticity, accuracy and/or worth of knowledge, claims and arguments." Critical thinking and information literacy skills are not obtained in a one-time classroom situation. Information literacy, as well as critical thinking, must be nurtured over time and enforced through lecture, questions, decision-making, assignments and everyday activities. For the purpose of this particular assignment, the assessment process can begin by noting the scores on completed assignments.

Sources:

Beyer, Barry K. "Critical Thinking: What Is It?" *Social Education* 49 (1985): 270–276.

Jones, Debra. *Exploring the Internet Using Critical Thinking Skills, A Self-Paced Workbook for Learning to Effectively Use the Internet and Evaluate Online Information.* New York: Neal-Schuman Publishers, 1998.

The Center for Critical Thinking: Colleges and Universities
http://www.criticalthinking.org/university/default.html

Teacher Talk at Capital–Critical Thinking and Information Literacy
http://capital2.capital.edu/faculty/afields/CRITTHNK.HTM

Critical Thinking in an Online World
http://www.library.ucsb.edu/untangle/jones.html

Supplementary Materials

The materials in this section have been placed on the accompanying disk so they can easily be copied and/or modified to fit the needs of individual libraries and instructors.

- Critical Thinking in an Information World
- Decisions, Decisions

Notes:

Section 2— Library and Research Skills and Strategies

Tour and Tell

Covering the Catalog

LC Potpourri

Library vs. Bookstore: Field Trip!

A Primer for the 2000 United States Presidential Election: An Integrated Approach to Presenting Library Resources in Information Literacy Activities

Translating a Citation

Teaching Print and Electronic Reference Sources Through Student Presentations

Writing Annotations

Evaluation of Sources Through Their Citations

Let's Play Telephone

Citation Scan; Scholarly or Popular?

Charting Your Research

Teaching First-Year Students Coping Skills for Information Overload in the Virtual Library

Different Types of Information Organizations (Including Libraries)

What's Wrong Citation Style Exercise

Six Sources in 30 Minutes

Using Questions to Evaluate, Or, If at First You Don't Deceive, Try, Try Again

Pick a Number, Any Number: An Information Review Activity

Tour and Tell

SARA BARON

Instructional Technology Center, Director
Coordinator of Library Instruction
UNIVERSITY OF MASSACHUSETTS BOSTON
sara.baron@umb.edu

JANET DiPAOLO

Reference Librarian
UNIVERSITY OF MASSACHUSETTS BOSTON
janet.dipaolo@umb.edu

Circumstances of the Instruction

This exercise, suitable for the first or second class of an information literacy course, gives students an active way to explore the library. The group component is designed to help students meet other classmates, increase comfort levels with "wandering around the library" (safety in numbers), and, also allows for peer instruction.
- Optimal number of students: 24
- Preparation Time: 10 minutes
- Activity Time: 45 minutes

Objectives of the Instruction

The students will:
- learn the physical layout of the library;
- locate service points/areas where they can get help;
- practice public speaking skills; and
- develop team-working skills.

Components of the Instruction

Preparation

The instructor brings to class copies of self-guided library tours or library floor plans.

Hands-on Activity

A. Create groups; each group should contain no more than 4 students.
B. Inform the students that they will be working in small groups that will require a report back to the entire class.
C. Distribute copies of a self-guided library tour or a library floor plan to all the students. Assign each group a portion of the self-guided tour or library floor plan. Instruct the group that they have 20 minutes to visit their assigned area of the library. While they are on tour, students should learn all they can about that area.

D. After the groups return to class, ask each group to tell the rest of the class what they found in their area. However, they must provide additional information that is not included on the tour materials. Questions to provoke discussion may include:

What did you see that was not on the tour?

Did anything in this area surprise you?

Did you find something you had no idea existed?

Did you see something you will use later in this class, or another class?

Was there anyone close by to help you?

Were there signs to help you?

E. End the discussion by encouraging the students to:

Explore other areas of the library.

Remember what they learned from their peers.

Evaluation

The instructor may choose to do all or a selection of the following evaluation methods.

- Ask the students to write a one-minute essay answering the following question: Do you have enough information to find your way around the library and get help if you need it? Please explain.

- Class vote: Have the class vote on the most exciting or unique thing they learned from the group presentations.

- Pop quiz: Have a brief pop-quiz of 10 questions related to library areas and service points. This can be done verbally or in writing. Questions might include:

The reference desk is on the 6th floor. True or False.

The music collection also has videos. True or False.

What are the three floors that have copy machines?

- Follow-up assignment: Have students complete the rest of the tour, as they will only have toured one area. Instruct them to write a very brief paper addressing the same questions raised in class (see Activity D).

Sources:

The Healey Library Self-Guided Tour may be viewed on the Library's web site—http://www.lib.umb.edu/LibraryTour/

Covering the Catalog

SARA BARON

Instructional Technology Center, Director
Coordinator of Library Instruction
HEALEY LIBRARY UNIVERSITY OF MASSACHUSETTS BOSTON
sara.baron@umb.edu

JANET DiPAOLO

Reference Librarian
HEALEY LIBRARY UNIVERSITY OF MASSACHUSETTS BOSTON
janet.dipaolo@umb.edu

Circumstances of the Instruction

This activity is designed to compliment a discussion of subject headings, keywords, and general library catalog searching. In small groups, students will sharpen their critical and creative thinking skills by brainstorming keywords and subject headings that best describe a particular book. They will discover that attributing keywords to a title is easier than attributing subject headings (controlled vocabulary). They will then search for their book in the library catalog using their keywords and subject headings.

- Optimal number of students: 24
- Preparation time: 10 minutes
- Activity time: 40 minutes

Objectives of the Instruction

The students will:
- learn the differences between subject heading (controlled vocabulary) and keyword searching;
- discover the complexity of Library of Congress subject headings;
- learn that books with a similar subject are shelved in similar call number ranges;
- discover the importance of complete citation information;
- practice critical and creative thinking skills;
- learn the basics of online catalog searching;
- practice public speaking skills; and
- develop team-working skills.

Components of the Instruction

Preparation

The instructor brings to class:
a) ten book jackets,
b) *Library of Congress Subject Headings*, and
c) copies of a one-page overview of the *Library of Congress Classification System*.

Hands-on Activity

A. Create groups. Each group should contain no more than 4 students.

B. Distribute one book jacket to each group.

C. Groups will have 10 minutes to answer the following, using only the information presented on the book jacket:

> What terminology describes this book? Select 2–4 terms.
> In which call number range do you think this book is located?
> How could you search for this book in the catalog?

D. After groups complete the questions, instruct them to search the library catalog for the book using their answers to the questions in the order presented.

E. During the discussion following the activity, students will discover if their perceptions of keywords and subject headings are correct.
- The instructor can illustrate the complexity of subject headings by showing a page from the *Library of Congress Subject Headings* on a document camera or overhead projector.
- Students will learn that books with a similar subject are shelved in similar call number ranges.
- Students will discover the importance of complete citation information. For example, it is easier to locate a book when you know an author's name or the title, rather than using a subject approach.

F. If there is time, introduce Boolean logic concepts. Have the students connect keywords from the first part of the activity. A more extensive discussion of Boolean logic could occur at a later time with references back to this activity.

Evaluation

The instructor may choose to do all or a selection of the following evaluation methods.
- Ask the students to write a one-minute essay answering the following question: What is the difference between searching by subject headings and searching by keywords? List two examples of when you would use each.
- Have students compare subject headings in the library catalog with subject headings in a subject database, for example, *Expanded Academic Index*. Why are the terms similar or different?

- Pop-quiz: Have students change keyword phrases and questions into Boolean statements. For example:
    1) "Why does pollution cause asthma?" becomes "pollution and asthma;"
    2) "Effects of violence and crime on kids" becomes "violence or crime and children;"
    3) "Artwork in Latin American countries other than Mexico" becomes "art? and Latin America? not Mexico."

Supplementary Material

The material in this section has been placed on the accompanying disk so it can easily be copied and/or modified to fit the needs of individual libraries and instructors.

- One-page Overview of the *Library of Congress Classification System.*

Notes:

70

LC Potpourri

SARA BARON

Instructional Technology Center, Director
Coordinator of Library Instruction
HEALEY LIBRARY UNIVERSITY OF MASSACHUSETTS BOSTON
sara.baron@umb.edu

JANET DiPAOLO

Reference Librarian
HEALEY LIBRARY UNIVERSITY OF MASSACHUSETTS BOSTON
janet.dipaolo@umb.edu

Circumstances of the Instruction

This activity, in which students are instructed to locate library material, is designed to follow an explanation of subject heading structure, call number order, and an explanation of the physical layout of the library.

The exercise gives students the opportunity to understand the relationship between library materials with similar call numbers appearing in different locations and in different formats. The activity is most suitable for freshmen at the beginning of a semester.

- Optimal number of students: 24
- Preparation time: 30 minutes
- Activity time: 1 hour

Objectives of the Instruction

- Students will understand the relationship between library materials with similar call numbers appearing in different locations and in different formats.
- Students will understand the differences between popular magazines and scholarly journals.
- Students will practice locating library material.
- Students will build team-working skills.
- Students will practice public speaking skills.

Components of the Instruction

Preparation

The instructor prepares and brings to class
- library location guides and
- packets of three or four index cards (see Supplementary Materials for an example of one packet).

Each packet covers one general subject area. Be certain that some packets include a mixture of popular and scholarly material while other packets contain only scholarly material. Record one title and call number on each index card. Each title should have a different location. For example, a circulating book; a reference book; a current periodical; a bound periodical; a video, etc.

Hands-on Activity

A. Create groups. Each group should contain no more than 4 students.

B. Inform the students that they will contribute to a group project that requires a report back to the entire class.

C. Distribute one packet of index cards to each group.

D. Instruct each group that they have 15 minutes to locate the items in their packet.

E. After the groups reassemble in the class, ask them to share with the rest of the class what they found. Questions to provoke discussion may include:
   - Did you find something of interest to you?
   - How does the reference book you found differ from the circulating book?
   - Did anyone find what they might consider to be a scholarly journal?
   - What is a scholarly journal and how does it differ from a popular-interest magazine?
   - Did you find something you would use for this class or for another class?

Evaluation

The instructor may choose to do all or a selection of the following evaluation methods.
- Have students e-mail five sources on their research topic to their professor. Sources must be from different library locations (reference, periodicals, etc.) and/or in different formats (book, video, etc.).
- Pop quiz: Have a brief pop quiz on identifying the differences between popular magazines and scholarly journals. Using a document camera or an overhead projector, display a list of magazine and journal titles. Choose a subject and ask the class which periodical would be most appropriate to use. For example: Which would you use to find a current research article on the treatment of sprained ankles on athletes? The periodicals to display could be *The Journal of Sports Medicine* and *Sports Illustrated*.
- Pop quiz: Have a brief pop quiz on the location of library material and on library policy. Questions may include:
   Where are periodicals located in the library?
   Does a bound periodical have the same call number as a current/unbound periodical?
   Can reference books be borrowed for home use?
   Will a main stacks book and an oversized book on the same topic have similar or different call numbers?
   Does the book, *Merchant of Venice* by Shakespeare, have the same call number as the video?
- Group activity: Give each group a selection of popular interest magazines and scholarly journals. Ask groups to explain the differences. For example: colors, pictures, advertisements, frequency of publication, length of article, etc.

Supplementary Materials

The sample index cards have been placed on the accompanying disk so they can easily be copied and/or modified to fit the needs of individual libraries and instructors. The Library Bookmark will only be found on http://library.albany.edu/usered/concepts.

- Packet of 3–4 Index Cards
- Library Bookmark

Notes:

Library vs. Bookstore: Field Trip!

SUE ANN BRAINARD
Reference/Instruction Librarian
SUNY GENESEO
brainard@geneseo.edu

KIMBERLY DAVIES
Reference/Instruction Librarian
SUNY GENESEO
davies@geneseo.edu

Circumstances of the Instruction

Recent articles in library publications have highlighted the phenomenon of college students preferring to use large bookstores to do research and as study space. Many students love bookstores and find using an academic library intimidating. In an attempt to illustrate the differences between bookstores and academic libraries, a field trip to the nearest "super" bookstore helps develop positive attitudes about, and a respect for, the academic library. Students discover for themselves differences between academic libraries and bookstores, besides being able to borrow books for free from the library and to obtain assistance from professional librarians.

This class trip works well with fifteen or fewer students, and is ideal with two instructors. It is probably best when the nearest large bookstore is within an hour's drive of the campus. An hour in the bookstore is enough time for students to complete the desired tasks and do some browsing as well. If possible, this trip can be combined with a meal at a restaurant; this really perks up students who are tired of eating in dining halls!

Objectives of the Instruction

- Students will understand that the lack of a catalog with subject headings to guide the user to a short list of books is a disadvantage in a bookstore.
- Students will understand that the lack of call numbers in a bookstore greatly impacts the time it takes to locate books.
- Students will articulate that the type of books and the number of books found in a bookstore differ from those on college library shelves.
- Students will recognize the difference in attitude, competence, and motivation between the staff at the bookstore and reference librarians.
- Students will articulate that the very nature of research, characterized by the consultation of many resources, hard thought, discussion, and writing and re-writing usually conducted under a time constraint, is different from the very nature of shopping.
- Students will interact with librarians in a social setting, which will dispel the pre-conceived ideas of stereotypical librarians.

Components of the Instruction

Preparation

The instructor must canvass the students to find a time when most can leave the campus for several hours. This will probably end up being at night, or possibly even on a weekend, since there will be fewer class conflicts at those times. It may be impossible to find a time when all will attend; choose the time when most can attend. Assign a make-up activity for those who miss the field trip (see Supplementary Materials).

A campus van should be reserved in advance. Prepare slips of paper with reference-type questions or research topics, one for each member of the class going on the trip (see Supplementary Materials). The instructor should have a stack of blank index cards ready to hand out at the end of the trip.

Presentation

Upon arrival at the bookstore, the instructor should refrain from explaining the layout, as it is best to let the students experience the unfamiliar bookstore the same way they experienced the unfamiliar academic library at the beginning of their first semester. Each student should be given a slip of paper on which a different research question or topic has been written. Without further ado, split the group up, directing each student to answer their question independently. Tell them to meet back at the front door in 30 minutes.

When the 30 minutes are up, either gather students at a quiet spot in the store or outside in the van if discussion is impossible in the store. The instructor should hand out blank index cards, and have each student write on the card three things they like about a bookstore and three things they like about a library. The instructor should collect these to use later in order to evaluate the learning experience. Students should one-by-one describe their experiences in the bookstore, and tell if they found the answer to the research question they were given. They should also explain how they found it, and if they asked for help. The instructor should take notes, determining by the student's words if the objectives were met. If the four key differences between bookstores and libraries (see Objectives of the Instruction) do not come up naturally in the discussion of their experiences, the instructor can guide the discussion by pointedly asking these questions:

- How easy was it to find the right section of the store? Were the signs easy to follow? Was the right section easier to find than in the library? Why do you think that is so?
- Once you were in the right section, how were the books arranged? How did you find what you were looking for? Browse? Flip through books? If you were in the library, how would you find what you wanted? Would you have used the online catalog first to find call numbers of appropriate books?
- Were the books on the bookstore shelves appropriate for research projects? In other words, were they scholarly? Were there in-depth, critical explorations of topics? How about in the library? Do you have difficulty understanding some of the scholarly books in the library?
- Did you ask for help? Was it easy to find someone to ask? Did they know how to help you? Were they pleasant? Are the librarians in the library pleasant, helpful, and easy to find? Do they usually know about the topics you ask for help on? Did the bookstore staff have some

knowledge of the topic for which you were searching? How much time did the bookstore staff dedicate to your question? How about the librarians at the library? How was your own attitude or mood as you searched through the store? Did you feel stressed? What did you observe in the others around you? Did anybody look stressed? How does the furniture and lighting compare to the library? How do you feel when you are searching for information in the library? Are the others in a library usually anxious about what they are doing? Does being around them cause you stress? Do you think having better furniture and lighting would naturally decrease the tension when using the library? Is it the activities of research that makes a library uncomfortable, or just the furniture, lighting, size, and signage?

After the discussion, drive back to campus.

Evaluation

To evaluate the success of the trip, the instructor should look at the index cards soon after returning to the campus when the discussion is still fresh in mind. Try to determine from the responses whether students learned some of the key differences between libraries and bookstores on their own, before the discussion took place. Next, the instructor should carefully consult notes taken while students were reporting. Determine if students met the objectives without being prompted by the instructor. That would be optimal, but the session should not be considered a failure if the students needed a lot of prompting by the instructor. Any issues that arise from the responses on the cards that did not come up in the discussion should be discussed in the next class session.

Supplementary Materials

The materials in this section have been placed on the accompanying disk so they can easily be copied and/or modified to fit the needs of individual libraries and instructors.

- Questions for Students to Answer at the Bookstore
- An Alternate Assignment for Students Who Cannot Attend the Trip

Notes:

A Primer for the 2000 United States Presidential Election: An Integrated Approach to Presenting Library Resources in Information Literacy Activities

CATHERINE COLLINS
Business Reference Librarian
TEXAS A & M UNIVERSITY - COMMERCE
catherine_collins@tamu-commerce.edu

Circumstances of the Instruction

Traditional library activities often treat library resources as isolated tools. Students are asked to locate some fact in one resource, then another fact using a different resource. The catalog, online databases, web resources, reference books, government documents, serials, and the main stacks are treated as independent resources. The result is that many students fail to see the relationship between all resources. Rather than evaluate resources and select the best resource(s) for the task at hand, students may rely on only a few resources for much of their university career.

This information literacy activity was designed for 24 students in a research course at a public university. This one-hour credit-bearing course is required for all entering freshmen and is co-taught by a librarian and a faculty member in the English Department. During the initial interview with the librarian, the professor specifically requested that this activity should go beyond the traditional library activity and that it should utilize the primary print and electronic resources available to students at the university. After a follow-up interview with the professor, the librarian determined that the activity must also require students to research an issue relevant to both their studies and their lives and, most importantly, require students to think critically about the resources that they use. Both the librarian and the professor agreed that if such an activity were to be of any benefit, it must also illustrate the relationship between library resources.

The resulting activity was a primer for the 2000 United States presidential election. The primer requires students to complete a series of tasks and to answer a series of questions that accompany each task. The questions and tasks that make up the activity are designed in such a way as to walk students through the research process and to require them to analyze, and then comment on, each resource. Tasks rely on multiple resources and each task builds on information gleaned from the previous tasks. While many of the questions are objective, some are subjective and cannot be "graded," although these questions can be used to evaluate the level of a student's understanding. The entire activity, including planning and grading, lasts five weeks.

Objectives of the Instruction

There are three primary objectives of the instruction, all of which support the goals of increased critical thinking and better understanding of the relationship between resources.

- Students shall utilize the key print and electronic resources available.
- Students shall be given some choice in the direction that their assignment takes so that the activity has relevance to the individual student.
- Students shall evaluate and comment on the resources that they use.
- Questions and tasks shall illustrate the relationship between resources.

Although this activity focuses on the 2000 United States presidential election, it can be easily tailored to fit other topics. Topics must be broad and controversial enough to have generated a vast amount of information in several different formats. Because students most likely already have an opinion on such topics as abortion, gun control, and prayer in school, these have been purposely avoided so that students cannot rely on pat answers.

Components of the Instruction

This activity consists of a librarian presentation, an in-library assignment, and optional post-assignment assistance.

Preparation

Week One—The librarian meets with the professor to discuss the goals and objectives of the activity, the librarian presentation, the in-library assignment, and any activity follow-up.

Week Two—The librarian designs and tests the assignment, making any necessary changes. The professor is given the opportunity to provide feedback before the assignment is finalized.

Presentations

Week Two—In class, the professor discusses with the students the upcoming presentation by the librarian.

Week Three—The librarian meets students in the library instruction room to demonstrate the online catalog and databases, discuss techniques for evaluating resources, and review the in-library assignment. At the conclusion of the class, the librarian distributes the assignment.

Assignment

Week Four—In place of their regular class time that week, students work on the assignment. The librarian is available in the Reference Department during these times to provide individual assistance. Students may also make appointments with the librarian. Students turn in their completed assignment to the librarian at the end of the week.

Week Five—The librarian grades the completed assignments, providing students with feedback on individual answers, including suggestions for improvement. The librarian returns the graded assignments to the professor, along with an analysis of class performance.

Evaluation

The effectiveness of the activity is determined by the assignment grades, the class performance analysis, and the post-assignment assistance provided by the librarian.

Assignment Grades

The librarian grades the completed assignments. Incorrect or incomplete answers are commented on fairly extensively. Assignments should not be downgraded for incorrectly answered subjective questions. Such questions can be used to evaluate a student's understanding of a particular task. The graded assignments are returned to the professor, who reviews the assignments with the students as a class.

Class Performance Analysis

The librarian prepares a spreadsheet with columns for student names, percentage of questions answered correctly, and comments. The third column can be used to note if a student had trouble understanding a task. Comments on the overall performance of the class can be noted at the bottom of the spreadsheet.

Post-Assignment Assistance

Students are given the option of meeting individually with the librarian to work on aspects that they did not master. In order not to take up more class time, students who opt to meet with the librarian must due so on their own time, but they may be rewarded with extra credit on their library assignment if the librarian believes that they have grasped tasks previously missed. If a large number of students require post-assignment assistance, particularly for certain sections, it may be a signal that the assignment needs to be adjusted.

Sources:

Commission on Presidential Debates
http://www.debates.org/

Evaluating Web Sites
http://multimedia.tamu-commerce.edu/Library/evalue.htm

Project Vote Smart
http://www.vote-smart.org/

Supplementary Material

The Assignment has been placed on the accompanying disk so it can easily be copied and/or modified to fit the needs of individual libraries and instructors.

- Information Resource & Evaluation Exercise

Notes:

Translating a Citation

ELIZABETH A. ELKINS
Director of College Libraries
SUNY COLLEGE OF ENVIRONMENTAL SCIENCE & FORESTRY
eaelkins@esf.edu

Circumstances of the Instruction

The library faculty at the SUNY College of Environmental Science and Forestry has taught a one-credit research methods class, now called Information Literacy, for over 20 years. The current syllabus for this class, including all the assignments, may be found at our library's web site— http://www.esf.edu/moonlib/cll300.html. The basic objectives of the course have always matched the ALA definition of information literacy. Students develop their ability to locate, evaluate, and use information effectively and efficiently by searching a topic of their choice, hopefully one they can use for another class. They work through a series of exercises that teach them a research process and create a bibliography on this topic.

The course, which is offered every semester, is a 200 level course open to all students (though most are juniors). The small classes, 15–20 students spread among up to seven sections, meet in a wired conference room where the students sit at tables and can work in small groups as necessary.

Objectives of the Instruction

The final product of the course is the creation of a bibliography. The last unit is devoted to this task with these specific objectives:
- evaluating and analyzing the sources located during the search and
- organizing and arranging a bibliography through the use of a style manual.

The activity that accompanies the final unit of this credit course could be used in a number of settings where students need help deciphering the information they have found in their search. The exercise can be done together in a class to practice the skill of interpreting the different styles of citations so that sources may be located and a complete and accurate bibliography compiled (see Supplementary Materials).

Students learn to find information in a wide variety of places: in the library's catalog; from bibliographic databases; through interviews; or from the Internet. References identified in these diverse sources are presented in a variety of formats and it is often difficult to decipher the information. Interpreting the components of the reference so that the source can be located and a bibliography ultimately created is more challenging than ever before.

Librarians have always spent time teaching the "anatomy" of bibliographic citations. Catalog cards were explained to be sure that students fully understood all the information on the card and learned as much about a book from it catalog entry as possible. There was comfort in knowing that the format of catalog cards was more or less standard and if you understood one card catalog you probably could understand them all. Students may have been taught to carefully record all the bibliographic information on a note card. Students learned to decipher the references found in printed indexes and record all the important components on a card. Today the formats of online catalogs differ, as do the hundreds of bibliographic databases that are available electronically. Students seldom write down or copy references. They print them out, collecting citations in the various formats in which they are found. Students often do not understand what they have found, cannot interpret the information they have collected, and consequently cannot find the source or write proper citations for a bibliography.

Components of the Instruction

Preparation

The exercise presents five references on a topic (e.g., urban trees) selected from five different sources (databases), such as: the library's local catalog, *Agricola*, *Expanded Academic Index*, *Agris*, and the Internet. It takes very little time for a librarian to locate these representative sample citations and cut and paste them onto a single page. The differences in their format and arrangement are striking.

Presentation

- Explain exactly what elements are necessary for a complete citation.
- Illustrate that an incomplete citation may mean that the book or article cannot be found. (For example, a letter with an incomplete address cannot be delivered.)
- Spend time explaining the need for a style manual in compiling a bibliography.
- Explain that there are many different styles and show the students several examples.
- Point out that they must be sure they are following a style that is appropriate for their courses (or for publication someday) and they must consistently follow the same style throughout their bibliography.
- Compare a style manual to a cookbook that explains how to assemble something to eat with a list of ingredients. A style manual explains how to take the information to assemble a proper bibliography.
- Make it clear that a style manual is a guide to the mechanics of assembling a bibliography.

Hands-on Activity

Give this list of prepared citations to the class and ask them to:
- Review the five citations.
- Translate the citation. Annotate each one by explaining what each line (section, field) means.
- Create a correct bibliography from these references following a specific style manual.

Divide the class into five groups to work on the citations. Provide copies of the popular style manuals (*Chicago*, MLA, *Council of Biology Editors*) for the class to use. Each group may pick one style manual to use and follow that format for all the citations.

Allow the students about 15 minutes to discuss these citations among themselves and identify the essential parts. Before they can locate a source and ultimately compile a bibliography they have to understand (translate) the information they have before them.

Ask one student from each group to put one of the citations on the board or overhead projector and explain it to the rest of the class.

Let the class discuss the citation under consideration. Ask if all the necessary elements are included? Is it clear what the citation is representing? Are all the elements presented in accordance with the selected style? Since each group used a different style the class will be seeing different styles represented on the board (which is part of the lesson, styles are different!) and each group has to explain the style they have used.

Evaluation

While interpreting citations is a skill librarians have mastered and revised over the years, it is very confusing to the student searcher. Librarians know what information is needed and how to pull it out of a citation. This is not always obvious to students and seeing these different citation formats illustrates this challenge very well.

This citation activity is difficult and confusing for many students. Nevertheless it helps them realize that while it is one thing to find a reference, it is something else to translate the reference and find the actual material it describes.

This exercise gives students an opportunity to practice deciphering citations and to compile a bibliography following a style manual, in a comfortable, supportive group of peers. Students should enjoy the hands-on experience, the discussion and working on this skill together, rather than an instructor's "show and tell" of the process. The ultimate success of this activity will be evident when students can locate sources for which they have citations and compile an accurate and attractive bibliography.

Supplementary Material

The material in this section has been placed on the accompanying disk so it can easily be copied and/or modified to fit the needs of individual libraries and instructors.

- Translating a Citation: What do all those pieces mean?

Notes:

Teaching Print and Electronic Reference Sources through Student Presentations

REBECCA FEIND

Reference Librarian
JAMES MADISON UNIVERSITY
feindrs@jmu.edu

Circumstances of the Instruction

The following activity is part of a semester-long course, RESEARCH AND INFORMATION, taught for the Honors Program at James Madison University. This is a 300-level course worth 3 credits aimed at juniors who will be conducting a literature review in support of their senior honors thesis. Course enrollment is capped at 20 students to ensure adequate time for class participation activities. The final project of the course is an annotated bibliography of 50 items, including a range of reference sources, books, journal articles, and other types of information sources as appropriate to individual topics. Students that represent a variety of majors enroll in the class, so it is useful to teach them a common set of major reference sources that will demonstrate the different types of reference tools.

Having the students give presentations to the class on the print and electronic versions of a reference tool draws on their ability to summarize the purpose of the tool, to know how to use it, and to communicate their understanding of the differences between the print and electronic formats. Asking students to compare the print and electronic versions of a specific source helps them to understand the limits of time coverage databases may have as well as the variety of access points available in the different formats. Using a peer-learning approach develops a collaborative learning approach to the class, as their knowledge of the sources will depend on their classmates' ability to present the information. In addition, it is enlightening to hear how the students describe the sources, and they do not get tired of the instructor raving about reference books and databases.

Objectives of the Instruction

- Students will understand criteria for evaluating reference sources.
- Students will understand how to teach themselves and others how to use a reference source.
- Students will demonstrate their knowledge of and ability to use specific sources.
- Students will be able to explain the capabilities or limitations of electronic sources in comparison to their print counterparts.

Components of the Instruction

Preparation

The instructor prepares a list of print and electronic resources from which students may select to do their presentations. It is useful to include a range of sources so students will be able to increase their knowledge of the different kinds/categories of reference sources. Include examples of encyclopedias, dictionaries, almanacs, statistical sources, and periodical indexes. Compiling the list can be time consuming, as it is important to verify the library still has print versions of reference tools, as many times a print subscription is cancelled if the library purchases the tool electronically. Students are allowed to sign up for the titles they want, but I do try to recommend titles that are related to a particular student's interest. A sample of titles is included in the Supplementary Materials.

Presentation

Students are assigned Chapter 2 of Deborah Fink's *Process and Politics in Library Research*. This chapter provides a detailed outline on how to evaluate reference tools and gives students specific examples of the kind of review I expect them to give on their sources. Modeling a presentation is also very important for demonstrating the kind of presentation I expect the students to give. I model a book talk using the *National Union Catalog, pre-1956 Imprints*, and demonstrate a database presentation using *WorldCAT*.

Hands-on Activity

Students are given a copy of the evaluation guidelines in advance in order to help them plan their presentations. Caution them that since they are responsible for teaching their fellow students the sources they are presenting, it is essential to give correct information. Add in a lighter tone that their presentations need to be accurate, as someone who uses these sources all the time will evaluate them! Students are given 5 minutes for a reference book presentation, 10 minutes for a database presentation (allowing for slow network time and comparison to the print source.)

Evaluation

The quality of the presentations will make it clear how well the students are able to negotiate learning a new reference tool. Their ability to explain how it works and when it would be relevant to use demonstrates their understanding of the nature of reference sources.

Sources:

Fink, Deborah. *Process and Politics in Library Research*. Chicago: ALA, 1989.

Supplementary Materials

The materials in this section have been placed on the accompanying disk so they can easily be copied and/or modified to fit the needs of individual libraries and instructors.

- Suggested Titles for Presentations
- Reference Book Presentation Guidelines
- Database Presentation Guidelines

Writing Annotations

REBECCA FEIND

Reference Librarian
JAMES MADISON UNIVERSITY
feindrs@jmu.edu

Circumstances of the Instruction

The following activity is part of a semester-long course, RESEARCH AND INFORMATION, taught for the Honors Program at James Madison University. This is a 300-level course worth 3 credits aimed at juniors who will be conducting a literature review in support of their senior honors thesis. Course enrollment is capped at 20 students to ensure adequate time for class participation activities. The students' final project is an annotated bibliography of 50 items, including a range of reference sources, books, journal articles, and other types of information sources as appropriate to individual topics. Writing accurate annotations is crucial to completing this project successfully. Learning to write annotations also draws upon students' ability to evaluate information and explain how sources are relevant to their individual topics.

Objectives of the Instruction

The students will:
- learn how to write accurate annotations;
- develop an academic tone for writing annotations; and
- be able to evaluate annotations.

Components of the Instruction

Preparation

The instructor selects a journal article for all students to read. In the past I have used "Umberto Eco On Libraries: A Discussion of 'De Bibliotheca'" by Michael F. Winter. The article is useful for this exercise as the topic is related to research issues. An abstract appears at the beginning of the article, which provides fodder for comparing the differences between abstracts and annotations.

Presentation

Students are assigned the following readings:
- Deborah Fink's discussion on writing annotations in her book *Process and Politics in Library Research*.
- James Harner's *On Compiling an Annotated Bibliography*.

The examples described in these readings are reviewed in class. The difference between an abstract and annotation is discussed.

Hands-on Activity

Students are assigned the common journal article to read and annotate. Each student is asked to e-mail his/her annotation of the article to the instructor a day in advance of the next class meeting. The instructor selects the best two or three annotations and prepares them for distribution by removing the students' names from the annotation and putting the two or three annotations on the same sheet. The sheets are distributed in class and students are given five minutes to read through the annotations and decide which one they think is the best. Students are asked which annotation they think is the best and to explain their reasoning. The discussion that follows should illuminate successful techniques of the writers for effectively annotating the same journal article. This activity helps students to understand that effective annotations meet certain standards yet it is possible for an individual writer's voice to still be heard. The students find it useful to see several examples of successful annotations that are not identical in word choice but that are consistent in meeting the guidelines.

Evaluation

The quality of annotations submitted by the students gives the instructor an early read on how well they understand the concept of writing annotations. In the discussion, it will be clear how well the class is able to understand the elements of a successful annotation.

Sources:

Fink, Deborah. *Process and Politics in Library Research*. Chicago: American Library Association, 1989.

Harner, James L. *On Compiling an Annotated Bibliography*. New York: Modern Language Association, 1985.

Winter, Michael F. "Umberto Eco on Libraries: A Discussion of 'De Bibliotheca'." *The Library Quarterly*. 9.2 (1994): 117–129.

Supplementary Material

The material in this section has been placed on the accompanying disk so it can easily be copied and/or modified to fit the needs of individual libraries and instructors.

- Annotated Bibliography Project

Evaluation of Sources through Their Citations

TIMOTHY H. GATTI

Head, Cataloging Services Department
UNIVERSITY AT ALBANY, SUNY
tgattti@csc.albany.edu

Circumstances of the Instruction

There have been many articles and activities designed for the evaluation of electronic resources using a "checklist" model. For example, if the author provides a bibliography, then the resource can be considered valid, while if a bibliography is not provided, the student researcher should be wary. This is a useful model, but students sometimes have difficulty making the same type of judgments when faced with bibliographic records in their library's online catalog. This activity is based in part on the article *"The Citation as Intertext: Toward a Theory of the Selection Process"* by Ross Atkinson. As stated in the title, the article provides a model for monographic collection development, and I believe that the same principles used by bibliographers can be relevant to students when they make a decision on whether or not to use a resource.

This exercise is designed for a credit-based information literacy course. The class size should be small enough so that ideas can be exchanged through discussion. The time for this activity is approximately 30 minutes, not including preparation.

Objectives of the Instruction

After the completion of this activity, students will:
- realize the importance of having a background in the subject that they are researching and
- make initial judgments about the validity of monographic works, based upon citation information found on library OPACs and databases.

Components of the Instruction

Preparation

The instructor will need to know the students' academic majors, or at least what the students' general areas of interest are (humanities, social sciences, sciences). The instructor can customize the evaluative Worksheet (see Supplementary Materials) to best mesh with the needs and interests of the students, if they so desire. Each student should receive a copy of the Worksheet.

Presentation

Atkinson describes the concepts of explicit and implicit citation. Explicit citations are those that the author of the work in hand provides – actual citations and references in their work to published works by other authors. Implicit citations are those that the reader makes between the work that they are studying and those works and concepts that they have encountered in the past.

Atkinson provides two examples of evaluation of resources through the examination of their citations. The first example can be used as a starting point. Atkinson states that if one had a book on the Jewish mercantile tradition, one would make radically different assumptions about the text of the citation if it concludes with "Berlin, 1942" rather than "Zurich, 1982." The explicit citations would be the actual references that the author has used. While the average undergraduate probably would not be able to recognize that the authors cited are pro-Nazi historians, they should be able to make the connection that this book was published during World War II in the heart of the Third Reich, thus the implicit citation between the text and past events.

The second example is a document dealing with the philosophical foundations of the Enlightenment. If instead of the 700 page (or multi-volume) text that would be appropriate for such a complex topic, the text is only seven pages long, one would have to doubt the reliability of the text. In this case, the explicit citation is the length of the text. The implicit citation is the realization of the student researcher that a complex topic of this nature could not be adequately presented in such a short format.

Such aspects of the citation, including author, title, place of publication, publisher, date of publication, and length, can provide clues as to the value of the source. Atkinson sees this influence as the syntagmatic context. Atkinson provides the definition of this context as "based upon nothing more than the realization that any part of the citation can influence and be influenced by the citation as a whole."

Discussion

Using the Worksheet (see Supplementary Materials), students should try to evaluate the citations based upon the information available. Does the work appear to be reliable? Why? Are there cases where these works could be used in research? I have attempted to provide some background for the sample texts in the Instructor's Version of the Worksheet (see Supplementary Materials).

Ideally students should bring some of their own ideas and biases to the discussion. A capitalist-minded business major might feel that Adam Smith's *Wealth of Nations* is a valid text, but consider Karl Marx's *Das Kapital* an unreliable text. But a radical-minded social history student might take the opposite approach.

Evaluation

After the discussion, the instructor should have an idea of the students' understanding of the relationship between bibliographic information and the intellectual content of the material. For additional evaluation, the instructor could assign students to find "unreliable" materials in the library and provide their own rationale for their selection.

Sources:

Atkinson, Ross. "The Citation as Intertext: Toward a Theory of the Selection Process." *Library Resources & Technical Services*. April/June 1984. 109–119.

Supplementary Materials

The materials in this section have been placed on the accompanying disk so they can easily be copied and/or modified to fit the needs of individual libraries and instructors.

- Evaluation of Sources Through Their Citations Worksheet (Student Version)
- Evaluation of Sources Through Their Citations Worksheet (Instructor Version)

Notes:

94

Let's Play Telephone

CAROL ANNE GERMAIN

Networked Resources Education Librarian
UNIVERSITY AT ALBANY, SUNY
cg219@albany.edu

Circumstances of the Instruction

Communication is a vital component of information literacy. Yet information often takes on a shape of its own when being communicated, mainly because it is extremely volatile. This instructional activity includes the transmission of information and quickly illustrates this point to students.

Objectives of the Instruction

The successful student will have the ability to:
- understand that information changes as it is transmitted and
- understand that the more complicated the information component the greater the likelihood it will change during exchange.

Components of the Instruction

Preparation

Write three statements that will be verbally passed around the room. These are put on index cards for the start point people. Try to include:
- one statement that is simple and contains some meaning for students,
- one statement that contains information that will probably contain little meaning, and
- one statement that is lengthy but includes material to which students can relate.

Examples

- The college has a radio station (call letters).
- Gladys Swarthout was an opera singer in the 1940s.
- Rage Against the Machine does a cover of Allen Ginsberg's "Hadda be Playing on the Jukebox."

Lecture

The lecture for this class period includes the evolution of communication tools (e.g., telegraph, telephone, etc.). This includes the technology changes as well as the social impact of these inventions. Quotes, anecdotes, and statistics about communication tools should be included to make the lecture more stimulating.

Hands-on Activity

This is a very short learning module—average time is about 12 minutes. Select three students in the classroom. It is best to pick students seated at the most extreme points in the classroom (i.e., first row, first seat or last row, last seat) and a person seated in the middle of the room. Give each of these participants one of the prepared index cards (I suggest giving the simplest statement to the middle person). These cards should be read by these individuals, who then pass the message on verbally (they keep the cards) to the person next to them. The extreme seats send the message in one direction, the middle participant sends the message in both directions. Let the messages either go to the opposite ends or set a time to stop. Using the white board or a visualizer, write down the reported statement. Underneath each statement write the original statements that the "starters" read aloud. A discussion about the results should follow.

Evaluation

Students' response to this exercise will let you evaluate its effectiveness. From my experience, students are anxious to participate in the follow-up conversation. If there is no response, prepare several statements for discussion.

What Do I Do Next?

JANICE R. HYLEN

Education Librarian/Assistant Instruction Coordinator
NEW MEXICO STATE UNIVERSITY
jhylen@lib.nmsu.edu

Circumstances of the Instruction

Students rarely spend time **thinking** about their research process. They think about the final product but they don't think about how they got there. This activity is designed to get them thinking about the process itself and the various steps involved in doing research. It also can introduce some new methods for conducting research that they may not have used before.

This activity is designed for an upper-level information literacy class of 24 students, but it would certainly work at all levels and with slightly larger classes because it involves either brainstorming as a large group, or dividing the class into smaller groups. It would not work very well with an extremely large group. It is designed to take place about a month into a course in which the students have a final project, but it would work in other situations as well.

The activity takes approximately 75 minutes but it could be adapted for either a shorter or longer time period.

Objectives of the Instruction

Students will:
- think about their own research processes,
- realize there are many different ways to do research,
- think about the many steps involved in doing research, and
- share their own researching experiences.

Components of the Instruction

Preparation

Preparation is minimal. The instructor will:
- think about the research process and the typical steps needed—
    these might include:
    - selecting a topic
    - getting a focus
    - preparing the outline
    - preparing the search strategy
    - gathering information
    - taking notes
    - formulating a thesis

- writing the paper
- documenting the sources
- revising and editing—
- make a list of questions for the students to answer and have answers to all the questions to "fill in" what the students may not say (see Supplementary Materials)

Presentation

This activity can be presented in two different ways. One way is for the instructor to do a little role playing and be introduced as a freshman with a research paper to write. The instructor/ freshman has been sent to this class because they are "experts" on research. Questions are addressed to the class as a whole, and students volunteer various answers. The instructor/ freshman can whine and be confused as much as is deemed necessary.

An alternate way (but not quite as much fun) to present this activity is to divide the class into groups to answer questions. Each group has two questions, but each group has different questions (see Supplementary Materials). The groups are given about half an hour to brainstorm and answer their questions. One person in each group is designated to write down their answers. They then share their results with the entire class in an order predetermined by the instructor and based on the typical steps of a research project. All students have the opportunity to share their thoughts on the questions from the other groups as the presentations are made.

The questions are the same no matter which way the material is presented.

Evaluation

Success is evaluated on the quality of the responses from the students. The instructor may have to present some additional ideas, particularly in the area of note taking.

Supplementary Material

The material in this section has been placed on the accompanying disk so it can easily be copied and/or modified to fit the needs of individual libraries and instructors.

- Questions for Small Group Discussion: What Do I Do Next?

Citation Scan: Scholarly or Popular?

JANICE R. HYLEN
Education Librarian/Assistant Instruction Coordinator
NEW MEXICO STATE UNIVERSITY
jhylen@lib.nmsu.edu

Circumstances of the Instruction

Although it is easy to judge the differences between popular and scholarly journals when looking at the actual magazines (layout, glossy pages, photographs, advertisements, etc.), most students will be trying to figure this out while looking at citations in article databases. When they are unfamiliar with the titles of scholarly journals, how do they determine whether the citations refer to scholarly journals or popular magazines? This activity is designed to give them the skills they need to make appropriate choices when looking at the citations in those online indexes.

Although used in an upper-level information literacy course with 24 students, this activity could certainly work with any level. It can also be modified for a slightly larger group, because the class is divided into small groups for discussion.

This particular activity is short, lasting approximately 15–25 minutes.

Objectives of the Instruction

By the end of the session students will:
- develop an understanding about the differences between scholarly and popular periodicals, and
- be able to judge, when using article databases, whether or not the citation is from a scholarly or popular periodical.

Components of the Instruction

Preparation

Preparation for this activity is minimal. The instructor needs to:
- decide all concepts to be covered,
- do a search in a database to find a topic appropriate for the follow up (see Evaluation), and
- bring in some scholarly and popular journals for the class to examine.

Presentation

- Divide the class into groups of 3 or 4.
- Briefly discuss information found in citations in article databases.
- Pass out journals to each group. Each group should receive at least one scholarly journal and one popular magazine.

- Have each group examine the journals and write down similarities and differences. Pay special attention to aspects that will be apparent in citations in an article database.
- Make sure all points are covered.

Hands-on Activity

Students examine the journals and have someone in the group record the differences between what they consider scholarly and what they determine to be popular. Since this will probably include the way the journals differ in appearance, it is necessary that they also include remarks that address qualities they would be able to look for in print indexes or article databases. This might be as simple as stating that most scholarly journals have article titles with subtitles. After approximately 15 minutes of small group discussion, group findings are presented to the class. The instructor clarifies or adds any points that the students may have missed.

Follow up by having students search an article database to see if they can pick out the scholarly journals. Have all students do the same search so that the discussion is less confusing. Allow them approximately 15 minutes to do this, and then have them discuss their answers in class.

A lecture and/or discussion on scholarly and popular journals and their uses is also needed. Since it will not cover the same material as the exercise, this could come before or after the activity.

Evaluation

From the discussion in class, the instructor should be able to tell whether or not students understand the concepts involved. The follow-up activity of having them practice their knowledge using actual databases would further confirm this.

Supplementary Material

The material in this section has been placed on the accompanying disk so it can easily be copied and/or modified to fit the needs of individual libraries and instructors.

- Concepts to be Covered in Class Discussion: Citation Scan—Scholarly or Popular?
  Note: This can be used as a handout *after* the discussion, but it would limit any brainstorming by the students if handed out ahead of time.

Charting Your Research

Janice M. Krueger

Instruction and Outreach Librarian
University of the Pacific
jkrueger@uop.edu

Circumstances of the Instruction

The following lesson plan and assignments are designed for students enrolled in an information literacy course at the undergraduate level. The discussion and activities facilitate student awareness of varying information needs when engaged in research. The assignments assist students in distinguishing between the quality of information available in print, electronic sources, and on the Internet. Since the research paper is a common assessment tool for credit-bearing classes, the library and its resources become the focal point for achieving these goals.

This session, which lasts approximately 45 minutes, works best with 10 to 15 students, and not more than 20. By using previously chosen student topics, greater effectiveness is achieved while searching a multidisciplinary or full-text database such as *Expanded Academic Index, EBSCOhost: Academic Search, Proquest Direct, Lexis-Nexis Academic Universe, or Dow Jones Interactive.* A database granting campus-wide access is preferred and recommended for hands-on activity. The example topic of Martin Luther King, Jr. and his "Letter from Birmingham City Jail" was used during an actual class with *Expanded Academic Index*, although the cited journal in the subsequent Presentation section is indexed in a number of databases. Sample forms and handouts as well as blank charts for additional topics and sessions will be found in the Supplementary Materials.

An alternative for those institutions without a formal information literacy course could be for the professor and librarian to work together in a basic writing course, English composition class, or other prerequisite course that integrates writing, research, and public speaking in a multitopic, multidisciplinary framework.

Objectives of the Instruction

Phase I

- To summarize the information already known about a topic
- To identify the information that is desired or needed for the assignment
- To develop a keyword list based on the needed information
- To itemize the information in a Know, Want, Learned (KWL) chart

Phase II

- To identify the differences between a popular publication and scholarly publication in print form

- To identify the differences between a popular publication and scholarly publication in an electronic form
- To identify appropriate sources for topic and desired information
- To recognize references and bibliographies
- To use references and bibliographies as pathways for further research
- To briefly summarize and categorize the new information according to areas defined in Phase I
- To complete the chart or outline begun in Phase I

Components of the Instruction

Preparation (Phase I)

Meet with the students and discuss the use of a KWL chart (see Sources for further reference and Supplementary Materials for a KWL chart). It is more beneficial if the students know their topics and can identify what information they need to find out prior to the library research session. The first two sections of the chart will aid in delineating between the information they already have and what they want or need to research. The students can complete it either in outline form or with a series of statements and questions within the blocks. A traditional outline without the chart can also be developed.

Student Activity/Assignment (Phase I)

Complete blocks one and two of the KWL Chart.

Preparation (Phase II)

Gather examples of popular magazines and scholarly or peer-reviewed journals. Use both types of publications that are referenced in the database or appear full-text. Select and search the databases for the chosen topic or topics, in this case, King's "Letter from Birmingham City Jail." Select a popular periodical, such as *Ebony,* and a full-text article from a scholarly publication that the library also subscribes to in print, for example:

> Gordon, D.B. (1998, November). Humor in African American discourse: Speaking of oppression. *Journal of Black Studies* [Online] 29(2), 254-276. Available: *Expanded Academic Index*/A21257394 [2000, October 11].

Also refer to the bibliography to select books containing the letter or to find another journal, such as the *Quarterly Journal of Speech,* which has an earlier article and must be reviewed in print.

Presentation (Phase II)

1. Direct the students to perform a keyword search in the database using "letter from Birmingham jail." Of course, this is just an example and other topics would produce other keywords discovered when completing the "Want/Need to Know" column of the Phase I chart.
2. Examine the list to find both types of publications, popular and scholarly.

3. Discuss the major points of differences for these publications. Also discuss how they appear in the print version and the online counterpart.
4. Refer to the bibliography at the end of the article by Gordon.
5. Show how his references can point to others. For instance, if a student needed to actually find a copy of King's work, he can readily see that it is available in *A Testament of Hope: The Essential Writings of Martin Luther King, Jr.* by J .M. Washington.
6. Point out the other journals that can be found in the library's collection, examples being the *Quarterly Journal of Speech* or *The Southern Communication Journal.*
7. Summarize the key points of the article together with the students.

Student Activity/Assignment (Phase II)

1. Complete the Phase II Chart with the article found in class.
2. Find at least two more sources in either the same or different databases and add to the Chart.
3. Finish last column of the KWL Chart with the applicable information.

Evaluation

Success can be ascertained by reviewing the class note sheets and entries in the student's charts at the end of the session and again after the completion of the paper. Reading and examining a sample of the finished papers along with the chart notations will reveal areas of strength and weakness. The instructor can then redesign the weak areas and plan for improved instruction and exercises.

Variations

1. If the discussion concerning the differences between popular and scholarly publications is not needed, then the sessions could focus on the scholarly publications in the multidisciplinary databases or subject specific databases, such as *JSTOR, Project Muse, American History and Life,* and *Historical Abstracts.* Of course, the database selection is dependent upon the scope of the research paper. The Phase II Chart could then be adapted as shown in the Supplementary Materials.
2. Comparing and contrasting web sites can also be accomplished this way. As the students are directed to examine pre-chosen sites, for example, those dealing with country information established by such bodies as:
   - the World Bank—www.worldbank.org,
   - the Library of Congress—http://lcweb2.loc.gov/frd/cs/cshome.html,
   - the U.S. Department of State—www.state.gov/www.background_notes,
   they can use the Phase II Chart to examine this type of information with that found on countries by searching arbitrarily on the Internet. The Phase II Chart could then be adapted as shown in the Supplementary Materials.

Sources:

Sebranek, P., Meyer, M., & Kemper, D. (1996). *Writers Inc.* Wilmington, MA: D.C. Heath & Company.

Supplementary Materials

The materials in this section have been placed on the accompanying disk so they can easily be copied and/or modified to fit the needs of individual libraries and instructors.

- Library Session Notes Sheet
- KWL Chart
- Phase II Charts:
  Selected Sources
  Selected Sources (variation with all scholarly publications)
  Selected Sources (variation for web sites)

Teaching First-Year Students Coping Skills for Information Overload in the Virtual Library

ALEXIUS SMITH MACKLIN

Assistant Professor of Library Science, User Instruction Librarian
PURDUE UNIVERSITY
alexius@purdue.edu

Circumstances of the Instruction

The activities and demonstration for this instruction session were developed to expand the first year student's experience with and understanding of virtual information sources such as online catalogs, electronic indexes, and the World Wide Web.

The session works most effectively with a group of 25–30 students. It is very interactive and fast-paced to keep everyone fully engaged for the entire 50 minutes. If you find yourself running short on time at the end, you might want to try combining the demonstration and segue with the evaluation activity.

Objectives of the Instruction

After engaging in the following hands-on activities, the students will be able to:

- explain the basic concept of information overload in the digital age of virtual information retrieval by sharing their own experiences of success and difficulty retrieving information;
- use the metaphor of the bags of mixed candies and PEZ™ to create sets or hierarchies for identifying their information needs;
- define and describe the functions of indexes, catalogs, and the World Wide Web;
- compare and contrast print and electronic versions of indexes and catalogs; and
- identify and access three kinds of virtual information sources available to them (electronic indexes, online catalogs, and the World Wide Web).

Anticipated Learning Outcomes

The activities in this instruction session were designed to help the students:

- relate finding relevant information to problem solving (creating sets and hierarchies with the candy), rather than relying simply on luck and a favorite search engine;
- define relevant information by identifying information needs prior to beginning a search;
- name the information sources available to find relevant information – both online and print versions; and
- access these sources physically and virtually using a proxy server when necessary.

Components of the Instruction

Materials needed for Hands-on Activities 1 and 2 are:
- re-sealable plastic bags, preferably sandwich-size, enough for each person in the instruction session plus a few extras;
- 5 – 6 different kinds of loose candies; and
- PEZ™ dispensers, one for each person.

Preparation

Prepare the individual bags of mixed candies for each participant before the instruction session. Each bag should contain some loose PEZ™, lemon drops, cinnamon buttons, and the like. The different amounts and kinds of candy in each bag represent various kinds of information and information formats available online today.

Hands-on Activity 1 (10 minutes)

1. After the bags are distributed, direct the participants to work in teams "organizing" the candy. Typically, a good number of people per team is 4–5. It is helpful to have tables/desks set up to accommodate teamwork ahead of time. Forming groups will then be as easy as saying, "This table is team 1," etc.
2. Allow the teams approximately 5 minutes to organize the contents of the bags. Explain that there are no rules to the organizing process. Each team is responsible for coming up with their own system.
3. As the teams organize the candy, watch how they work together. You should notice that some of the teams are organizing according to a particular hierarchy, i.e. the same kind, the same color, etc. Some may be organizing according to likes and dislikes. Others may be creating a pattern or design. There is no right or wrong way to "organize" the candy. The point of this activity is simply that each group is thinking about order in a unique way. This organizational thought process is also very important to understand when considering how we look for and select information.
4. After the participants have completed the organization task, describe the relationship of this activity to information overload. Take an extra bag of candy and describe the metaphor of the contents in the bag to the contents on the WWW. For example, you might want to use the following comparison statement, "Finding useful information is kind of like organizing this candy. You don't know what you have until you sort it out."
5. Now ask: "So, how do you know if what you have sorted out is any good?" Give the participants a few moments to answer this question, and then describe the term "relevance." Explain that there are tools we can use to find what belongs and what does not belong. In this case, we are going to use a PEZ™ dispenser as our measuring device.

Hands-on Activity 2 (5 minutes)

1. Pass out the PEZ™ dispensers and tell the teams to use these "tools" as a way to capture the "relevant" candy.

2. After the teams finish putting the selected candy in the dispensers, ask the following questions:
   - What did your team select to put into the dispenser? Why?
   - Did you put your selection into the dispenser in any particular way?
3. Unless your instruction program has a lot of money, you might want to collect the PEZ™ dispensers and reuse them. The bags of candy are a bonus for the participants!

The goal of Activities 1 and 2 is to provide a visual way of thinking about relevancy and the selection of information sources.

Segue (3–5 minutes)

1. As you are completing the second activity, segue into the next part of the instruction session by asking, "How many of you are affected by information overload?"
2. Allow a few moments for the participants to respond to the question. Explain that information overload can be more than simply getting too many returns on a particular search engine. Information overload may occur because there are literally too many choices. With so much attention focused on the capabilities of the Internet, some participants may be confused by the functions of various electronic resources.
3. Discover what is already known about different information resources by asking, "Who can describe what a catalog is?" "Who can describe the function of an electronic index?"

Preparation for Hands-on Activity 3

Collect the following:
- 1–2 scholarly journals
- 1–2 popular magazines
- 1 *New York Times* newspaper issue
- 1 *New York Times* print index that covers the selected issue
- 4–5 print copies of indexes that correspond to the online versions
      (I used the following)
      1 print copy of the *Applied Science and Technology Index*
      1 print copy of the *Humanities Index*
      1 print copy of the *Reader's Guide to Periodical Literature*
- 1 card file drawer from the old card catalog – Author, Title *(If available)*
- 1 card file drawer from the old card catalog – Subject *(If available)*

Hands-on Activity 3 (10 minutes)

1. Pass out 1–2 items listed above to each team.
2. Allow approximately 3–4 minutes for the teams to study the item(s) they were given in preparation for a one-minute lecture.
3. Ask each team to present their item(s) to the whole group and explain what functions their item(s) serve in finding or retrieving information.
4. As the teams present, ask specific questions, such as: "What is the difference between the journal and the magazine?" "What does the "see also" mean in the printed indexes?" "How is an index organized?"

Demonstration and Evaluation Activity

Preparation for Demonstration and Evaluation Activity

The following materials are needed for this activity:

- computers with Internet connections for each team;
- a computer with an Internet connection and an LCD projector for the instructor; and
- annotated citations of information sources, written on index cards, for each resource presented (i.e., one citation for an article in the newspaper, one citation for a journal article from each of the printed indexes, one citation for a book from each of the card files, etc.).

Demonstration (10 minutes)

1. Explain that all of the printed items presented are currently available electronically. "Today we are going to transfer what we know about these items physically to what we need to know to use them in the virtual library."
2. Tour the virtually-owned information resources in your library. Keep the demonstration very specific and simple by showing only the online catalog and the electronic indexes that correspond to the printed ones the teams presented.
3. Explain the function of each electronic database as it is introduced, and compare the online version to its physical counterpart from Hands-On Activity 3.

Segue and Evaluation Activity (10 minutes)

1. Log each team onto the library's web site at your institution.
2. Pass out annotated citations – one index card to each team.
3. Ask each team to answer the following questions about the citations:
   - Is this resource a: book; journal article; web site?
   - Your team found a matching citation using: the catalog; an index; a URL

The goal of this demonstration and evaluation activity is to assess the participants' knowledge of the virtual information sources available to them, and to test their ability to connect the right resource to the right source (i.e., books go to catalogs like articles go to indexes).

Different Types of Information Organizations (Including Libraries)

KATE MANUEL

Physical Sciences Librarian, Instructional & Interpretive Services
CALIFORNIA STATE UNIVERSITY, HAYWARD
kmanuel@csuhayward.edu

Circumstances of the Instruction

This activity has three parts, each with its own specific purpose, as listed below. The three parts are, however, intended to work together as a unit with the overall objective of introducing students to various types of information organizations and helping them begin to make determinations of what organizations are best for what types of information needs.

- Part 1—Students draw upon their prior knowledge of community organizations to list the types of places/persons collecting and providing access to various types of information resources corresponding to scenario(s) given to them.
- Part 2—Students work through the implications (strengths and weaknesses) of various frameworks for organizing things in their personal lives to understand better, by analogy, the ways in which different types of information organizations differ in providing access to resources.
- Part 3—Students collaborate with the instructor in mapping out relationships between different types of information organizations, with special focus on what types of organizations provide what and how they can best be accessed.

This activity works best if students have already been introduced to "information" and "information needs" in a broad sense. Students should not be limiting their understanding of information to scholarly texts written on paper as books or journal articles, nor should they view an "information need" as something arising only in relation to school or work assignments. They should, instead, be primed to think of "information" as anything meeting a need to know, to think of non-written information sources, and to think of information needs in people's personal lives.

This is intended to be a three-part unit constituting a single 50-minute class; however, it is modular in that each of these three parts can stand as its own unit should less time be available. Each part should take approximately 16 minutes.

Objectives of the Instruction

- Students will learn about various types of information organizations.
- Students will make determinations of what information organizations are best for what types of information needs.

Components of the Instruction

Hands-on Activity

Part 1—Each student is given a colored index card. Depending upon the size of the class and the space available, there may be anywhere from two to four cards of a particular color distributed to the group. On each color of card is a scenario describing a different "information need." By finding another student(s) with the same colored card, students find others with the same scenario, and small discussion groups are formed. Students read their scenario(s) and discuss various places within the community where one could find information corresponding to the need.

A sample scenario is as follows (see Supplementary Materials for a full page of scenarios):

> *Consider the situation described below and then think of some places where this information could be found.*
>
> **The Situation:**
>
> LaShawn works for an independent newspaper and is researching a feature article about the likely effects of national cigarette advertising upon the long-term health of African-American teens in her community.
>
> **Places where information could be found:**

After approximately five to seven minutes, the instructor reads each scenario aloud and asks the groups to identify the information organizations that would help to meet the information need(s) described in the scenario. As the students talk, the instructor lists the information organizations mentioned by the students on a whiteboard, chalkboard, easel with paper, or overhead transparency. (It is easiest if facilities can be arranged so that the listing remains visible to the class throughout the session. In a classroom with a single whiteboard or chalkboard, this may mean dividing the board into two segments, or using an easel with paper or an overhead transparency for part of the session.) While listing the information organizations suggested by the students, the instructor begins to push the students toward voicing how these organizations work and to what they provide access.

Part 2—The students are then told that their next exercise is designed to help them think about the different ways information organizations arrange things. Specifically (1) how the type of information being organized determines how it is arranged and (2) that there are pluses and minuses to every organizational scheme. Each student is presented with a worksheet with a graphic organizer. They are asked to think of one type of thing they own and could organize, five different methods that could be used for organizing this type of thing, and an advantage and a disadvantage of each organizational method (see Supplementary Materials).

Students can work individually or with a partner to complete their worksheets. Most students select either their music CDs or their clothing as things to be organized. Less commonly, students select books, cooking herbs and spices, or automobile repair tools. After giving students seven to ten minutes to work on this, the instructor asks them to share examples of the types of things being organized, the different organizational schemes, and the strengths and drawbacks of each organizational method. For example, a student might respond that the type of thing being organized was music CDs. That possible organizational methods were by CD title, by singer, by how much the CDs are liked, by what type of music they are, and by how recent they are. And, that if CDs are organized by how much they are liked, this is "good" because it enables the person to get to their favorites first but "bad" because they will not play some of the things in the back and because the favorites will change over time. Students can be questioned further, if need be, to get them to recognize arrangement by format, by size, by title, by author, by "subject" (what things are about), by timeliness, by person/group issuing them (e.g., record company), and by popularity. These organizational methods are listed on the board for latter mapping (in Part 3) to the types of information organizations listed in Part 1.

Part 3—The third part of this exercise draws upon the two listings
- of types of information organizations and
- of organizational methods

that the instructor has made and left on display for the class. The instructor engages in directed questioning with the entire class to make connections between the types of information organizations and organizational methods listed on the whiteboard, chalkboard, easel with paper, or overhead transparency. The connections are indicated by colored lines, pictures, or other visual means. Each student then completes a cluster map corresponding to the things being discussed by the entire class. The cluster map gives students a framework within which to take notes, a way of structuring their attention, and a record of the class discussion for later reference.

For example, the class should begin to recognize that governmental agencies are an information source, but one (largely) limited to information by/about that agency; that public libraries are (generally) more concerned with new popular resources (i.e., the latest best sellers) than academic libraries are, and that academic libraries (commonly), unlike school or public libraries, use call numbers/subject descriptors even for fiction books because they have more books – and thus more books with the same title or author's last name, etc.

Evaluation

Students' understanding of the information addressed by these activities can be assessed by multiple choice and true/false quizzes or by open-ended essays. An open-ended, five-minute paper asking students to write down the ways in which a public library differs from a university library or from a museum works well. Student responses can be evaluated based upon the number of differences they address, as well as the accuracy and thoroughness with which they do so.

Supplementary Materials

The materials in this section have been placed on the accompanying disk so they can easily be copied and/or modified to fit the needs of individual libraries and instructors.

- Information Scenarios
- Organizational Methods
- Information Organizations

What's Wrong Citation Style Exercise

ANNE MOORE

NEW MEXICO STATE UNIVERSITY
annemoor@bellsouth.net

Circumstances of the Instruction

Summary—In a classroom with several white or chalk boards, students practice detecting errors in citations for bibliographies, reference lists, or works cited prepared according to the desired style manual, e.g., American Psychological Association, Modern Language Association, or *Chicago Manual of Style*.

Importance—The purpose of this activity is to provide the students with hands-on practice to increase comfort with citation style. Students typically have difficulty mastering citation style because it requires attention to detail and strict adherence to a set of precise rules. This exercise gets students actively involved with detecting errors in citations. Students develop an awareness of the information required in a citation, therefore they are more likely to gather all the required elements while they conduct their research. Small group practice with citation style helps students understand what is involved when they have to construct and proofread their own citations.

Level—This activity is appropriate for all information literacy courses.

Size—The class may consist of up to 36 students.

Length—The activity takes approximately 30 minutes.

Objectives of the Instruction

The students will:
- develop an awareness of the information required in a citation,
- practice citation style for works cited lists or bibliographies,
- work in small groups to analyze and correct citations, and
- instruct and learn from one another.

Components of the Instruction

Preparation

Before the session, the instructor prepares a handout covering the desired citation style (*APA* and *MLA* versions available in Supplementary Materials). Many libraries have posted their guides on the Internet (see Sources for examples). In addition, the instructor prepares a worksheet, a sheet of numbered citations prepared according to the desired style, but containing errors, plus a key to the worksheet (*APA* and *MLA* versions of both documents available in Supplementary Materials). The instructor makes sufficient copies of the worksheet, key, and handout to distribute to each student in the class. The instructor brings the selected official style manual to class:

Gibaldi, Joseph. *MLA Handbook for Writers of Research Papers*. 5th ed. New York: Modern Language Association of America, 1999.

   or

American Psychological Association. (1994). *Publication manual of the American Psychological Association*. 4th ed. Washington, DC: APA.

Presentation

As the class arrives, the students receive the handout and worksheet. The instructor discusses the basics of the selected citation style and refers to the handout.

Hands-on Activity

The instructor breaks the class into 2-person teams and assigns each team one or more of the numbered citations on the worksheet for correction. The teams analyze the assigned citations for errors, consult the handout or official style manual for clarification, and then write the correct citation on the white or chalk board. The instructor circulates through the room to monitor and advise the groups. After 15 minutes, the class reassembles. Each team explains the errors in its assigned citation(s) and how to correct them. Students record the corrections on their worksheets and retain the handout to refer to when they create their own bibliographies.

Evaluation

As a homework assignment, students complete the remainder of the worksheet. During class on the due date, students exchange papers, the instructor distributes the key to the worksheet, and students mark the errors on the paper they are grading. Since there are many errors, the instructor should assign the final grade to each paper. A possible grade breakdown might be:

     "A" 15 or fewer errors
     "B" 16–30 errors
     "C" 3145 errors
     "D" 46-60 errors

Sources:

APA

APA style examples from or based on the 4th edition of the publication manual of the American Psychological Association. (1999, November 19). Allentown, PA: Muhlenberg College, Trexler Library. Retrieved December 12, 2000, from the World Wide Web— http://www.muhlenberg.edu/library/ref/acad/s_apa.html.

Electronic reference formats recommended by the American Psychological Association. (2000, August 22). Washington, DC: American Psychological Association. Retrieved December 12, 2000, from the World Wide Web—http://www.apa.org/journals/webref.html.

MLA

Lee, I. "Chapter 12: How to Write a Bibliography: Examples in MLA Style." *A research guide for students*. July 1998. 12 Dec. 2000— http://www.geocities.com/Athens/Troy/8866/12biblio.html.

Purdue University Online Writing Lab. *Using Modern Language Association (MLA) Format.* 1995. West Lafayette, IN: Purdue University. 12 Dec. 2000—http://owl.english.purdue.edu/handouts/research/r_mla.html.

Supplementary Materials

The materials in this section have been placed on the accompanying disk so they can easily be copied and/or modified to fit the needs of individual libraries and instructors.

Handouts
- *APA* Style Handout
- *MLA* Style Handout

Keys
- Key to *APA* Style Worksheet
- Key to *MLA* Style Worksheet

Worksheets
- Correct the Errors in the *APA* Style for These Citations
- Correct the Errors in the *MLA* Style for These Citations

Notes:

116

Six Sources in 30 Minutes

ANNE MOORE

NEW MEXICO STATE UNIVERSITY
annemoor@bellsouth.net

Circumstances of the Instruction

Summary—In a classroom with several white or chalk boards, students practice detecting errors in citations for bibliographies, reference lists, or works cited prepared according to the desired style manual, e.g., American Psychological Association, Modern Language Association, or Chicago Manual of Style.

Importance—Students apply the research skills conveyed in the information literacy course under time pressure, through group and individual work, and in a written assignment. The time lag between when students attend information literacy training and apply the concepts in their schoolwork and personal life leads to a lack of retention or mastery of the material. This exercise gets students actively involved in finding information sources. The students apply the concepts as they learn them. This helps the students retain and transfer the concepts to later experience.

Level—The activity is appropriate for all information literacy courses.

Size—The class size may range from 12 to 24 students.

Length—The activity requires one 50-minute session.

Objectives of the Instruction

The students will:
- practice the research process;
- practice searching online for information sources;
- work in small groups to apply research techniques and develop interpersonal skills;
- practice evaluating information sources;
- analyze the process of searching for information sources; and
- practice their writing skills.

Components of the Instruction

Preparation

The instructor makes sufficient copies of the evaluation criteria used by the instructor, department, or library (see Sources for examples) and the Source Evaluation Rubric (see Supplementary Material) for each student. At the preceding class meeting, the instructor divides the class into groups of three students and assists each group in selecting a practice research topic. Likely candidates for group topics are one student's paper topic in another course or the topic for an upcoming assignment or class session. Each group identifies keywords, phrases, and subject terms in advance.

Presentation

The instructor distributes the copies of the evaluation criteria and the evaluation rubric as the class enters the lab. The group members sit together when the class assembles in the computer lab. The instructor teaches or reviews: finding books, government documents, web sites, and other materials in the online catalog; locating scholarly, popular, and newspaper articles in the online databases to which the institution subscribes; and searching efficiently for relevant web sites on the Internet. The instructor demonstrates the search process and systems with a pre-selected topic (not a topic selected by one of the groups). Instruction in evaluating information sources improves the quality of student performance during this exercise. Optimally, this instruction occurred in previous class sessions. If so, the instructor provides a quick review.

Hands-on Activity

The groups spend 30 minutes locating two items from the online catalog, two articles from online databases, and two web sites that are justifiably relevant to their topic and appropriate as sources for citation in an academic paper on the subject. The groups organize the research process as they wish although it is most efficient if one student searches in the online catalog, one in the online databases, and one in Internet directories or search engines. The instructor circulates through the room to monitor and advise the groups.

The groups then collaborate for the remainder of the class session to discuss and take notes on each source as they apply the evaluation criteria (see Sources for examples) to them.

Evaluation

As a homework assignment for the next class meeting, each student writes a paragraph on two of the sources his or her group found. In the paragraphs, the student describes why each source is appropriate for the topic and meets the evaluation criteria. The instructor grades these reports according to the Source Evaluation Rubric (see Supplementary Material). The class meeting when the instructor returns the Source Evaluation Rubrics presents another opportunity to discuss the evaluation of information sources.

Sources:

Alexander, J., & Tate, M. (1996). *Evaluating web resources*. Chester, PA: Widener University, Wolfgram Memorial Library. Retrieved December 11, 2000, from the World Wide Web—http://www2.widener.edu/Wolfgram-Memorial-Library/webevaluation/webeval.htm

Beck, S. E. (1997). *The good, the bad, & the ugly: Or, why it's a good idea to evaluate web sources*. Las Cruces, NM: New Mexico State University Library. Retrieved December 11, 2000, from the World Wide Web—http://lib.nmsu.edu/instruction/evalcrit.html.

Grassian, E. (2000). *Thinking critically about World Wide Web resources*. Los Angeles, CA: UCLA College Library. Retrieved December 11, 2000, from the World Wide Web—http://www.library.ucla.edu/libraries/college/help/critical/index.htm.

Henderson, J. R. (1999). *ICYouSee: T is for thinking*. Ithaca, NY: Ithaca College Library. Retrieved December 11, 2000, from the World Wide Web—http://www.ithaca.edu/library/Training/hott.html.

Jacobson, T., & Cohen, L. (1996). *Evaluating Internet resources.* Albany, NY: University at Albany Libraries. Retrieved December 11, 2000, from the World Wide Web—http://www.library.albany.edu/internet/evaluate.html.

Ten C's for evaluating Internet sources. (2000). Eau Claire, WI: University of Wisconsin Eau Claire, McIntyre Library. Retrieved December 11, 2000, from the World Wide Web—http://www.uwec.edu/Admin/Library/Guides/tencs.html.

Supplementary Material

The material in this section has been placed on the accompanying disk so it can easily be copied and/or modified to fit the needs of individual libraries and instructors.

- Source Evaluation Rubric

Notes:

Using Questions to Evaluate: Or, If at First You Don't Deceive, Try Try Again

GREGORY SZCZYRBAK

Assistant Professor, Reference Librarian
YORK COLLEGE OF PENNSYLVANIA
gszczyrb@ycp.edu

Circumstances of the Instruction

Evaluation is a key component of information literacy. According to the American Library Association, "To be information literate, a person must be able to recognize when information is needed and have the ability to locate, evaluate, and use effectively the needed information."[1] The importance of proper evaluation becomes even more apparent as more of our students turn to the World Wide Web for their research needs. While the World Wide Web can contain valid and accurate information, its very nature encourages quick and easy self-publication without editorial or academic review. Therefore, the content on the World Wide Web often becomes automatically suspect.

The following activity introduces the importance of careful and critical evaluation of all resources. Students will recognize the need to ask questions about resources in order to perform an accurate evaluation. They will develop their own evaluation plan, which they will be able to use for a variety of information resources.

Allow 30 minutes to complete the activity, more if you decide to follow up with further examples. I designed this lesson for use in my class, which has 24 undergraduate students ranging from freshman to seniors. It is can easily be adapted for students of any level.

Objectives of the Instruction

The students will:
* understand the importance of careful and critical evaluation of all resources;
* recognize the need to ask questions about resources in order to perform an accurate evaluation; and
* develop a plan for evaluating a variety of information resources.

Components of the Instruction

Presentation

Begin by explaining the importance of evaluating information, especially in the context of the huge amount of available information and the questionable quality of some.

Present a scenario in which the class has an information need. Tell them that you have found some information that you think may be helpful in answering their need. Then present the class with some foreign or unfamiliar object. For instance, play a song in a foreign language, show an abstract painting, or display an unrecognizable artifact. If you will be using music, you will need a playback device that can be heard from all parts of the room. Likewise, if you are presenting a work of art, it will need to be viewable from all seats in the room.

Without further explanation, ask the class to evaluate the unfamiliar item. Ask them to consider the typical evaluation criteria such as bias, timeliness, accuracy, and audience. Have the students consider the evaluation in small groups, and write their collected responses on a sheet of paper. This admittedly difficult task will provoke some strange observations. Collect the responses and share a few of the more common ones with the class.

Now enlighten the class by translating the lyrics or explaining the concept behind the foreign object. This is particularly effective when the translated content is surprising in some way. For instance, I play a hard rock song, which is sung in German and purposefully arranged to sound like a propaganda speech, spoken by a Hitler-esque character.[2] The translation, however, is merely a recipe for cookies.

Ask the students why they think their own evaluations were successful or unsuccessful. Common responses are "I did not have enough information;" "I relied on my gut feeling or instinct;" I made an assumption;" or "I had preconceived notions or ideas." Reinforce their responses by discussing the importance of having or finding enough information to evaluate both the source and the content contained within it. Remind them not to rely on their first impression or gut instinct.

To further reinforce the lesson, follow up with further discussion about evaluation. You may wish to demonstrate further by showing some hoax websites.[3] Discuss critical thinking skills and how they apply to evaluation.

Hands-on Activity

Now its time for the students to apply their new found knowledge. Remind them that they said they did not have enough information about the source to do a proper evaluation of it. A good way to obtain information is to ask questions. Therefore, have the students make a list of evaluation questions that they can ask about sources of information.

You might choose to offer some headings as a starting point: Author, Publisher, Date of Publication, Scope, Audience, and Edition, etc... Have the students prepare their own list of questions to ask about a source. Help them along by giving an example in each category. Encourage them to make their own categories. Collect the lists so that you may assess the quality of the questions.

Evaluation

Evaluation of the lesson is simple. What are the students' responses to the question about the successfulness of their initial evaluation of the unfamiliar object? If they are thinking critically, they will know right away that they need more information. This is the major theme of the lesson. Also, consider their evaluation questions. What kind of questions did they ask? Do they scratch the surface, or do they delve deep into evaluation?

Endnotes

1.	American Library Association. Presidential Committee on Information Literacy. 11, Dec 2000—http://www.ala.org/acrl/nili/ilit1st.html

2.	Tool, *Die Eier Von Satan*, BMG/Zoo/Volcano/Pavement/CZ 1996

3.	There are several websites that have lists of hoax websites. Here are a few:
	a.	http://www.ycp.edu/library/ifl/etext/ycpeval.html
	b.	http://www2.widener.edu/Wolfgram-Memorial-Library/webevaluation/examples.htm
	c.	http://lib.nmsu.edu/instruction/evalexpl.html

Notes:

124

Pick a Number, Any Number: An Information Review Activity

NANCY B. TURNER

Electronic Resources Coordinator
NEW MEXICO STATE UNIVERSITY LIBRARY
nturner@lib.nmsu.edu

Circumstances of the Instruction

One of the many challenges that undergraduate students face as they begin library research in today's environment is vocabulary that is specialized and may be foreign to them. Their comfort level searching on *Yahoo!* may be high, but their overall exposure to the concepts of information literacy may be limited. The differences between subject versus keyword searching and bibliographic citation versus full-text article databases are unfamiliar distinctions to many students.

This exercise is appropriate for an information literacy course in which a good comfort level with the vocabulary is necessary. The activity is easy to prepare and provides a fun method for in-class sharing of information. Class time required is 20–30 minutes.

Objectives of the Instruction

- Students will gain a better understanding of new concepts in information literacy
- Students will review new vocabulary

Components of the Instruction

Preparation (10–15 minutes)

Create numbered 3x5 index cards. Number at least as many cards as there are students in the class. On each card write a single vocabulary word.

Examples might be:
controlled vocabulary
field
database
Boolean operator
URL
IP address
HTML

The instructor should prepare a handout that includes each word and its definition.

125

In-Class Activity (20–30 minutes)

The instructor holds the cards and calls upon each student to "pick a number, any number." The student then receives the card with that number on it. The student must define the word on the card for the class. If they are unsure of the word, they may pass the card on to a neighbor.

A fun variation on this activity is to prepare a few cards with numbers, but no words. It is the lucky student that picks these numbers!

At the end of the activity, the instructor should distribute to the class the handout that includes all the words with their definitions.

Evaluation

Students will demonstrate increased enthusiasm for review of material. Students will be engaged with one another and have fun. Students will be more successful in quizzes and examinations that require them to demonstrate knowledge of vocabulary and concepts associated with information literacy.

Sources:

Reitz, Joan. *ODLIS: Online Dictionary of Library and Information Science*
http://www.wcsu.edu/library/odlis.html
This online dictionary, with its short definitions, provides some assistance to the instructor in preparing the handout for review.

Section 3—Hierarchy of Learning, Publication Flow, and Formats

Five W's of the Scholarly Communication Process

Exploring the Definition(s) of Information

Primary and Secondary Sources Presentation and In-Class Exercise

Publications Hierarchy: Question Authority!

Defining, Identifying, and Understanding the Difference between Data, Information, and Knowledge

Primary vs. Secondary Sources

Production and Transfer of Information in the Sciences

Around the World of Information

The Five W's of the Scholarly Communication Process

COLLEEN BELL

Library Instruction Coordinator
UNIVERSITY OF OREGON
cbell@darkwing.uoregon.edu

Circumstances of the Instruction

In this lesson plan, students explore the scholarly communication process and try to determine the who, what, when, where, and why of the process. They conduct an inventory of their information environment, noting the variety of sources they use to solve their information needs, then compare these to the academic research environment. During the class discussion, students also link the process to the publication cycle and consider who produces the information they use. Finally, they interview a scholar in a field of interest about the scholarly communication process to see how the process is adapted to a particular discipline.

This lesson could be used with undergraduate students at any level, although freshman may find the concept of "scholar" difficult and need help identifying someone to interview. Because students work individually as well as taking part in a larger class discussion, this activity works well in both small and large classes. For larger classes, you might want to consider having students work in pairs on the interview assignment. The discussion should not take longer than one 50-minute class period.

Objectives of the Instruction

- Have students make the link from their own information environment to the scholarly information environment.
- Make students aware that there are established channels for disseminating scholarly information in each discipline.
- Teach students the language of the scholarly communication process.
- Make students aware of the variety of information producers, and the publication cycle.

Components of the Instruction

Student Preparation

About a week before you plan to do the activity described below, students are assigned a reading on scholarly communication. An example is Michael W. Giles' November 1995 address to the Southern Political Science Convention which describes the "traditional" scholarly communication process in political science, and forecasts how that model might change in the age of electronic information. [Giles, M. (1996). From Gutenberg to gigabytes: Scholarly communication in the age of cyberspace. *The Journal of Politics* 58, 613–626.]

Students are also asked to keep a journal for 3 to 5 days [see Journal Assignment, below], in which they record the variety of information needs they are confronted with each day and how they solved them. The number of days can vary, depending on your class schedule. The purpose of the assignment is to give students an opportunity to examine what their own sources of information are. These will be used to begin the class discussion on scholarly communication.

Instructor Preparation

Prepare a transparency showing a diagram of the scholarly communication process; it should include a timeline, show formal and informal channels of communication, and provide opportunities for a discussion of concepts such as peer review, societies, and the invisible college. Ideally, it would also adapt itself to a discussion of how the Internet changes the traditional model of the scholarly communication process. I have adapted a diagram from an article on scientific communication in psychology [Garvey, W.D., & Griffith, B.C. (1971). Scientific communication: Its role in the conduct of research and creation of knowledge. *American Psychologist* 26, 349–362.] Make copies of the transparency for each student.

Presentation/Discussion

Begin the class by asking students to list out loud the resources they used in their journal. As students list the resources, record them on a whiteboard (or blackboard or flip chart, whichever is available). Next, ask students to define the various channels of communication discussed in the article they read. If you used the Giles article, students should be able to identify informal channels, informal peer review (e.g., presentation at conferences), and publication (or formal channels). Finally, ask students to look at the resources they used, and classify them by the channels of communication they identified from the article they read. Ask several students to explain why they chose each of these communication channels in solving their own information needs.

Next, use the transparency you prepared to present a model of how scholars communicate. Ask students to identify the different channels of communication on the diagram. Discuss the role of the invisible college and professional societies. Discuss the timeline; how long it takes to get something published? Explain why it takes so long; this is a good time to introduce peer review. Link the publication process to the people involved—commercial publishers, professional societies, peer reviewers (or referees), and editorial boards—and discuss the role that each of these plays in the process. Do not forget to talk about indexing and abstracting services, annual reviews, and professional society bulletins and reviews. Note that there may be differences depending on the discipline involved; for example, literary scholars often do research in isolation, eschewing many informal channels of communication as well as preprints, while astronomers rely heavily on these informal channels.

Finally, ask students to consider more recent communication methods, such as e-mail and the web. How might these affect the communication process for scholars or the timeline? If you have time, you might ask students to help you diagram a new model of the scholarly communication process that incorporates both traditional and newer forms of information dissemination.

Evaluation

Students are given an assignment in which they interview a professor with a record of research and publication about the professor's scholarly communication process. Students should be able to demonstrate with this interview their understanding of the information dissemination process by applying the elements of the class discussion to a professor's individual area of interest.

Supplementary Materials

The materials in this section have been placed on the accompanying disk so they can easily be copied and/or modified to fit the needs of individual libraries and instructors.

- Journal Assignment: Information Environment Inventory
- Transparency: Diagram of the Scholarly Communication Process
- Assignment: The Five W's of Scholarly Communication

Notes:

Exploring the Definition(s) of Information

COLLEEN BELL

Library Instruction Coordinator
UNIVERSITY OF OREGON
cbell@darkwing.uoregon.edu

Circumstances of the Instruction

This activity encourages students to think about how the word "information" is used (or perhaps overused) in our vocabulary, and to consider whether information is different from data and knowledge, as well as how these terms are related to each other. It has been used quite successfully as a way to introduce the idea of classification (as it refers to the division of knowledge) and classification systems. Because students work individually as well as taking part in a larger class discussion, this activity works well in both small and large classes. It usually takes 30–50 minutes to complete.

Objectives of the Instruction

- Students will develop a definition of information.
- Students will identify the characteristics that distinguish information from data.
- Students will determine the relationships between data, information, and knowledge.

Components of the Instruction

Preparation

Prepare a transparency showing 2–3 definitions of the word "information." I use relevant pieces of the definitions from *Merriam-Webster's Dictionary*—http://www.m-w.com/—and the *Oxford English Dictionary*—http://dictionary.oed.com/—as well as the definition from *The ALA Glossary of Library and Information Science* (in that order), because each presents a different picture of the relationship between data, information, and knowledge.

Also prepare several examples using numbers and alphabetic characters that, when punctuation is added, take on meaning. For example:

544970168	544–97–0168	Social Security number
5413461817	(541) 346–1817	North American phone number
290364	29/03/64	date
567947028044064	$5,679,470,280,440.64	U.S. national debt at 4:45 pm on Dec 19, 2000
974031299	97403–1299	U.S. zip code
987654333	987–654=333	arithmetic expression

Use examples that are appropriate for your particular geographic area or institution. Prepare another set of examples that, when described in a particular context, take on meaning. For example:

+33 1 44 32 30 00	international phone number (a phone number in Paris)
cbell@darkwing.uoregon.edu	e-mail address for someone who works at an academic institution in Oregon
V0K 2E0	Canadian postal code
45, rue d'Ulm	street address in a French-speaking country
NaCl	chemical formula for sodium chloride, or table salt
2r=d	formula for the diameter of a circle

Again, use examples that are appropriate for your particular geographic area or institution, and that are examples your students are not likely to guess immediately.

Presentation/Activity/Discussion

Do not provide an introduction, except perhaps to explain that you will be looking at what information is. Give students 1–2 minutes to write a definition of the word "information." Ask them to share their definitions with the class. As they read their definitions out loud, write down the salient points on a whiteboard (or blackboard or flip chart, as appropriate for your setting). Ask your students if they agree with the definition they developed as a group; if not, ask them to revise the definition until they are satisfied with it.

Present each definition you prepared, one by one. Ask students if they agree or disagree with any part of the definition, and revise the definition they developed as you go along, using different colored markers. Note any parts of these prepared definitions that students disagree with, as well as any words that are used in the definitions that students feel do not fit with the definition they developed. Ideally, students would take exception to "information" being used synonymously with terms like "data" and "knowledge." Leave the definition on the board.

Next, present the first set of examples you prepared, one by one. Write the numbers on a second whiteboard (or blackboard or flip chart, as appropriate) without punctuation, and ask students to guess what the number means. Once students have made several guesses (one of which may or may not be the correct one), add the punctuation to make it clear. Does everyone understand the meaning now? Ask students if the first number fits their definition of information (ideally, the answer would be "no"). What about the second number? Ideally, the answer would be "yes." Ask them if they can articulate the reason why (e.g., information must be meaningful; a string of numbers is not meaningful, because we can only guess at the context).

Next, present the second set of examples and ask students to guess at their meaning. Some will be easy, others will not. After students have made several guesses (one of which may or may not be the correct one), ask them if it fits their definition of information. Ideally, the answer will be "yes." Ask them if they can articulate the reason why they could or could not identify the meaning of the phrase (e.g., information is contextual or has perspective; we automatically place it within a context shaped by our social, cultural, and educational experiences).

Finally, return to the definition the class created earlier and ask students if they are still satisfied with the definition. Ask them to think about the pieces of the prepared definitions and other terms that they felt were incorrectly used. How do these terms fit together? Are they synonymous? Are they related? How are they related?

Evaluation

One way to evaluate student learning in this lesson is to ask students to diagram the relationship between information and any other terms they identified in the activity (e.g., "data," "information," and "knowledge").

Sources:

Young, H. (Ed.). (1983). *The ALA glossary of library and information science*. Chicago: American Library Association.

Suggested Readings:

Roszak, T. (1994). Information, please. In *The cult of information: A neo-luddite treatise on high-tech, artificial intelligence, and the true art of thinking* (2d ed., pp. 3–20). Berkeley: University of California Press.

Shedroff, N. (2001). An overview of understanding. In Wurman, R. S. *Information Anxiety 2* (pp. 27–29). Indianapolis, IN: QUE. To provide a broader context for information as a concept, you might want to assign the entire chapter in which this brief article appears, which is entitled "The Business of Understanding" (pp. 23–52).

Wurman, R.S. (1994). The non-information explosion. In *Information anxiety: What to do when information doesn't tell you what you need to know* (pp. 31–50). New York: Bantam Books.

Notes:

Primary and Secondary Sources; Presentation and In-Class Exercise

GREGORY BOBISH

User Education/Reference Librarian
UNIVERSITY AT ALBANY, SUNY
gbobish@albany.edu

Circumstances of the Instruction

The concept of primary and secondary sources is a very important one for undergraduates to master. As students begin to conduct research in their own fields, they find that they must decide which source out of many is the best for a specific project. Many undergraduate students have never been exposed to the mass of scholarly and popular research that exists on practically every subject, and so they might assume that one source is as good as another. Combined with additional sessions on the evaluation of various sources of information, an understanding of primary and secondary sources will provide students with essential tools needed for academic success.

The following instruction session was developed for use in a quarter-long (seven weeks) information literacy class taught in a university library setting. It should take 20–30 minutes to complete depending on the level of student participation. Since the course meets a general education requirement, and the students come from various backgrounds and disciplines, the material is designed to have the widest possible application.

Objectives of the Instruction

Students will:
- Understand the difference between a primary and a secondary source.
- Recognize that the researcher's point of view may affect whether a source functions as primary or secondary.
- Understand the relationship between the publication cycle and primary and secondary sources.
- Be able to determine whether a given source is primary or secondary.

Components of the Instruction

The instruction consists of an instructor-class interaction, followed by an in-class exercise, each lasting 10–15 minutes.

Instruction (10–15 minutes)

1. Solicit ideas from the class about primary and secondary sources. Have they heard the terms before? If so, what definitions can they come up with?

2. Provide students with the first handout, "Primary and Secondary Sources and the Research Process," and go over definitions and examples of both types of sources. Ask students to suggest other possible primary and secondary sources.

3. Point out the recommended web sites at the bottom of the handout for further information.

4. Discuss the relationship between primary/secondary sources and the publication cycle. (What type of information is published first, what next, etc.?) Point out that items published at the same time an event occurs are more likely to be primary sources, but that this is not always the case.

In-Class Exercise (10–15 minutes)

This exercise can be done using handouts or presentation software such as Microsoft PowerPoint, depending on the instructor's preference and available facilities. When using a presentation program, the list of sources may be enhanced with images or sounds illustrating the source in question.

1. Present the students with a handout listing various primary and secondary sources (see "In-Class Exercise for Primary and Secondary Sources" in the Supplementary Materials) or display the list on a screen.

2. Ask students to offer their opinions about whether each source is primary or secondary. If they seem reluctant to respond ask them to vote for one or the other, or suggest an answer and ask them why it is correct or incorrect.

3. A sample list of sources is provided, but this can be altered based on the focus of the class. It is helpful to provide one or more sources that could fall into both categories depending on the researcher's goals.

Evaluation

In the University at Albany's Information Literacy course, the students are required to provide one primary and one secondary source on a topic of their choice as part of an annotated bibliography. Their success in doing this can be used as one measure of the success of the instruction session. Often students are more willing to discuss their difficulties in class if they have first tried to find a source on their own. Follow-up discussion in the next class is therefore highly recommended to reinforce the ideas as well as to answer any questions that may have arisen while completing the assignment. This discussion greatly assists the instructor in improving the effectiveness of the instruction by highlighting areas that may not have been adequately explained or understood.

Supplementary Materials

The materials in this section have been placed on the accompanying disk so they can easily be copied and/or modified to fit the needs of individual libraries and instructors.

- Primary and Secondary Sources and the Research Process
- In-Class Exercise for Primary and Secondary Sources

Publications Hierarchy: Question Authority!

Sue Ann Brainard

Reference/Instruction Librarian
SUNY Geneseo
brainard@geneseo.edu

Kimberly Davies

Reference/Instruction Librarian
SUNY Geneseo
davies@geneseo.edu

Circumstances of the Instruction

Students frequently have a difficult time distinguishing between scholarly and popular publications. Their professors tell them to only use scholarly works in their papers, yet students inevitably include sources from more popular literature. This is true with both print and web materials. It is necessary, then, that students know the specific criteria for evaluating sources and adopt a skeptical attitude when deciding whether a publication is scholarly or not. By asking students to sift through a pile of different types of material and filing them in the right categories —**scholarly, trade, popular, and tabloid**—by applying specific criteria to each, they will have a better understanding of the publications hierarchy. Additionally, students who are given a number of web sites to evaluate for content and design with help from an instructor will be able to decide whether or not a site is scholarly.

This lesson works well with a class of 15–20 students. There are two class sessions dedicated to the Publications Hierarchy lesson. In the first, students will break into groups of three or four to allow for enough input and evaluation from each student. They will work together and discuss why one publication fits under a certain category and not another. The second class will require students to work independently. Students should complete their tasks within 30 minutes, leaving 15–20 minutes remaining at the end of each class to discuss the results and their impressions on evaluating the sources given to them.

Objectives of the Instruction

- Students will be able to distinguish between popular magazines and scholarly, professional, and trade journals.
- Students will be able to identify web sites that are scholarly or popular; intended for a certain audience or geared toward the general public.
- Students will understand that some articles go through a strict "peer review" process before getting accepted for publication in a subset of scholarly journals known as "refereed," and how this affects the database selection stage of their research.
- Students will understand that successful academic use of the web depends on their own thoughtful analysis of what organizations and institutions might have the information they are seeking, and then searching for that organization's web site.

- Students will be able to define the word "authority" as it pertains to the information seeking process.
- Students will be able to determine who is intellectually responsible for a web page.
- Students will have a sense of under what circumstances it is appropriate to include popular materials in their research.

Components of the Instruction

The Publications Hierarchy lesson consists of two class sessions that do not have to be scheduled in sequential order. The two sessions are described below, beginning first with class 1 and followed by class 2.

Class 1

Preparation

For the first lesson, which involves student evaluation of scholarly, trade, popular, and tabloid print and electronic materials, the instructor should prepare individual signs that list the criteria of each publication type (see Supplementary Materials). A bulleted list of the criteria set in a large enough font, that makes the signs easy to read, is one way to design the visual. The instructor should also gather a variety of different sources from the library's collection including materials such as books, full-text articles from computer databases, newspapers, magazines, journals (bound and current), videos, compact discs, and printouts of web pages. A collection of these materials (a variety of 15–20 sources) should be placed on four or five tables around the classroom, depending on how many students are in the class, along with the five signs listing criteria for the different publication types. In other words, there should be four or five tables set up with a variety of 15–20 sources and the five criteria signs on each table. These tables will serve as the students' workstations.

Presentation

Before the students form their groups of three or four, the instructor should give a brief description of the activity and run down the lists of criteria, while illustrating specific examples. Students will then have an initial sense of what they must look for in each publication.

Hands-on Activity

During the first activity, students will break into groups and sit down at a table where the different materials have been placed. With a limited amount of help from the roaming instructor, students will discuss each item, fitting the different criteria to each, and determine the type of publication. They will gradually build piles in front of each sign indicating the publication type. Students may need quite a bit of assistance from the instructor at the beginning of the activity but should increasingly work amongst themselves to complete the task. Once the 30-minute period is over and the students have finished categorizing their sources, the instructor will move the class from one workstation to another. Students within a specific group will tell the rest of the class why they classified certain sources the way they did. Questions are bound to arise and the instructor should first let the students try to answer their peers' questions based on their experiences in this activity. If students are stumped on a particular issue, the instructor should then add insight.

Class 2

Preparation

The second class focuses on student evaluation of pre-selected web sites. The instructor should create a web page that lists the main criteria for scholarly, trade, popular, and tabloid publications and provides examples of web sites for each publication type (see Supplementary Materials). The instructor should add different examples of popular and scholarly web sites that the students will evaluate linked from the course web page. This will allow the class to have one main source from which they can access each web site.

Presentation

Before the students begin to work independently, the instructor should give a brief description of the activity and run down the lists of criteria, while illustrating specific examples. Students will then have an initial sense of what they will be looking for in each web site.

Hands-on Activity

The class on web evaluation is set up so that students will be given two different web sites linked from the course page that they will have to analyze and classify as scholarly, trade, popular, or tabloid. After 30 minutes of evaluating, the instructor will call on each student to demonstrate their sites and discuss the criteria they found that would categorize the site as scholarly or popular. A projection or control system where the class can focus in on one student's workstation would be ideal for this situation. The instructor should ask pointed questions and highlight certain aspects of a site that a student might have overlooked. The instructor should also provide helpful hints that go beyond the evaluation of one site depending on the type of research that might use a more popular or biased site.

Evaluation

As the students teach the class what they have learned through evaluation of their assigned materials, the instructor should listen for clues that demonstrate students have achieved the various learning objectives.

Sources:

Sue Ann Brainard's web page, "Finding Web Sites for Academic Research," http://library.geneseo.edu/~brainard/fws.htm.

Sue Ann Brainard's web page, "Tips for Evaluating Web Sites," http://library.geneseo.edu/~brainard/tipsevaluating.htm.

Supplementary Materials

The materials in this section have been placed on the accompanying disk so they can easily be copied and/or modified to fit the needs of individual libraries and instructors.

- Signs listing the criteria for types of publications. Post the signs on tables in the classroom.
  - Refereed
  - Scholarly
  - Trade
  - Popular
  - Tabloid
- Worksheets that guide students through the evaluation of web sites.
  - Web Evaluation Checklist
  - Criteria for Evaluating Web Documents
  - Evaluating Web Sites

Defining, Identifying, and Understanding the Difference between Data, Information, and Knowledge

GERALD T. BURKE

Humanities Bibliographer
UNIVERSITY AT ALBANY, SUNY
gtb03@csc.albany.edu

Circumstances of the Instruction

With the development of digital technology, the production and distribution of data and information has increased dramatically, and many students equate quantity with quality. In addition, many print resources have been making the transition to digital format, and with the development of the Internet, in particular the World Wide Web, a great deal of the responsibility for determining value and authority has shifted to the individual user. This question of determining value and authority is an issue that students must be made aware of, but first they need to be aware that all things digital, or print for that matter, are not created equal. They need to be aware of the distinction between data, information, and knowledge.

Generally, the difference between data and information can be recognized easily, but the difference between information and knowledge frequently is more difficult to discern. Students need to be aware of the process of analysis, synthesis, and critical thinking that transforms information into knowledge. This exercise is designed to introduce them to the basic categories of data, information, and knowledge so they can begin their own process of creating knowledge and, at some point, transforming that knowledge into wisdom.

Students will be introduced to basic definitions, form groups, and identify examples of each category. Then each group presents to the class their example with a brief explanation. The use of a national newspaper is a good vehicle because of its diversity, currency, and familiarity to most students. Finding examples of data is usually easy, while examples of information and particularly knowledge is more difficult. Still, this difficulty can provoke discussion and provide an excellent instance of the sometimes vague distinctions when value and authority is added to data and information.

The exercise is best with a class of 10–15 students, although larger classes could be accommodated with the use of additional newspapers. Overall the exercise should take 30–60 minutes, but the time can be adjusted by using selected group examples.

Objectives of the Instruction

- Introduce basic definitions and distinctions between data, information, and knowledge.
- Show that these distinctions generally are consistent regardless of the content being examined.

- Show instances where the boundaries between data, information, and knowledge can be blurred.

Components of the Instruction

Preparation

1. Prepare a handout of straightforward and relatively simply definitions of data, information, and knowledge. A useful resource is the *ODLIS: Online Dictionary of Library and Information Science* by Joan M. Reitz located at —http://www.wcsu.edu/library/odlis.html. Key words or phrases are highlighted to emphasize basic concepts.
2. Prepare a handout that allows each group to fill in a "citation" to identify each instance of data, information, and knowledge, and additional space for the group to briefly explain why each instance qualifies as an example of each category.
3. Make enough packets of the definitions and worksheets for each group.
4. Purchase (or borrow) a copy of a current national newspaper like the *New York Times*, *Washington Post*, or *Los Angles Times*. A national newspaper will have enough sections to be sufficiently diverse and in-depth for the assignment, covering national and international news, sports, business, arts, science, dining, etc.

Presentation

After distributing the definitions handout to all students, go over them with one or two brief examples of each. Then have a few students volunteer examples of their own to reinforce the concept.

Hands-on Activity

- Break the class into groups of three or four students and give each group a citation/explanation handout.
- Next, give each group a section of the newspaper. Explain that the group must cite and explain one example each of data, information, and knowledge.
- Rove the class answering questions and making sure students have a clear understanding of the definitions and overall assignment.

When the groups are done, have them present their findings. Have each group identify their example of data and read their explanation. Do the same for information and then knowledge. Since these last two topics are more complex, some of the examples may seem to fit the other definition and vice versa; you can ask other students to comment and this may provoke discussion.

Evaluation

This exercise works well on two levels. Generally it will turn up clear examples of data, information, and knowledge; on the other hand, the examples that are not so clear-cut show how sometimes what appears as data can, in certain circumstances, be labeled as information and vice versa, and this is also true with information and knowledge. In the end, students will have a basic understanding of the concepts and an understanding that definitions can, at times, be problematic requiring an analysis of context or point of view for clarification.

Supplementary Materials

The materials in this section have been placed on the accompanying disk so they can easily be copied and/or modified to fit the needs of individual libraries and instructors.

- Definitions Handout:
  Definitions: Data, Information, and Knowledge
- Evaluation Worksheets:
  Identifying Data, Information, and Knowledge in a National Newspaper (Data)
  Identifying Data, Information, and Knowledge in a National Newspaper (Information)
  Identifying Data, Information, and Knowledge in a National Newspaper (Knowledge)

Notes:

Primary vs. Secondary Sources

CAROL ANNE GERMAIN

Networked Resources Education Librarian
UNIVERSITY AT ALBANY, SUNY
cg219@albany.edu

Circumstances of the Instruction

By the end of a student's college experience, they will be required to use primary and secondary resources for papers. Teaching the difference between these sources is often challenging. This session is preliminary instruction.

Objectives of the Instruction

The successful student will have the ability to:
- explain what a primary source is and provide examples;
- define what a secondary source is and provide examples; and
- differentiate between a primary and a secondary source.

Components of the Instruction

Preparation

Packets containing different sources with specific topics need to be prepared. In each packet include:
- Two primary sources
- Two secondary sources
- Research topic
- Four worksheets to be filled out, soliciting the following information for each item in the packet:
    - What is the source?
    - Primary?__   Secondary?__
    - Why primary/secondary?

Packet Examples

Packet #1
Topic – Techno musician Moby

Primary sources:	Cover from Moby's CD *Play*
	Lyrics to the song Honey printed from an Internet
Secondary sources:	Review of Moby's CD *Play* from the *New York Times*
	Review of same CD printed from *Amazon.com*

Packet #2
Topic – Spike Lee movies
Primary sources: *Do the Right Thing*, movie by Spike Lee
                       Malcolm X, movie by Spike Lee
Secondary sources: *Spike Lee's Do the Right Thing*, a book by Mark A. Reid
                       "Spike Lee and the American Tradition" from *Literature Film Quarterly*
                       24.1 (1996): 26.

Lecture

Primary and secondary sources are the core of this lecture. Definitions for each are provided. For many, this concept is **very hard** to grasp. I emphasize to students that primary is original and secondary is interpretation. Many examples are given for each type of source following the same theme for each.

Examples of this include:

Declaration of Independence
An article reviewing the Declaration of Independence

The car manual from my Honda Civic
An article from *Consumer Reports* critiquing the Honda Civic

Roe v Wade, 410 U.S. 959
An analysis of Roe versus Wade

Hands-on Activity

The class is broken up into groups of 3–4 people. Each group receives a packet (described above). The groups are given 5–7 minutes to review the sources in the packet and to fill out the four worksheets. Each group will have a "reporter" who will inform their findings to the rest of the class.

Evaluation

Students' response to this exercise will let you evaluate its effectiveness. If students paid attention to the lecture, they will be able to make the distinctions with the sources. You will need to correct mistakes and provide explanations for your evaluation.

Production and Transfer of Information in the Sciences

KATE MANUEL

Physical Sciences Librarian, Instructional & Interpretive Services
CALIFORNIA STATE UNIVERSITY, HAYWARD
kmanuel@csuhayward.edu

Circumstances of the Instruction

This activity is designed to introduce students to the main patterns and tempos of information production and communication in the sciences, especially the physical sciences, while laying the groundwork for introducing students to the types of information tools used to access the characteristic products of the different stages of the information flow. Students should gain awareness of the time between an idea/basic research and its communication in certain types of publications, as well as the likelihood of finding various types of information in distinct types of sources.

This activity consists of a story-telling session, accompanied by handouts presenting a visual encapsulation, as well as a textual summary, of the story's main points, followed by a crossword puzzle giving students clues related to the story and handouts. The crossword puzzle asks students to recall the meanings and applications of particular terms from the story, as these terms serve as the "answers" to the puzzle's clues. Students work well in teams of two or, at most, three students. The entire session can take place in 50 minutes, with approximately 20–25 minutes being spent telling the story and looking at the accompanying visual aids, and another 25–30 minutes being spent by students working on the crossword puzzle.

This activity works best in the 3rd or 4th week of a quarter or semester, after the students have had time to develop a better sense of their peers, the instructor, and the group's dynamics. The reason for this is that the story can be told with involvement of and participation by the students at crucial junctures, provided that the teacher is able to "read" the students and the students are comfortable with the teacher and with each other. It is often less distracting to the students if the story is told first, before the handouts are presented; the story that has been told can then be mapped to the handouts after it has been told. Storytelling can work well with students who are not native speakers of English provided that the instructor takes care to select an appropriate example, to speak clearly, slowly, and with appropriate vocabulary, and to allow pauses for questions related to comprehension of the story.

The crossword puzzle/activity works best if students are allowed to work individually for a few minutes before being partnered with one or two others to check their work and answer each other's questions.

Objectives of the Instruction

- Students will learn the main patterns and tempos of information production and communication in the sciences, especially the physical sciences.
- Students will learn the types of information tools used to access the characteristic products of the different stages of this information flow.

Components of the Instruction

Hands-on Activity

The Story (briefly): This is the story of a man named Andy. One weekend, on a summer afternoon, Andy is in the backyard with his buddies drinking beer and barbecuing hamburgers. Everyone agrees it's too hot out to be grilling with charcoal or gas, and Andy proposes a solar barbecue, which would use the sun's heat to grill the food. Andy does not abandon plans for his solar barbecue when the workweek comes. He builds a device, tests it, and mentions it to friends and co-workers. He gets a workable device and patents it. Over time, other people researching solar technologies hear of Andy's ideas. Andy is invited to present a paper at the annual solar technologies conference. Andy writes the text of his presentation for the conference. In addition to giving this paper to the conference organizers for inclusion in the published conference proceedings, Andy posts a copy of his text to the Department of Energy e-print server, thinking that other scholars researching alternative energy sources will be interested in what he has to say.

Some of his fellow attendees at the conference really like what Andy had to say. They encourage him to do some research studies and write up his findings in an article for the journal *Solar Technologies*. Andy spends several years researching and writing – not only does this scholarly work take lots of time; Andy is also busy founding his own company to manufacture solar barbecues. Once Andy submits the article to *Solar Technologies*, the journal editors send it out to other solar researchers for review (a process called "peer review"). The review takes about six months, and by the time Andy completes making the changes to his article that were suggested by the reviewers, more time has passed. Andy's article is finally published in *Solar Technologies* about 12 months after he submitted it and several years after his presentation at the solar technologies conference.

Once the article is published, Andy gets back to the work of running his company and making money. Meanwhile, a researcher named Julie begins writing a book on solar technologies. She finds Andy's article listed in an article database, reads it, and devotes a chapter of her book to solar cooking methods – with most of it being about solar barbecues. Julie spends 12–24 months researching her book. Once she has finished writing, it takes another 12–16 months for the editors at the company publishing her book to review it for mistakes. Julie's book is finally published, though, in both print form and electronically in a "digital library." (The electronic version is not available freely on the web though, only people paying for that "digital library" get access to Julie's book.) Julie goes on to do other research and write other things.

Then along comes Jamal, an expert on technology. Jamal has a contract with a publishing company to produce an *Encyclopedia of Innovations*. He finds Julie's book in a library, reads it, and learns a bit about Andy's invention from it. Jamal spends years in compiling his encyclopedia. In it, he includes an entry on solar technologies, using and citing Julie's book as a source. He very briefly mentions the solar barbecue as an example, without naming Andy or citing Andy's article.

Meanwhile, Andy has become rich and famous because of his solar barbecue. He sells his company and retires early to an island in the Mediterranean. Before leaving for his island, Andy bundles up all his personal papers – letters, notes, and e-mails relating to his work on the solar barbecue, to his company, and to his personal life – and donates them to the library of the university from which he got his bachelor's degree. The university's library makes Andy's papers available in the archives. A few of Andy's most important papers relating to the solar barbecue are digitized by the library and posted on their web site.

Finally, 85 years after her book was published, the copyright expires on Julie's book. (Copyright protection lasts for the life of the author plus 70 years.) The Association of Inventors is free to post this classic text on their web site, and researchers using search engines can find the site by searching on the topic of "solar power."

Evaluation

Students' understanding of the information addressed by these activities can be assessed by multiple choice and true/false quizzes or by open-ended essays. A sample open-ended question is as follows: You need to find the latest, most current research on filtering technologies as the research is in progress, as well as preliminary findings of this research. Is an encyclopedia article a good place to look for this? Why?

Sources:

Nancy Lane, Margaret Chisholm, and Carolyn Mateer, *Techniques for Student Research: A Comprehensive Guide to Using the Library* (pp. 4–5). New York : Neal-Schuman Publishers, 2000.

Supplementary Materials

The materials in this section have been placed on the accompanying disk so they can easily be copied and/or modified to fit the needs of individual libraries and instructors.

- Production, Communication, and Organization of Information
- How Scientific Information Is Communicated and Published
- Crossword Puzzle

Notes:

Around the World of Information

ANNE MOORE

NEW MEXICO STATE UNIVERSITY
annemoor@bellsouth.net

Circumstances of the Instruction

Summary

In small groups and during a visit to the library (with a computer classroom), students practice locating the different types of information sources found in a library and online to support a course research paper or project.

Importance

Students apply the research skills conveyed in the information literacy course in group work and oral presentations. The interactive practice of locating and evaluating information sources makes the process easier to replicate when the students conduct their own research. Although in this class meeting students practice finding just one type of information source, they hear about finding other types of sources during oral presentations.

Level

The activity is appropriate for all information literacy courses. The activity is especially effective when conducted in smaller and undergraduate libraries.

Size

The class size may range from 12 to 24 students.

Length

The session requires one 50-minute class session plus an additional class for oral presentations.

Objectives of the Instruction

- Students practice the research process.
- Students learn to locate materials from one category of information source.
- Students work in small groups to apply research techniques and develop interpersonal skills.
- Students practice evaluating information sources.
- Students analyze the process of searching for information sources.
- Students practice their oral presentation skills.

Components of the Instruction

Preparation

The instructor makes sufficient copies of the evaluation criteria used by the instructor, department, or library (see Sources for examples) and Source Evaluation Rubric (see Supplementary Materials) for each student. The instructor selects a controversial and intriguing (but narrow, e.g., should the Electoral College be abandoned?) topic on which sources from a variety of categories of information sources are available in the library, through electronic databases, and on the Internet. The instructor plans to divide the class randomly into evenly sized groups of three to five students (e.g., distributing slips as the students arrive). Each group will search for relevant materials from a single category of information source. For example, these categories might be reference sources, books, scholarly journal articles, web sites, newspaper articles, government documents, etc.

Presentation

As the class arrives, the instructor distributes the copies of the evaluation criteria recommended by the instructor, department, or library (see Sources for examples). Using a different aspect of the topic the students will research (e.g., background information on the Electoral College), the instructor briefly reviews how to find each type of source and how to apply the evaluation criteria. This demonstration should not exceed 20 minutes. If not already accomplished, the instructor divides the class into groups and assigns each group one of the categories of information sources.

Hands-on Activity

Students work in their groups for 20 minutes to find several relevant, high quality sources from their assigned category. They may work anywhere in the library and might retrieve an actual source (e.g., a book or government document from the collection). The instructor circulates through the area to monitor and advise the groups.

Each group gets together for an additional five to ten minutes to evaluate the sources and select the best one to present to the class. Each group appoints a spokesperson and prepares a brief oral presentation.

The class assembles in the computer classroom for the next class meeting. Before the oral presentations, the instructor distributes the Source Evaluation Rubric to which the students will evaluate the source presented by each group. Each group's spokesperson shares the selected source or whatever documentation the group located about the item (e.g., online catalog record, full-text article, web site). The spokesperson displays an electronic source either by coming forward to the instructor workstation or from his or her workstation if the lab has a control system. The spokesperson explains why this item is the best example of that type of information source on the topic and justifies the choice with the evaluation criteria. The instructor guides the presentations by probing for subjective analysis of the process each group used, what they learned from the experience, and perhaps for a noteworthy source the students rejected.

Evaluation

One member of each group must complete the Source Evaluation Rubric for the source presented by one of the spokespersons. The instructor collects these forms at the end of the session. After the session, the instructor assigns a grade to each source presented using the student evaluations as reminders. All the members of the group receive that grade on the assignment, except for the spokesperson that receives extra credit.

Sources:

Alexander, J., & Tate, M. (1996). *Evaluating web resources.* Chester, PA: Widener University, Wolfgram Memorial Library. Retrieved December 11, 2000, from the WWW— http://www2.widener.edu/Wolfgram-Memorial-Library/webevaluation/webeval.htm.

Beck, S. E. (1997). *The good, the bad, & the ugly: Or, why it's a good idea to evaluate web sources.* Las Cruces, NM: New Mexico State University Library. Retrieved December 11, 2000, from the World Wide Web— http://lib.nmsu.edu/instruction/evalcrit.html.

Grassian, E. (2000). *Thinking critically about World Wide Web resources.* Los Angeles, CA: UCLA College Library. Retrieved December 11, 2000, from the World Wide Web— http://www.library.ucla.edu/libraries/college/help/critical/index.htm.

Henderson, J. R. (1999). *ICYouSee: T is for thinking.* Ithaca, NY: Ithaca College Library. Retrieved December 11, 2000, from the World Wide Web— http://www.ithaca.edu/library/Training/hott.html.

Jacobson, T., & Cohen, L. (1996). *Evaluating Internet resources.* Albany, NY: University at Albany Libraries. Retrieved December 11, 2000, from the World Wide Web— http://library.albany.edu/internet/evaluate.html.

Ten C's for evaluating Internet sources. (2000). Eau Claire, WI: University of Wisconsin Eau Claire, McIntyre Library. Retrieved December 11, 2000, from the World Wide Web— http://www.uwec.edu/Admin/Library/Guides/tencs.html.

Supplementary Material

The material in this section has been placed on the accompanying disk so it can easily be copied and/or modified to fit the needs of individual libraries and instructors.

- Source Evaluation Rubric

Notes:

Section 4—OPACs, Databases, and Indexes: Content and Searching Techniques

Human Database

Search Scenario

Let's Go Fishing!

Translating English into Computerese

Creating Effective Search Strategies

Print Periodical Indexes CAN Be Useful

Effective Databases Searches; Setting the Stage and Evaluating Learning

Teaching Students the Concept of Controlled Vocabulary

Using Tatooing to Teach Boolean Searching

Understanding Controlled Vocabulary; A Thesaurus Exercise

Boolean Logic

Empowering Students: Encouraging Peer to Peer Learning

Human Database

SUE ANN BRAINARD

Reference/Instruction Librarian
SUNY GENESEO
brainard@geneseo.edu

Circumstances of the Instruction

Successful searching of research databases depends on the understanding of crucial concepts such as adjacency, proximity, Boolean operators, keyword searching, subject heading searching, field searching, and truncation. These are difficult concepts for most students to comprehend. A fun, lively demonstration of how a computer processes these commands can teach the meanings of the concepts, and teach why it is beneficial to use them when searching databases.

The focus should be on concepts, not specific databases. It is preferable to teach students concepts and how the use of a technique could benefit them rather than try to teach specific databases and their screen arrangements. Ideally, after a student understands Boolean operators, truncation, etc., they will be motivated to search for tips about using these techniques in whatever database they are searching.

This activity works best with 15–20 students, but can be adapted for as few as 10 and as many as 40 by using fewer of the film database records, or by handing more than one record to each student. Depending on the complexity of the students' questions, the activity could take up to an hour and fifteen minutes to complete. (It will take less time if there are few questions.) It can conceivably be broken into two sessions, with the break happening after the last use of the film database and before the class starts looking at real databases. The activity is designed to be used with anyone who is new to database searching or unhappy with the quality of their own database searching attempts. (This activity was first used with an older audience, so older films were used to create the database. With a younger audience, new popular films could be added to pique their interest.)

Objectives of the Instruction

- Students will understand basic computer capabilities and database construction.
- Students will understand subject heading and keyword searching, proximity and adjacency, and truncation.
- Students will successfully use Boolean operators AND, OR, NOT to refine a search.
- Students will navigate search screens and help screens of databases to find out how the database allows the building and refining of search strategies.

Components of the Instruction

Preparation

The instructor should prepare index cards with information about films arranged into fields, with common field names (see "Film Database Records" in Supplementary Materials). This becomes the "Film Database" used during the session. The instructor should make overhead transparencies of these cards as well so that the entire class will be able to see a copy of the card one student is holding. The instructor should also create a poster (large enough to be seen by everyone in the room) with the list of database searching terms and phrases that will be discussed throughout the class (see "Database Searching Terminology (poster)" in the Supplementary Materials.) It should be placed near the front of the classroom, as it will be referred to often during the session. The instructor should have an overhead projector available for showing the transparencies made of the cards in the database. A computer with projection capabilities is necessary to connect the "human" database that the students are creating to the actual research databases available on campus. Various databases should be used as examples, which may mean an Internet connection if the libraries' databases are online. Finally, a dry erase board or blackboard is needed so that the instructor can write commands for the human database to perform. (Blank transparencies on the overhead projector can be used to write on if a board is not available.)

Presentation

At the beginning of the session, the instructor should direct students' attention to the poster listing words and phrases to be defined during class. This serves as an outline of the session for the students and is a visual reminder for the instructor of what terms to define, demonstrate, and review at the end of the session.

The instructor should give each student a card on which there is a record from the film database. The instructor should define the word **database** briefly, saying that databases are made up of records that are made up of fields, where data is located. Using a sample record from the Film Database on the overhead projector, the parts of a record, such as field names, should be discussed. It should be stressed that each student in the room has a record (has "become" a record in a database) with exactly the same field names, but different data. *Data* should be discussed. The instructor should remind students that, to a computer, a word is just a string of letters followed by and preceded by spaces. A computer is simply following the commands given to it and cannot discern the intent of the searcher!

The instructor should begin demonstrating database searches with a query that directs the students to pass their eyes over the data on their card looking for the words **Alfred Hitchcock**. Write the words on a dry erase board, blackboard, or blank transparency. Several students should respond, and the instructor should ask each to tell the name of the film whose record contains the words **Alfred Hitchcock**. The instructor should put the corresponding transparencies on the overhead pointing out where the words occur. Eventually, the student holding the card that has **Alfred Hitchcock** in the summary but not as director is mentioned. The instructor should point out that the query just performed was a **keyword search**, which allows the words to appear anywhere on the record.

The instructor should then announce, and write on the board, the second query, **Director: Alfred Hitchcock**. The total number of students who respond to this query should be fewer, since only those students whose cards mention **Hitchcock** as the director should respond. It should be pointed out that this is an example of field searching, and that all of the fields on the cards can be searched in this way, resulting in more precise searches than a keyword search. In other words, students can tell the database where, or in what field, they want to look for their specified terms.

Using the computer and research databases, the instructor should discuss and demonstrate how a typical database screen is arranged. For example, many databases don't allow you to change any fields at the basic search level; the importance of getting to the advanced screen should be stressed. The instructor should demonstrate that the advanced database screens are usually set up to search keyword (in other words, the default is a keyword search). Most have drop-down menus that allow the searcher to change the fields to be searched. The instructor should point out that if the database on the screen was the computerized version of the human database of film information, the drop down menu would contain the field names of Director, Title, Actor, Genre, Summary, Date, and so on. Several different databases should be demonstrated to illustrate to students that even though each database's search screen looks different, the main elements are always there: search box and drop-down menus to change fields. The instructor can query the students every time a new database screen is displayed asking them to point out how to change the field being searched.

Next, refer to the poster of vocabulary words, pointing to the words already defined: database, field, record, keyword searching, field searching, text box, and drop-down menu. Attention should then be drawn to the concepts that will be defined next, Boolean operators AND, OR, NOT.

Write on the board **Director: Alfred Hitchcock and Actor: Jimmy Stewart** and direct the students whose records answer the first part of the query **Director: Alfred Hitchcock** to raise their hands. The rest of the students should be told that they are ignored for the rest of the search, since ONLY those records that fit the first part of the query will be searched for the second part, **Actor: Jimmy Stewart**. Direct those students with **Director: Alfred Hitchcock** to scan the actor field looking for the words **Jimmy Stewart**. Only one should respond since the film *The Man Who Knew Too Much* is the only one that matches the criteria. It should be pointed out that using the Boolean operator AND narrowed the search, and actually requires that the computer do two searches. The part of the search statement to the left of the AND is done first, and the second part of the statement to the right of the AND is applied only to the results of the first search. The results must satisfy both sides of the equation. The instructor should demonstrate this using Venn diagrams for those students who are visual learners (see "Venn Diagrams" in the Supplementary Materials.) Again, only the student holding the card that matches the left side of the search statement, **Director: Alfred Hitchcock**, AND the right side of the statement, **Actor: Jimmy Stewart**, should respond. It should be the student holding the record for *The Man Who Knew Too Much*.

Point out that with AND searches, it does not matter which statement comes first, the results will be the same. Demonstrate this by saying **Actor: Jimmy Stewart** and pause while hands go up. (There will be other students responding than with the preceding search, since all the students with cards naming **Jimmy Stewart** as actor should respond). Now add AND **Director: Alfred**

Hitchcock. The search will narrow to the same results as before when the second part of the statement is applied.

The instructor should continue in this manner, using the following searches to demonstrate the concepts not yet discussed.

To demonstrate Boolean operator OR
> **Director: Alfred Hitchcock OR Director: Frank Capra**

To demonstrate a complex search that uses both AND and OR
> **(Director: Alfred Hitchcock OR Director: Frank Capra) AND Actor: Jimmy Stewart**

To demonstrate the Boolean operator NOT
> **Actor: Harrison Ford NOT Genre: Action**

In order to tie what has been happening thus far to real databases, the instructor should show two examples of database screens. Point out and demonstrate two ways that database screens allow you to use Boolean operators. One requires the user to type the search statement with AND, OR, or NOT directly into a text box, much like the way the instructor has been writing on the board during the session. The other requires the user to change a drop-down menu, with the options being AND, OR, and NOT, situated between text boxes.

Draw the students' attention to the poster listing the database terminology and point out that they have demonstrated Boolean operators AND, OR, NOT. Next, the class will focus on adjacency (phrase searching), subject headings, truncation, and proximity.

Adjacency should be discussed briefly before demonstrating it. The instructor should point out that in some databases two words together are automatically considered a phrase but in most databases, an AND is automatically inserted whenever two words are typed into a search box. In these latter databases, quotation marks placed around two words will cue the computer into searching for those two words in exactly the order they are typed. This can be demonstrated by writing the words **"John Bates"** in quotes and directing only those students with cards where the two words fall next to each other in that exact order to respond. This will result in one film, *Beloved*. Removing the quotes results in another film, *Primary Colors*, in addition to *Beloved*. This is because **John Bates** without the quotes becomes **John AND Bates**. This search retrieves *Primary Colors* because of **John** Travolta and Kathy **Bates**. In should be pointed out that some phrases should be separated out into separate words. An example would be **"alien spacecraft"** which retrieves one film, *E.T.* Putting it in quotes, however, misses the film *Star Wars*, whose summary mentions **"aliens** in a **spacecraft."** Students should be cautioned, then, that careful thought must go into constructing the search statement.

The subject heading field should be pointed out on the overhead in an example record from the film database. The instructor should discuss how subject headings are used in most databases, and that they are assigned by indexers to tell what the film, article, or book is all about. Those words or phrases are not assigned randomly, however, but from a controlled vocabulary list. This

162

concept should be described briefly, perhaps by pointing out that the English language has many words to describe the same things (such as lawyer and attorney, or teenager and adolescent). A controlled vocabulary list means that indexers have agreed on which word to use when talking about a subject. That word becomes the official term, called the subject heading, in a database. Give some examples, such as the use of the word neoplasm instead of the word cancer in medical databases.

The benefits of searching by subject heading should be demonstrated by first doing a keyword search for the word **war**. Many of the student's hands will go up, as the word **war** is used in many of the records, in many different fields. The instructor should put some of the successful records on the overhead, pointing out that though a few films are really about **war**, most use the word **war** to describe behavior ("**war** between the races") or as a descriptor, as in "World **War** II gunboat." At this point, say and write **Subject Heading: war** on the board. Now only a few hands will go up, and all will be about the subject of **war**: *Gone with the Wind*, *M*A*S*H*, and *Saving Private Ryan*.

To further demonstrate subject headings, use
      school (as keyword).
Then use
      school (as subject heading) and compare the results.

Next, the difficulty in coming up with the right subject headings should be demonstrated along with the search technique called *truncation*. Begin by describing the common use of the asterisk (*) after the stem of a word in order to retrieve the plural and other forms of the word. For instance, in most databases **teach*** will retrieve **teach, teaches, teacher, teachers, teaching**, etc. Also mention internal truncation, perhaps using **wom?n** as an example. At this juncture, say and write **Subject Heading: teenager***. This will retrieve no results. The instructor should explain that when controlled vocabularies are used, the "wrong" word frequently retrieves nothing. If the searcher cannot think of another subject heading, it is possible to discover the "official" heading by doing a keyword search. The instructor should say and write the word **teenager***. Several students will respond. Some will have cards with the word **teenage**, others will have the word **teenagers** or even **teenaged**. The students should be directed to look at the subject heading field on their record to see what the official subject heading is. The answer will be adolescents or adolescence. The group should then be given the command **Subject Heading: Adolescen***. Several pertinent films result, including *Wizard of Oz, Rebel Without a Cause*, and *To Sir With Love*, some that have **adolescence** as a subject heading, and some that have **adolescents** as a subject heading.

Now discuss full-text databases, telling the students to imagine that the cards in their hands actually have the full-length movie script attached to them. Unless they are searching for a very unique word that is rarely used or has only one distinct meaning, searching by keyword is almost useless. It will search hundreds of pages of text, and many words will appear over and over again. Subject headings and other field searches should be used whenever possible. However, it should be pointed out that there are times when subject heading searches fail, and keyword searches are necessary. In these cases, proximity may be helpful. The instructor should point out that in many databases, the proximity operator is NEAR, and allows the searcher to find the words

163

they specify near each other in the text. In some databases, NEAR means "within a set number of words," such as ten. In others, the searcher has to designate how many words apart the words can be.

Demonstrate proximity by asking students if they thought the full-text of their movie script contained the word **death**. Many should respond positively. Now ask if they thought the following search would be successful in their script: **death near angel**. There should only be one, *It's a Wonderful Life*.

Finally, the instructor should construct a complex search on the board, asking students again to imagine the full-text of their film to the best of their knowledge: **(death or suicide or murder) near (angel or spirit or ghost) and Director: Hitchcock and Genre: drama**. One film should result: *Rebecca*.

Turning back to the computer, demonstrate a full-text database with the capability to do a complex search such as the one above, where periodical articles are used instead of film information. Specifically, the students should be shown how to use the proximity operator NEAR in the database as well as how to use truncation. By investigating the help screens, show how to find information about all of the search techniques that have been discussed in class. Stress that students should always consult help screens because symbols and options will vary from database to database.

A handout entitled Database Searching Troubleshooting Guide can be given to help students remember when to use the different database searching techniques covered during the class (see Supplementary Materials). A handout called Database Searching Terminology can be given out so students can take with them the definitions of the terms discussed in class (see Supplementary Materials).

The instructor should direct students' attention back to the poster with the word list. By this time, all of the words should have been discussed, so use this review as a way to evaluate the session.

Evaluation

The instructor should randomly pick students to define the database terminology from the posted list. Students should also be asked when it is useful to use the technique. This will give the instructor a good idea of the success of the session.

Supplementary Materials

These materials are not included on the accompanying disk but will be found on the following web site—http://library.albany.edu/usered/concepts.

- Film Database Records
- Venn Diagrams
- Database Searching Terminology (poster)
- Database Searching Terminology (handout)
- Database Searching Troubleshooting Guide

Search Scenario

SUE ANN BRAINARD

Reference/Instruction Librarian
SUNY GENESEO
brainard@geneseo.edu

Circumstances of the Instruction

This activity helps teach students how to refine a search strategy using advanced search techniques like Boolean operators, truncation, adjacency, and subject headings. It also helps them learn to read and evaluate citations and abstracts, and think about the suitability of sources for specific research projects.

The class session needs to be held in a computer lab with projection capabilities. An overhead projector is also necessary. The activity works well whether students are working by themselves or with a partner. It should be used with students who have previously had a basic database searching lesson and have seen several demonstrations of database searches. They should already be familiar with the library's web site and how to use it to access research databases.

Objectives of the Instruction

- Students will demonstrate their knowledge of Boolean operators (AND, OR, NOT), truncation, subject heading searching, keyword searching, and limiting by year.
- Students will demonstrate their ability to analyze the search screen and help screens of a database in order to determine how to perform the most effective search possible.
- Students will determine whether a set of search results is appropriate or not for a particular research problem, and will demonstrate the ability to correct the search to yield better results.

Components of the Instruction

Preparation

Prepare a search scenario for each student or pair of students. The search scenario presents an unsuccessful attempt to find articles on a topic, along with a printout of the actual search results, and space for the student to report the improvements they are suggesting. The scenario consists of a sheet of paper with a research topic at the top, the name of a research database below it, and a search screen from the database (screen capture works well) filled out with search terms. The bottom of the sheet should consist of a blank search screen where students will write the revised search statement once they figure out a way to improve the search. Attach the printout of the results of the search which should show that the search produced too few articles, too many articles, or articles inappropriate to the search topic.

Create search scenarios using topics that are complex and do the initial search in the most suitable database for the topic. (Other class sessions might be devoted to choosing the best database for a task; this activity focuses on improving search results.) The scenario should include a flawed search statement that fails to use advanced techniques like truncation, Boolean operators, subject headings, or phrase searching. The instructor should choose search words that are unscholarly (*teenager* instead of *adolescent*, for instance), and should use words that have multiple meanings. This will force students to use subject heading searches when they try to improve the search. The results of each of these initial flawed searches should either be too few results (such as one or two), too many results (more than 40), or inappropriate results (such as articles that only briefly mention the search words). Make sure that these flaws are well represented among the students so that multiple students or groups of students are grappling with the same issues.

Presentation

Place a sample search scenario on an overhead projector. Tell the students that today's session will be devoted to improving an unsuccessful search. (Students can be told to imagine that a friend is asking for advice and they should make improvements to the friend's search strategy.) Guide the class through the process of improving a search, using the example on the overhead. Show where on the sheet to find the name of the research database used in the scenario and show the search as it appears on the first sheet of the search scenario. The results of the search should be looked at and a decision made about why the results are unsatisfactory. The students can then recommend ways to improve the search, which the instructor demonstrates until all agree that the search is as much improved as can be. This should take no more than ten minutes.

Now hand out the search scenarios to individuals or groups, announcing that each scenario uses a different database and research topic. Tell students to work through the assignment just as the class did together with the example scenario. Roam around the room, suggesting improvements or just observing the work.

With 20 minutes remaining in the session, each student or pair of students should be asked to demonstrate for the class what their original search was, what was wrong with the results, and how they were able to improve it.

Evaluation

In the last few minutes of the session, students should anonymously complete a matrix (see Supplementary Materials). The matrix lists search problems encountered in the search scenarios on one side and techniques for correcting those problems along the top. For each problem, they should put a check next to the technique that could help solve it.

Supplementary Materials

The materials in this section have been placed on the accompanying disk so they can easily be copied and/or modified to fit the needs of individual libraries and instructors.

- Example Scenario
- Search Scenario Matrix

Let's Go Fishing! Introducing Library Databases and Basic Keyword Search Techniques

JANET DAGENAIS BROWN
Education Librarian & Associate Professor
WICHITA STATE UNIVERSITY
jbrown@twsuvm.uc.twsu.edu

CONNIE DALRYMPLE
Life & Health Sciences Librarian & Assistant Professor
WICHITA STATE UNIVERSITY
dalrympl@twsuvm.uc.twsu.edu

Circumstances of the Instruction

This activity introduces students to the concept of library databases—what kinds of information they contain, how they are constructed, the great number and wide variety that are available to researchers, and how to make effective use of them by developing keyword search statements using Boolean logic. The instructor can stress that keyword searching will be a good technique for students to use in almost any database they choose.

The activity is geared to beginning researchers, or those who are unfamiliar with the concept of searching databases using keyword search techniques. We use it during the second week of our 8-week, one-credit-hour course, Introduction to Library Research, just before we begin to introduce students to the library catalog and other databases they will be using for their research. This activity takes approximately one hour.

Objectives of the Instruction

- To introduce students to the concept of library databases and to the types of information they contain
- To alert students to the wide variety of databases that are available, and to the fact that they will need to make informed choices about which databases they choose to use
- To help students learn to differentiate between bibliographic and full-text databases
- To introduce the concept of Boolean logic by providing students with a ready-made database, and having them create sets of items based on search statements created first by the instructor, and then in groups by themselves

Components of the Instruction

There are two parts to this instructional activity. The first part includes the discussion of databases, and the second covers the concept of keyword searching using Boolean operators.

Part 1—Defining and describing the concept of a library database

Preparation

For the discussion of databases, the instructor should be prepared with some ideas of several different types of databases with which students will already be familiar. For example, databases of medical records kept by doctors' offices, or college financial aid applications, such as the FAFSA (Free Application for Federal Student Aid), stored in databases by the federal government.

The instructor should purchase two regular size candy bars for the discussion of the differences between bibliographic and full-text databases.

Construct several different types of "databases" to illustrate the many kinds of databases that are available. Place similar items together in plastic bags to represent the various databases. Below are four ideas for databases that you might use–you can probably think of several others. Plan to have students return all but the Candy databases at the end of the class session. The databases will also be used in Part 2, and students usually enjoy consuming them at the end of class!

1. **Fasteners**

   paper clips of various sizes and colors, including metal and plastic

   staples, binder clips, etc.

   rubber bands of various sizes and colors

   brads, thumbtacks, etc.

   roll of tape

2. **Writing implements**

   pens of various types–ballpoint, fountain, gel, etc.

   pencils of various kinds

   crayons

   felt-tipped markers, highlighters, etc.

3. **Coins**

   pennies, nickels, dimes, quarters

   arcade game tokens

   foreign coins

4. **Candy**

   [at least one piece of each–this can get expensive if you're too generous!]

   miniature chocolate bars (include some that are plain chocolate as well as some that contain
     peanuts, almonds, crisp rice, caramel, etc.)

   miniature peanut butter cups

   chewy candies—fruit, chocolate, honey, or toffee flavored caramels or anything else you
     might choose to add

Presentation

The session begins with the definition of a "database" as "Any electronically-stored collection of data." Make the point that students use a variety of databases every day, and give a couple of examples. The overhead below may be used to facilitate the discussion. Ask students to think of other databases that they use, and then write their ideas on the overhead, too. A version of this overhead suitable for copying is available in the Supplementary Materials.

Overhead 1

What is a database?
 "Any electronically-stored collection of data."
  Freedman, Alan. *The Computer Glossary*. New York: AMACOM, 2001.

Examples of databases we encounter every day:
  Telephone number databases accessed by directory assistance
  Airline flight arrival and departure information available over the Internet

A discussion of what the word *database* means in libraries should follow, stressing that library databases typically contain *descriptions* of items in a particular collection or subject area. Each database that students might choose to use to search for information represents a group of possible information sources. At this point, the instructor should pass out the four different kinds of databases. Give one of each kind of database to every student if you have a small group. If you have a larger number, have them pair up and give each pair a set of databases. Ask the students to identify what kinds of materials each database contains.

Continue the discussion by stating that each library database is made up of a collection of words that describe the items included in the database. The items described could be books, videos, periodical articles, maps, cassettes, Internet sites, etc. The words used to describe the items may come from titles, authors' names, summaries or abstracts, additional descriptive subject words that are added to the database, or even, in some databases, from words in the actual text of the items.

It is useful to make the point here that most databases describe a selection of items within a particular category (such as all items in a library's collection) or within a specific subject area (such as medicine or psychology). This is a good time to begin stressing the point that not all databases describe items available in your own library. Most databases, in fact, describe items that exist out there in the world, and *some*, but not all, of those items will be available in your library. Point out there are even databases, such as *WorldCat*, that help researchers identify exactly which libraries own specific items they wish to use. The overhead below could be used to facilitate the discussion of databases. See Supplementary Materials for a version of this overhead suitable for copying.

Overhead 2

What is a library database?
    A collection of *descriptions* of textual, visual or audio items:
        books
        videos
        periodical articles
        maps
        cassette tapes
        Internet sites
    Most databases describe items within specific categories or subject areas:

The library catalog	All items in the library's collection
PsycINFO	Psychology and the social sciences
ERIC	Education
MEDLINE	Medicine
Historical Abstracts	History
Compendex	Engineering

Next, the instructor should discuss the differences between *bibliographic* and *full-text* databases, indicating that bibliographic databases contain only *descriptions* of items, but full-text databases contain the complete or full text of some or all of the items described in the database. Two regular size candy bars make a good prop or illustration for this concept. Remove the wrapper from one candy bar. This wrapper will represent the bibliographic database, in that it contains only a description of the candy bar, but is not the candy bar itself. Mention the different types of descriptive information found, such as ingredients, weight, number of calories, manufacturer, etc. Then, show the other candy bar that is still wrapped, and let this illustrate the full-text database— it includes both the descriptive information *and* the "full-text" or actual item itself. The following overhead could be used in this discussion. See Supplementary Materials for a version of this overhead suitable for copying.

Overhead 3

Libraries provide two main types of databases for researchers:

Bibliographic databases
        Contain ***descriptions*** of books, periodical articles, maps, videos, music, etc.

Full-text databases
        Contain both ***descriptions*** and the ***complete text*** of periodical articles, books, newspaper articles, etc.

More detailed information should be presented briefly about both types of databases. To help describe a bibliographic database, show the candy bar wrapper again to illustrate the different kinds of descriptive information that can be discovered. Make comparisons to similar pieces of information that are used to describe books or other materials, such as the name of the candy bar (similar to a title), the manufacturer's name and location (author, or publisher and place of "publication"), the weight or size of the bar, number of calories and grams of fat (physical description), and the ingredients (descriptors or keywords). It is important to point out here that each description of an item in the database is called a **record**, and that each record is made up of a number of *fields* which contain the various descriptive pieces of information, such as author, title, etc. Stress that each database students use will be made up of similar records with various fields of information. Give examples of some of the bibliographic databases available in your library, and ask if students are already familiar with any of them. The overhead below might help direct the discussion. See Supplementary Materials for a version of this overhead suitable for copying.

Overhead 4

Bibliographic databases
      Contain *descriptions*
Each *description* in the database is called a ***record***
Each *record* is made up of numerous *fields* of information, such as:
      author's name
      title
      publisher
      publication date
      abstract or summary
      additional descriptive subject words

Examples of bibliographic databases include:
      The Library's catalog
      ERIC
      PsycINFO
      Social Sciences Abstracts

More detailed information about full-text databases should also be provided. Show the wrapped candy bar again to illustrate the fact that full-text databases include the actual items as well as the descriptions. A copy of an article that has been printed from a full-text database might provide further illustration. The overhead below could be used to facilitate the discussion of full-text databases. Include examples of full-text databases available in your own library. See Supplementary Materials for a version of this overhead suitable for copying.

Overhead 5

Full-Text databases
Contain *descriptions* and *complete text*

Some full-text databases also include the *graphics or illustrations* that accompany the text

Examples of full-text databases include:

InfoTrac Web

Full-text of articles from approximately 1,000 periodicals

Lexis-Nexis Academic Universe
Full-text of articles from newspapers and periodicals, radio news broadcasts, state and federal legal cases, etc.

Part 2—Constructing search statements to "fish" for information in the database

Preparation

Make copies of the page available in the Supplementary Materials called "Let's Go Database Fishing!" It is designed to be copied onto legal size paper so that there is plenty of room for students to work. (The version of the page shown in Figure 1 has been altered to fit on an 8 ½ x 11" sheet of paper). Make a copy of the page for each student, or, if you would like to have the students work in teams, one copy for each team. The page has a small fishing pond at the top that represents a database. A fishing net at the bottom of the page will be used to "search" or sweep through the database gathering up only the items we want in each search that we execute.

Presentation

Have students dump the contents of their candy databases onto the fishing pond at the top of the page. Mention that each database they use is like a pond with descriptive words floating around in it, and that they are going to go fishing! Explain that the pond represents their database and the pieces of candy are the contents or descriptions of the items in the database. To reinforce the earlier discussion on the differences between bibliographic and full-text databases, ask the students which type of database their candy database represents. Ideally, they will recognize that they are working with a full-text database. Explain that we are now going to search or sweep through the database with our fishing net to "catch" only the items that have the specific qualifications we are looking for. This is similar to what a "search engine" will do for them in an electronic database.

Hands-on Activity

First, have the students sort through their databases and find all of the items that contain *chocolate*. Have the "search statement" with the word *chocolate* on an overhead for the students to view. Have them "fish out" the chocolate items from their ponds and slide them down into their fishing nets, leaving the rest of the items that do not fit that criteria in the pond. There should be several different pieces of chocolate in their nets–plain miniature chocolate bars, those with nuts or crisp rice or caramel, and maybe a chewy chocolate roll as well.

Tell the students they are going to further qualify their search. Ask them to now keep only those items in their fishing nets that have *both* chocolate and rice, and to throw the remaining items back into the pond as they no longer fit the specified search criteria. Use this search to illustrate the concept of using the Boolean operator AND. Point out how it narrows or further refines their search. Have the search statement *chocolate and rice* showing on the overhead.

Have students return all items to the pond. Next, have them gather all of the items in the fishing net that contain either peanuts or peanut butter. Use this example to illustrate the concept of using the Boolean operator OR. Describe how using OR expands the search to include one or the other or both of the criteria. If you can find chunky peanut butter cups, they might make a good example of an item that actually contains both peanuts and peanut butter. Have the search statement *peanuts or peanut butter* showing on the overhead.

Using the same items already caught up in the fishing net, have students find only those that have either peanuts OR peanut butter AND chocolate. Once again, they will see that they will need to throw a few items back into the pond, and that AND narrows their search. Have the search statement *chocolate and (peanuts or peanut butter)* showing on the overhead, and explain how it describes the items remaining in the fishing net. Also, mention the concept of nesting or enclosing similar or synonymous terms in parentheses.

Finally, have students return all of their items to the pond once again. Have them gather all of the items that are candy but NOT chocolate into the fishing net. They will see that the chocolate items remain in the pond. Explain that the Boolean operator NOT serves to eliminate items from a search.

At some point during this activity, it might liven things up a bit to ask students to search in the database for items that will not be there, such as paper clips or colored pencils. When they respond that those items are not included in the candy database, ask them what they would have to do to find those items. Ideally, they will respond that they would have to choose a different database–one that included those items, such as the databases that were passed out earlier. This will help make the point that not all databases will be appropriate for all of their topics. They will have to choose databases based on what they know about the kinds of materials that are included.

Now, have the students make up their own searches. Ask each student or group to come up with at least two new searches for the rest of the class to try. Have each student or one group member come to the overhead projector and write down the search statements they have devised. Then, have the rest of the class conduct each search.

Wrap up the discussion by reminding students that the way they have just combined search words to get only the candy items they want in the database is exactly the same way the computer will sift and sort through the items in any database they will be searching. Tell them that the concept they've just learned is called *keyword searching* and is one of the most effective ways of searching any database that they might use. Remind them that keyword searching employs the Boolean operators AND, OR, NOT. At the conclusion of the exercise, tell the students they may now eat their words!

Evaluation

We have not tried a formal evaluation of this activity. It is fairly easy to tell whether or not students understand the concepts when they propose and carry out their own keyword search combinations. But be careful--you may find that students are more observant than you are during this exercise! We were taking a fairly simplistic view of what the chocolate candy bars contained. If you could see peanuts, we counted them as items that contained peanuts. However, our students noticed that, although peanuts weren't visible on the chocolate-coated cookie bars, they *were* listed as an ingredient on the wrapper, and rightfully belonged in our search results. We had totally missed this piece of information!

Supplementary Materials

The overheads have been placed on the accompanying disk. The graphics will only be found on the following web site—http://library.albany.edu/usered/concepts/

Overheads:

- What is a database?
- What is a library database?
- Libraries provide two main types of databases for researchers
- Bibliographic databases
- Full-text databases

Graphics:

- Let's go database fishing! (8½ x 11" version)
- Let's go database fishing! (8½ x 14" version)

Notes:

176

Translating English into Computerese: An Exercise in Building Keyword Search Statements for Library Databases

CONNIE DALRYMPLE
Life & Health Sciences Librarian & Assistant Professor
WICHITA STATE UNIVERSITY
dalrympl@twsuvm.uc.twsu.edu

JANET DAGENAIS BROWN
Education Librarian & Associate Professor
WICHITA STATE UNIVERSITY
jbrown@twsuvm.uc.twsu.edu

Circumstances of the Instruction

Due to the popularity of Internet search engines and metacrawlers, library users increasingly do not understand why they cannot simply enter words in natural language or in any format and get reasonable results in library databases. Their tendency is either to type in a single term and grudgingly sort through the resulting avalanche of hits, or to type in a string of search terms WWW search engine-style and leave frustrated with no results. We felt that understanding the necessity of properly constructed search statements and how to build them was one of the most essential concepts to teach to library users.

This exercise is designed to take library research neophytes through the process of developing a proper Boolean search statement starting with a research question stated in English. This exercise is used during week two of our eight-week, one-credit class called Introduction to Library Research. It can also be used in longer (two or more hours) instruction sessions geared to a specific subject area. The exercise takes approximately 30 minutes to complete.

Objectives of the Instruction

- Students learn to develop and articulate a research question rather than a one-word topic.
- Students learn to identify keywords and weed out irrelevant terms.
- Students learn the importance of alternate, narrower, and broader terms in the research process.
- Students learn how to identify alternate, broader, and narrower terms.
- Students learn to recombine (translate) the identified terms into search statements the computer can understand using Boolean operators, truncation, and nesting.

Components of the Instruction

This exercise is an instructor-led activity involving the entire class and is interspersed with mini-lectures.

Preparation

You will need:

- Previous lesson on Boolean operators, truncation, and nesting.
- A possible research question to use for the class in case students do not volunteer one.
- An overhead transparency of the *Translating English into Computerese* worksheet (see Supplementary Materials).
- Transparency markers.
- An overhead projector and screen.
- Two paper copies of the *Translating English into Computerese* worksheet for each student (one copy on which to take notes and one copy for them to use in future research).

Presentation

The first step is a mini-lecture to make clear to the class the reason they are participating in the exercise. Ask the class, "Are any of you familiar with the Internet search services *AskJeeves* or *WebCrawler*? They are advanced search engines that allow users to search for information on the Internet using natural language inquiries. For example, if you want to know what makes the sky blue you can type in "Why is the sky blue?" in *AskJeeves* or *WebCrawler* and the search engine will come up with a list of web sites that might answer the question. Library databases, on the other hand, are not that sophisticated. You need to phrase your searches carefully in order to get meaningful results. Luckily, this is fairly simple once you get the hang of it and this exercise will show you how."

The next step is to solicit a research topic to use as an example. Saying, "Does anyone have a research project that they have to do this semester that we can use for our example? This is your chance for some free research advice!" is usually enough to tempt someone to volunteer a topic. If the class is unwilling or unable to come up with a topic, the instructor should be prepared with an emergency back-up topic.

Usually the class will respond with a one-dimensional topic like "smoking" or "global warming." This allows the instructor to talk about giving some more thought to what they want to know about the topic. Questions like "What specifically interests you about smoking?" or "What would you like to find out about smoking?" can draw the student out and give you more information with which to work. We also like to stress phrasing topics as questions that can then be "answered" by doing research. Once the class has come up with a research question that you think is reasonable, it can then be transcribed into the Research Question (English) line of the *Translating English into Computerese* chart as in Figure 1.

Figure 1.

Research Question (English): Do people who begin smoking as teens have a greater risk of developing cancer than people who start smoking later in life?

Next, help the students identify the most important words (keywords) in the research question. If students are reluctant at this stage, the instructor can begin by saying something like, "Let's cross out some of the obviously unimportant words. Do you think using the word 'a' or 'as' in the database will give us meaningful results?" This is usually a good ice-breaking approach and gives students the confidence they need to warm up to participating. At the end of this part of the exercise, the class will have led the instructor to either cross out all of the unimportant words or circle all of the keywords in the research question. These keywords can then be written into the Keywords line of the chart as in Figure 2.

Figure 2.

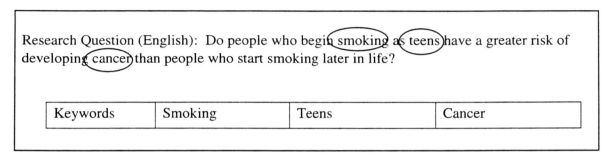

Explain to the class that, "In some cases, you could go directly from the step of identifying keywords to using Boolean operators, nesting, and truncation to build search statements in computerese. This can sometimes lead to problems, however." Propose the following scenarios, "What if you find thousands of records in the databases under your search? Do you want to read through thousands of records to find good sources or would you rather narrow down your search to find fewer, but more relevant items? Or, what if you don't find any items in the databases? Are you going to give up on a topic that interests you, or should you broaden your topic a little to try to include a wider range of possibilities or choose synonyms or alternate terms for the same concept? Having thought ahead of time about these broader, narrower, and alternative terms will make your job much easier when you're actually working in the databases themselves."

The next step is to solicit the students' help in filling in the chart as in Figure 3. It can sometimes be useful to play dumb at this point and say something like, "I always have a hard time thinking of these possibilities. My mind always goes blank. Does anyone have any ideas?" Occasionally one can run into long silences during this step. The instructor can break these, if so inclined, with a serendipitous, "Hey, what about X. Would that work?" We generally let them fill in the chart in any order, not asking that they concentrate on a particular area before the rest. Allowing the creative juices to flow freely can be very helpful in getting the students involved.

Figure 3.

Keywords	Smoking	Teens	Cancer
Alternative Terms (Synonyms)	Smoke Smoker Smokers	Teenagers Teen	Cancer Cancerous Neoplasm Neoplasms Neoplastic
Broader Terms	Tobacco use	Youths Young adults Child Children Minors	Health problems Health issues Health concerns Mortality Death
Narrower Terms	Cigarettes Cigars	Teenage boys Teenage girls 13-15 year-olds 15-19 year-olds	Lung cancer

When you are satisfied that the chart is filled out sufficiently, you can stop the group and give another mini-lecture. "I think this is probably sufficient for our purposes. If you're really stuck on this step, you might even consider consulting a thesaurus. Also, as you read database records you'll probably get more ideas about other terms to search. You may even find some subject headings assigned by the people who built the database that you can just click on that lead you to interesting information. You should keep your worksheet nearby so you can record these subject headings and ideas as you go along."

The next step is to translate the raw keywords from the chart into a search statement in computerese. In addition to the keywords from the chart, they will need some tools for building search statements. These tools are Boolean operators, nesting, and truncation. This exercise assumes that this topic has been covered in a separate session. Review these topics briefly. As a summary to the review, we find that it is good to mention that almost all databases will have some sort of help function, which will allow them to look up the proper use of these tools in that specific database. Then say it is time to apply these tools to their example, starting with truncation.

The first step is to look at the terms in the chart to see which ones have truncation possibilities. After the instructor gives an example or two, "Hey, what do you think about truncating or shortening "smoking" to smok*?" the class will usually respond with other possibilities. Choose a method to indicate the truncation possibilities on the chart. We usually put a slash at the truncation point or cross out the ending of the word. Figure 4 depicts the chart as it will appear after this portion of the exercise.

Figure 4.

Keywords	Smok/ing	Teen/s	Cancer/
Alternative Terms (Synonyms)	Smok/e Smok/er Smok/ers	Teen/agers Teen/	Cancer/s Cancer/ous Neoplas/m Neoplas/ms Neoplas/tic
Broader Terms	Tobacco use	Youth/s Young adult/s Child/ Child/ren Minor/s	Health problem/s Health issue/s Health concern/s Mortalit/y Death/
Narrower Terms	Cigar/ettes Cigar/s	Teenage boy/s Teenage girl/s 13-15 year-olds 15-19 year-olds	Lung cancer/ Esophageal cancer/ Tracheal cancer/ Laryngeal cancer/ Skin cancer/

Constructing the search statement is fairly quick once the groundwork has been laid. The instructor says, "Next, we will use parentheses, or nesting, to group like terms together. We will use a set of parentheses for each basic keyword concept column in our chart. How many sets of parentheses will we need?" The instructor then takes the cues from the class and writes the parentheses with plenty of space within and between them as in Figure 5.

Figure 5.

Then place a Boolean "and" between each set of parentheses as in Figure 6 and explain, "Now it is time to use one of our Boolean operators. We are going to connect each of these concepts with "and" so that the database knows to look for only records which have Concept A AND Concept B AND Concept C together in the same record."

Figure 6.

Search Statement (Computerese): (   ) and (   ) and
(   )

Then solicit from the class the most likely choices among the keywords, alternative, broader, and narrower terms to place in the parentheses, using truncation, explaining that this is just a preliminary search statement and that it may be necessary to revise what you include as you work in the databases. "Now we're going to fill in some search terms representing each concept. We just came up with lots of great possibilities in our keyword chart. Let's concentrate on the most likely alternatives right now and we can come back to the chart later if we find our searches aren't working in the databases." As you write the words into the parentheses, leave plenty of room between words as we have in Figure 7.

Figure 7.

Search Statement (Computerese): (smok?   cigar?   tobacco) and (teen?
child?   minor?) and (cancer?   neoplasm?)

Next, put a Boolean "or" between each set of words in the parentheses as in Figure 8. Explain, "We are going to connect each of these concepts with "or" so that the database knows to look for records with either Keyword A or Keyword B or Keyword C and Keyword D or Keyword E, etc."

Figure 8.

Search Statement (Computerese): (smok? or cigar? or tobacco) and (teen? or child? or minor?) and (cancer? or neoplasm?)

The final step is to sum up the activity, "Let's take a look at what we've done. First, we came up with a good, concrete research question that we can answer by looking in the databases and finding literature. Then we chose the most important concepts about our question to look for in the databases. Next, we chose alternate, broader, and narrower terms so that we'd be prepared if the database responded with too many or too few records on our topic. Finally, we used the database tools (which are Boolean operators, truncation, and nesting) to build a search statement that the computer can understand. In this case the computer is going to be looking for anything having to do with smoking or cigarettes or tobacco and teens or children or minors and cancers or neoplasms." A completed chart will be found on the accompanying disk in the Supplementary Materials.

Variations

One possibility for more class involvement is for the instructor to call for a volunteer to do the writing as the class works through filling out the chart. If no one volunteers, you can just select a student and cajole him or her into participating, promising that it will not be hard. You can then sit among the students and add your suggestions in a less leading way than if you were standing up and doing the writing at the overhead projector.

This method could be used to more quickly work through a topic of the instructor's devising and then as an individual or small-group activity where the class was broken down into pairs to work on their own research ideas. The instructor can circulate among the groups or individuals as they work and give individualized instruction.

Assignment

When using this as a guest lecturer in another professor's class, we usually just make extra copies available and encourage them to follow the same procedure when they attack their own research projects. It also is a good opportunity to encourage them to take advantage of reference service, where they can have help with any aspect of the chart or just have someone look it over to spot any trouble areas.

When we use this in our Introduction to Library Research class, it allows students to work on a research project for another class or other topics of interest to the individual student. The assignment is to fill out the chart for the research project they'll be working on during the course of the semester. We collect the assignment the next week and give them counseling on more possibilities. We also encourage them to keep the chart near them while using the database so that they can use it as a tool and fill it out with more search possibilities that they discover along the way.

Evaluation

There are two possibilities for evaluation. Students can take the chart home as an assignment, whether it is for a credit class in library research or as an assignment for a class where you served as guest lecturer, and you can grade the assignment when it returns and give the students counsel about their research. Another method is to turn the students loose on the chart during class time and circulate among the students to see how they are doing and to give them feedback.

Conclusion

We enjoy this exercise because it is very realistic. The instructor avoids the temptation to come up with canned search examples that work in every database. Almost every time the search statement resulting from the exercise is tried in the library catalog, it results in no hits because the search statements tend to be very specific. This is a wonderful opportunity for students to learn how to be flexible as they search the databases. In a very conversational way we say, "It looks like our search hasn't found any records in the library catalog. I guess that isn't terribly surprising, since our search statement was very specific. This library probably just doesn't own a book that is specifically about the incidence of lung cancer in people who started smoking in their teens. Maybe the library has books dealing with the incidence of lung cancer in people who smoke. Let's broaden our search by eliminating the concept dealing with ages. Maybe books from this search, while they wouldn't be solely about our topic, would at least mention people who started smoking early in life." Sometimes it will be necessary to broaden the search even more.

In the above example you might need to resort to looking for books about the health effects of smoking. Although this approach is not as comfortable as canned search examples that always work, and is more time consuming, we feel that seeing this kind of exercise, and the reasoning behind it, is very valuable to the true understanding of the research process.

Supplementary Materials

The materials in this section have been placed on the accompanying disk so they can easily be copied and/or modified to fit the needs of individual libraries and instructors.

- Translating English into Computerese worksheet (sample copy)
- Assignment – Developing a Search Statement
- Translating English into Computerese worksheet (blank copy)

Creating Effective Search Strategies

CELITA DEARMOND

Reference Librarian and Bibliographer
UNIVERSITY OF TEXAS AT SAN ANTONIO
cdearmond@utsa.edu

ANGELA DUNNINGTON

Reference Librarian and Bibliographer
UNIVERSITY OF TEXAS AT SAN ANTONIO
adunnington@utsa.edu

Circumstances of the Instruction

This activity is designed to assist students in creating effective search strategies for any research topic at any educational level. An appropriate class size is between 25–30 students to allow for both individual and small group participation. This activity preferably takes place in a computer classroom with workstations that have access to library online databases, but portions of this activity can take place in any type of classroom setting. Classroom supplies include a whiteboard, chalkboard, or similar writing surface. The time required for this activity can last between 50–75 minutes, including the warm-up exercise.

Objectives of the Instruction

- Students will identify key concepts and keywords for a research topic.
- Students will construct a variety of search statements based on keywords.
- Students will perform, compare, and evaluate various search statements in a selected database.
- Students will evaluate search results for relevance to a research topic.

Components of the Instruction

Preparation

The instructor pre-selects a research topic that relates to the subject matter and matches the scope of the class research assignment. Pre-searching the topic in several databases is recommended in order to become familiar with which search language works best for the topic.

The Search Strategy Worksheet (see Supplementary Materials) must be prepared for in-class use. The instructor may wish to include the names of specific search tools in the "Select a Search Tool to Use" section of the Search Strategy Worksheet.

Presentation/Hands-on Activity

Warm-up exercise: This exercise gives students time to consider how they would actually search for and evaluate information for a particular topic. It can be done either in a previous class, or allow for time at the beginning of class. Pass out note cards or have students use their own paper.

Introduce the pre-selected research topic to the students and ask them to answer the following questions:
- How would you find information on this topic?
- What type(s) of information would you use?
- How would you know if an information source is appropriate for this topic?

Allow 15 minutes to complete this warm-up exercise, giving students:
- 5 minutes for individual reflection and answers,
- 5 minutes for to share answers within a small group of 5–6 students, and
- 5 minutes for each group of students to share answers with the rest of the class. (Each group selects a spokesperson, with a maximum of five groups sharing for 1 minute per group.)

1. The class creates a basic keyword search strategy: 5–10 minutes.
    During the warm-up exercise, draw the boxes from the "Create a Basic Keyword Search Strategy" section of the Search Strategy Worksheet onto a whiteboard or chalkboard. You may also want to write the research topic above the boxes. Pass out the Search Strategy Worksheet. Ask the students to help you fill in the boxes with primary keywords from the research topic going across with AND in the middle. Lead students in discussing why it might also be a good idea to help you write in alternate keywords, synonyms, or related keywords for the primary keywords going down with OR in the middle.
    (Note: You may consider briefly mentioning that while basic AND searching works well most of the time, there are ways to search for keyword phrases and various keyword endings as well. Consider introducing these specific techniques in section 3 below.)

2. The instructor discusses search tools: 5–10 minutes
    Briefly discuss how academic information could be organized hierarchically into three main categories:
    - background information;
    - in-depth information; and
    - information that highlights specific aspects of a topic.

    Relate the organization of this information to the selection of search tools:
    - background information = library catalog to find encyclopedias;
    - in-depth information = library catalog to find books; and
    - specific aspects = periodical index to find articles.

    Refer to the names of specific search tools if they were included in the "Select a Search Tool to Use" section of the Search Strategy Worksheet.

3. Small groups search for information and evaluate search results: 15–20 minutes
    Allow each small group of students to either select a search tool on their own or have all groups use the same search tool. Each small group performs 3–5 different searches and answers the last three questions in the "Evaluate Your Search Results" section of the Search Strategy Worksheet. If there is more than one computer being used within a group, encourage them to work together to share search results.

(Note: At this point, you may consider sharing specific advanced searching techniques such as adjacency and truncation with each group for the search tool they are using.)

4. Small groups share their answers with the class: 5–10 minutes
   Each group selects a spokesperson, with a maximum of five groups sharing for 1–2 minutes per group. Each group shares the following:
   - which search statement worked best and why?
   - which item (book? article? other?) best fits the research topic and why?
   - which subject headings were listed in the item's description and how these subject headings might help them with their search strategy?

5. The instructor does wrap up and/or evaluation forms for library session: 5–10 minutes
   Wrap up: Discuss the difference between keyword searches that find keywords anywhere in an item's description and subject searches that find items which are about a particular topic. (You may consider demonstrating at least one subject search using the subject headings collected by one of the small groups.)

Evaluation

The goal of this activity is to encourage students to create and evaluate their own search strategies for any particular topic. The quality of the students' group discussions should determine if they understood the concepts that were presented and practiced in class.

Supplementary Material

The material in this section has been placed on the accompanying disk so it can easily be copied and/or modified to fit the needs of individual libraries and instructors.

- Search Strategy Worksheet

Notes:

Print Periodical Indexes CAN Be Useful

JANICE R. HYLEN
Education Librarian/Assistant Instruction Coordinator
NEW MEXICO STATE UNIVERSITY
jhylen@lib.nmsu.edu

Circumstances of the Instruction

Most students use article databases (online indexes) and have never used print indexes. To better understand how those article databases are constructed, they begin with a look at print indexes, so that later they can compare the differences between print and online indexes. Ideally this will take away some of the "magic" attributed to online indexes, and students will better understand them, thereby using them more effectively. Some students may not even know of the existence of print indexes, and since some of these are very specialized and some of them are necessary for historical research, introducing them to these print indexes can prove very beneficial.

This activity is designed as part of a unit in an upper level information literacy class of 24 students. However, it can be used with all levels, and easily adapted to a larger group. The activity takes approximately an hour to accomplish, including some follow-up discussion of the different indexes.

Objectives of the Instruction

By the end of the session students will:
- become familiar with the nature, function, arrangement and use of print periodical indexes and abstracts;
- acquire search techniques and methods in searching print periodical indexes;
- understand when it is necessary to use print indexes; and
- understand how periodical indexes are constructed and transfer that information to article databases.

Components of the Instruction

Preparation

The instructor needs to:
- Write questions that students will answer based on the print index they will be given. Since each student will have a different index, these questions need to be generic. Some examples follow. What do the citations include? For what purpose would a researcher use this index?
- Collect a wide variety of print indexes, some general, some subject-specific. It is also a good idea to include indexes with abstracts and citation indexes.
- Make copies of the worksheet "Print Periodical Indexes Can be Useful" (see Supplementary Materials).

Presentation

The class begins with a brief lecture on the importance of periodical literature and how to find it. The instructor should cover a range of aspects, such as the recent coverage located in article databases, the need to sometimes use the print indexes for earlier information as well as the existence of very special print indexes that cover specific subjects.

The instructor will hand out worksheets (to be filled out), as well as a print index to each student. One way to hand out the indexes is to call out the titles one at a time and have the students come to the front of the class and get the one they are interested in. For example, the golfer in the class might want the *Physical Education Index* and the special education major might want *Education Index*.

Evaluation

The success of the activity can be judged in two ways: the number of questions asked during the activity ("What does it mean...") and by looking over the completed worksheets. If there are a lot of questions during this activity, the instructor may want to pause and explain some of the typical features of print indexes.

Supplementary Material

The material in this section has been placed on the accompanying disk so it can easily be copied and/or modified to fit the needs of individual libraries and instructors.

- Worksheet: Print Periodical Indexes CAN be Useful

Effective Database Searches: Setting the Stage and Evaluating Learning

TRUDI E. JACOBSON

Coordinator of User Education Programs
UNIVERSITY AT ALBANY, SUNY
tj662@csc.albany.edu

Circumstances of the Instruction

This lesson is intended for novice database searchers and is designed to be used in a computer classroom. Students often do not appreciate the effectiveness of Boolean operators and other search tools unless they can see the "before" and "after" results. This activity sets up a teaching moment by showing students how erratic and unreliable unfocused searches can be. This activity can be used as part of discipline-based one-shot instruction sessions as well as within a class on database searching for a lower-level information literacy credit course. The initial activity takes only 5–10 minutes, and the evaluative exercise that finishes the segment can take as little as 5 minutes, depending on how you structure it. The content of the lesson between these two pieces varies on the search tools you introduce and the techniques you use. The entire class may take between 30–55 minutes.

Objectives of the Instruction

- Make students aware that searches conducted by novices can be unsuccessful despite the fact that appropriate material exists in the database.
- Teach students to develop successful strategies using a few key tools.
- Reinforce student learning and recall of search strategies.

Components of the Instruction

Preparation

Select a multi-faceted topic and an appropriate database that is applicable to the class that you are teaching. Be sure that the topic includes terms that have synonyms. Also make sure that the terms you are using are not all descriptors/subject headings and that you are not using Boolean operators in the logical places. As an example, "violence in urban high schools" works well in ERIC. Search the topic yourself so that you are aware of what the equivalent subject headings would be and so that you can determine that a well-constructed search on the topic retrieves a reasonable number of hits.

Make copies of the evaluation worksheet for each student (see Supplementary Materials).

Presentation/Hands-on Activity

Do not give much of an introduction to this lesson. Just tell students the topic of the day and show them how to access the database you have chosen. Give students the topic you have selected, and ask each one to enter the search in whatever way they see fit. Emphasize that it does not have to be entered as you have expressed it. You may want to write the topic on the board or provide it to students on sheets of paper. These techniques will reduce spelling errors. Ask students to stop searching once they have gotten a results set, even if it is zero.

At this point, ask students to announce to the rest of the class the term they entered and the number of results they obtained. Typically, they will use a variety of search statements and the responses will range from zero to several hundred or more. This is a very dramatic way for students to see that all search statements are not created equal.

I continue with the lesson on searching techniques, explaining the use and results of Boolean operators, the existence and usefulness of descriptors/subject headings, and the use of truncation. I also teach students how to read their results, and how to find the material they have identified as useful to their search. This part of the class can be taught in any way desired. I generally give students several more opportunities to enter searches and investigate the results.

Evaluation

The evaluation component of this class is couched in the form of another activity. I give each student a copy of the worksheet shown here. When I initially used this worksheet, all the boxes were filled in. However, that approach did not encourage student learning, nor was I able to determine how much learning had taken place.

The worksheet can be used in a variety of ways. You can ask each student to fill one in by him or herself. You can ask small groups of students to work on filling in the sheet together. Or you can ask the entire class to brainstorm ways to broaden or narrow a search. Each of these methods will take varying amounts of time, with class brainstorming generally the quickest. However, the other two methods give you a better sense of how much each student learned. Allow enough time at the end of the class for this exercise and discussion, if needed, of the responses students are contributing.

Supplementary Material

The material in this section has been placed on the accompanying disk so it can easily be copied and/or modified to fit the needs of individual libraries and instructors.

- Improving Electronic Database Search Results Worksheet

Teaching Students the Concept of Controlled Vocabulary

TRUDI E. JACOBSON

Coordinator of User Education Programs
UNIVERSITY AT ALBANY, SUNY
tj662@csc.albany.edu

Circumstances of the Instruction

This lesson is used with novice researchers in a variety of different classes, including an undergraduate information literacy course. In this activity, students learn very directly the difficulty of selecting subject headings and the need to be flexible in their selection of search terms. This unit does not need to be taught in a hands-on classroom, but it might logically be paired with another database-related lesson or activity that might require student use of computers. In addition, the activity below does include two optional sections where student computers can be utilized.

Objectives of the Instruction

- Raise student awareness of the complexity of identifying search terms.
- Teach students to appreciate the need for indexer-assigned subject headings.
- Teach students to use subject headings when searching databases.

Components of the Instruction

Preparation

Find a short article (less than one page) on a topic of general interest to students or on a topic related to the course work. Also find the record for this article in a database such as EBSCO or *Expanded Academic Index*. Make enough copies of both so each student will have their own. [An article I have used successfully is "Valley of the Doll-Less: Surfing the Web for Dates in America's Tech Zone," by Brad Stone.]

Presentation

Begin the class with an explanation of databases and effective searching using Boolean operators, or allow the students to work on activities that will lead to this understanding. You might use the activities in other lesson plans in this book, such as "Effective Database Strategies: Setting the Stage and Evaluating Learning" and "Using Tattooing to Teach Boolean Searching," before beginning this activity. Students should have some knowledge of why they would use databases for this activity to be meaningful.

Hands-on Activity

Pass out the photocopies of the article you have selected and ask students to read through it quickly. As they read (or once they have finished), they should circle terms or words in the article that they think they could use in database searches to find similar articles. I also encourage them to jot down additional terms they think would be useful that are not found in the article itself. This part of the activity will take 5–10 minutes, depending upon the length of the article you have selected (assuming it is one page or less).

Ask for volunteers or call on students to give you just one of the terms they selected. Write it on the board, then ask how many other students selected that term. Continue adding terms to the list until you have 6–10 different ones. Keep a tally next to each term of how many students chose it. When I have used this activity, anywhere from one student through a majority of students will have selected any given term. Once you have a variety of terms with widely differing numbers on the board, hand out the second sheet with the actual record from a database. Ask students to compare the terms from the record with those they had chosen. Ask them if they would have chosen any of these terms to search under; their responses will vary depending on the indexing. [I use EBSCO's record for the above-mentioned article, in which the headings assigned are not intuitive, and students always say no.]

At this point, if you are in a room with computers or a demonstration system, show students how to find subject terms in the database you used as an example, either through the subject search option, or using an online thesaurus.

Discussion

Talk with the students about the way articles are indexed and the use of subject headings. Explain that subject headings can vary from database to database because of the way they are selected. Ask the students what they have learned about subject headings in order to search efficiently—they frequently will note that they have to be flexible in selecting search terms. Raise the point if they do not. Ask students how full-text databases with the capability to search the entire text affect the selection of subject headings. Do subject headings still serve a function, if a full-text database includes them?

Evaluation

If you are teaching in a hands-on classroom, you might ask students to select a topic and then use the database's subject listing or thesaurus to find three appropriate subject headings. If your students do not have access to computers, this might be given as a homework assignment.

Sources:

Stone, Brad. "Valley of the Doll-Less: Surfing the Web for Dates in America's Tech Zone." *Newsweek* 134.7 (August 16, 1999) 59.

Using Tattooing to Teach Boolean Searching

Michael Lorenzen

Library Instruction Coordinator
Michigan State University
lorenze1@msu.edu

Circumstances of the Instruction

Knowledge of Boolean searching techniques is important for undergraduates to be successful in constructing searches in the catalog, databases, and on the Web. Therefore, it is important to introduce it to college students early in an information literacy course or during a bibliographic instruction session. This lesson uses active learning strategies to interest and teach students basic Boolean strategies. This is achieved by having students write and talk about tattooing. Ideally, the class will have between 15–25 students to allow for both small group work and a larger class discussion. The lesson detailed here takes about 50 minutes to conduct. The lesson works best with undergraduates who are in their first or second year of post-secondary education. It also works well with high school students.

Objectives of the Instruction

- The student will learn the importance of narrowly defining the search early in the search process.
- The student will learn how to use AND in a Boolean search to narrow a search.
- The student will learn how to use NOT in a Boolean search to exclude a term from a search.
- The student will learn how to use OR in a search to expand a search.
- The student will learn that although databases are constructed differently, the basics of Boolean searching can be applied in all of them.

Components of the Instruction

It has been my experience that students do not arrive at information literacy courses very excited or motivated to learn. The student may be enrolled in an information literacy course as a graduation requirement and may have low expectations towards the course or the student is at the session because an instructor arranged for a class to receive library instruction. Either way, grabbing the attention of the students can be extremely difficult. As such, I have been using the concept of tattooing at the beginning of all basic class sessions dealing with online searching.

Begin the class by asking each student to write down on a piece of paper the types of people they believe get tattoos. It is important to have some extra sheets of paper and some pencils available for the students as many of them will come unprepared to write or take notes. Give the students a minute or two to write down their responses. Some of the students are going to be surprised that the instructor is asking about tattoos and requiring them to actually participate by writing. Look around for these students and strongly encourage them to write down a few responses. This is a basic use of the idea of the minute paper and it is a good way to let students know that they will be expected to participate in class.

At this point, break the class down into five or six groups. Try not to have more than three students in any one group. If possible, make the default groups work in such a way that no counting off or moving is required since this takes time and will distract the students. For example, if the room has three rows of seats divided by an aisle, use the six resulting areas as groups. Ask the groups to discuss with each other the responses to the question. Let them know that each group will be asked to pick one example to share with the entire class. Be sure to let them know that each group must share an original answer so that back-up answers are a good idea. Let the groups work for several minutes. Try not to cut off the discussions until they start to drift off topic.

Bring the class back to attention and begin asking each group for an example. As you get the answers, write them down for all of the students to see. A flip chart, blackboard, or whiteboard at the front of the class works well for this. Continue until all of the groups have provided a response. When finished, ask if any of the students would like to share additional answers. Usually, you will be able to write down a few more suggestions. Most of the responses will be standard and you will hear them each time you teach this way. Bikers, sailors, prisoners, and athletes will be popular. Monks, students, and even librarians will be thrown in occasionally as well!

This is the opportunity to emphasize how important it is to narrow down a search. The students will have demonstrated by their examples that even a simple topic like tattooing can be about a bunch of different things and people. A broader topic like abortion, war, poverty, Shakespeare, etc. is going to have even more words that may be relevant. Getting good results in a library is not always dependent on how hard one works. It is possible to work hard and get bad results. You can also work for an hour and have all that you need. Thinking about what you want, what words may be used to describe it, and how you may narrow down your search will save the student time and results in better research. This point is easy to make at this point in the lesson. And the students, still deeply interested from the tattooing discussion, will listen.

An explanation of Boolean searching can be added at this point. Refer back to where you have written down the suggestions from the students. Explain what AND, NOT, and OR are and how they are used to construct searches. Use the words the students gave you as examples. For instance, when explaining the use of AND, write on the board "bikers AND tattoos" to demonstrate. This can be done with all the Boolean terms using the tattoo related words the student shared. You will find this much more effective than the use of Venn diagrams or straight lecture.

After explaining the Boolean concepts, go ahead and demonstrate the database or databases the students need to learn about. If possible, use the tattooing examples that the students gave you when demonstrating a search. Whatever searches you use to demonstrate the database, be sure to point out when you are using Boolean operators in a search. A few examples where you do bad searches compared with some good Boolean searches is a nice way to reinforce the importance of using AND, NOT, and OR. Showing more than one database is a good idea. Try to get two databases that look different to show that regardless of the database, Boolean searching still works although variations in the databases may require the user to make some modifications.

It is important to have the students conduct their own searches as soon as possible. Ideally, you will have a classroom where each student has their own computer and can follow along with you as you demonstrate searches. This is a highly effective method of active learning that will reinforce what you teach and immediately let you know when a student is having difficulty. If a room with computers for the students is not available, try to leave time to take the students out to an area with computers to help them do a few searches. The small assignment provided with this lesson can also be used.

Evaluation

The easiest way to assess the learning of the students is to have them complete the Boolean Searching Assignment (see Supplementary Material) or one similar to it. Do the students do well? Are they grasping the concepts they were taught? If so, this lesson is successful. If not, it will need to be revised to meet the learning needs of the students at your institution.

Try teaching this lesson with an example other than tattooing. Do the students do better with a more serious example? Do the students pay attention and interact with the librarian and other students with other examples? Experiment with ideas and methods of delivering this lesson until you find one that both works for you as a teacher and delivers the results with the students that are desired.

Supplementary Material

The material in this section has been placed on the accompanying disk so it can easily be copied and/or modified to fit the needs of individual libraries and instructors.

- Boolean Searching Assignment

Notes:

Understanding Controlled Vocabulary: A Thesaurus Exercise

MARY SELLEN

Assistant Director for User Services
UNIVERSITY AT ALBANY, SUNY
msells@csc.albany.edu

Circumstances of the Instruction

The key to successful database searching at any level is choosing the appropriate terms that match the vocabulary of the database. While students have the option in most databases to use natural language, understanding the way vocabulary is structured and used in specific databases enables students to become more effective searchers. OPACs and sophisticated databases such as *ERIC* and *PsycINFO* have published online thesauri. EBSCO and the UMI databases have subject lists that function like online versions of thesauri for the advanced level searcher. Having students construct mini-thesauri based on a subject that is familiar to them can reinforce theoretical concepts of controlled vocabulary and thesaurus construction.

When instructors are ready to discuss advanced searching skills, an entire session on the use of language in database searching is necessary. After a lecture on the theoretical concepts of thesauri has been given, assigning students to write a small thesaurus based on a subject of interest to them reinforces the idea of language control and provides proof that the concepts of controlled language have been understood.

Objectives of the Instruction

- Make students aware that usage of vocabulary identified by the database results in more effective search strategies.
- Teach students the hierarchical structure of thesauri.
- Expose students to the variety of published and online thesauri.

Components of the Instruction

Preparation

A lecture on the theories of thesaurus construction is necessary. The concepts of:
- broader,
- narrower,
- used for, and
- see also

must be minimally explained. Showing examples from the *ERIC Thesaurus* and *Library of Congress Subject Headings* are good examples of established works and ones that many students will use in their academic career. Demonstrating the online subject lists of EBSCO or a similar general database is a good exercise and of practical benefit as students rarely venture into the

"Advanced Searching" part of this highly used database. Doing a search in a database with controlled language and comparing it to one done with natural language will also demonstrate the effectiveness of using controlled vocabulary.

Following the lecture, it is helpful to engage in a discussion by posing a general subject and have students suggest "broader," "narrower," and "used for" words for the subject. This is a good test to see if they have comprehended the concepts of the lecture and can result in a lively discussion if a subject that engages them is used.

Assignment

Students can now be assigned to construct their individual thesaurus. Specifying an exact number of terms and urging students to choose a subject they are interested in and familiar with will result in a thoughtful exercise. An effective strategy is to ask students to develop a thesaurus of a minimum of fifty terms. Specify the number and type of terms. For example, requiring a specific number of "broad" terms and "used for" terms will reinforce to them that all four categories must be used for a passing grade. The usage of the names of specific people or proper nouns as terms should be discussed. Specific numbers of such terms might be stipulated. If these precautions are not discussed there is a good possibility that the student will simply hand in a list of 50 terms with no organization.

Another useful suggestion is for students to identify 50 terms on their subject and write them on 3x5 cards. They can then arrange them in an appropriate hierarchy, and write the thesaurus. This allows for variations that will naturally occur as the student thinks about the meaning of the word in the context of the subject.

Evaluation

Good thesauri will contain terms that embody all the concepts of "broader," "narrower," "used for," and "see also." The use of these concepts will indicate if the student has really thought through the vocabulary of a specific subject. The lists of terms under "narrower" should not make up most of the 50 terms. Good papers will contain more than the minimum of 50 terms.

Boolean Logic

MARTHA STEPHENSON

Bibliographic Instruction Coordinator
UNIVERSITY OF WISCONSIN – WHITEWATER
stephenm@mail.uww.edu

Circumstances of the Instruction

This activity is designed to aid students in understanding the function of each Boolean operator and how they change the number of results and when to use each one or a combination of several. It is important to understand the concepts behind Boolean logic; use of these operators will result in receiving the most useful and appropriate results to an online (or CD-ROM) search. The user will avoid wading through many irrelevant responses just to find one useable result.

This exercise is geared toward inexperienced and beginning online researchers. A basic knowledge of typing and computer use is required. Knowledge of other search tools such as truncation and phrase searching would be helpful. Boolean operators may be used in most proprietary indexes and other databases as well as many Internet search engines.

It is important to have no more than twice the number of students as computer workstations. An example would be 20 computers for a maximum of 40 students. Working with more than 20 students, or pairs of students, may not allow for sufficient time to assist those with questions. Working in pairs often aids in the learning process, a more informed student would be able to assist a less knowledgeable one. Both students should have time for some hands-on practice.

This unit will take one class period of 50 minutes if students have already received instruction in the use of databases: 50% of the time for instruction and 50% of the time for hands-on practice. If students have not yet received instruction in the use of databases and will not be using the computers, allow 25–30 minutes. Later, preferably soon, when instruction in the use of databases is given, allow 25–30 minutes for a quick review of Boolean logic and hands-on practice.

Objectives of the Instruction
- Students will determine when to use Boolean logic.
- Students will use the appropriate Boolean operators for the tool at hand.
- Students will think more expansively about search terms.

Components of the Instruction
Preparation
- Find out if students have previous online or database searching experience to determine length of activity.
- Review Boolean logic examples in the context of your student body. Choose the most appropriate one. Some adjustments may need to be made for schools with uniforms, stringent dress codes, adult learners, etc.

- Perform searches to make sure they will work in your electronic resources.
- Create a Microsoft PowerPoint presentation, overhead slides or drawings on a blackboard, whiteboard or easel paper of the Boolean logic examples.
- Make handouts of the Boolean logic examples and the Search Diagram and put them on the class web page.

Presentation

This demonstration involves these learning processes—verbal, visual, and kinesthetic.
Ask who in the class knows what Boolean operators are. Select a student from the raised hands to explain. Augment the student's explanation as needed or provide one if none was proffered. For example: "Boolean operators are the connecting words that make searching faster and more efficient by using a combination of search terms."

Verbally present these definitions while showing slides of the graphical representations:

OR is used to expand the results set of a search. Sometimes it is used to include synonyms or near-synonyms for a concept, other times it is used to express several different concepts.

AND is used to reduce the results set of a search. The searcher will **AND** terms representing new concepts.

NOT is used to reduce the results set of a search. Use this operator when search terms have multiple disparate meanings or to eliminate a subset of results.

Nesting guarantees that statements created with Boolean operators occur in the correct order. Some databases have programming that automatically does this, but most do not.

Students will next participate in a demonstration of Boolean operators.

During this exercise the students will repeat what they have just learned about Boolean operators. Repetition is key; people tend to only remember 10% of what is said, so repeat important points. Also, repetition allows the instructor to find out if she has conveyed the intended meaning and then to clarify as necessary.

Explain to the class that you are going to do a demonstration of Boolean logic, and that you will need their cooperation.

First, ask all the students wearing jeans to stand up. Make sure all those who are able are up. Tell students to look around at the group. Say that this is an example of a single term search. Students remain standing.
Example: jeans

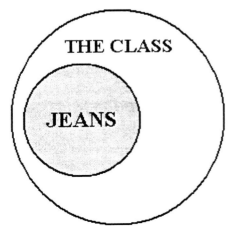

Reiterate when to use an OR search and what happens to the results set. Ask all the students wearing a skirt to stand up and join those wearing jeans. Ask for a volunteer to explain what has happened to the size of the group (results set). Everyone may sit down. Example: jeans or skirt

Ask for a student to explain what to do to make their results set smaller. Augment the student's explanation of AND or NOT as needed. Ask the students wearing jeans and a t-shirt (or jeans, but not blue jeans) to stand up. Remark that the set is smaller than the jeans only set. Everyone may sit down. Example: jeans and t-shirt

Ask for a student to explain the other way to make their results set smaller. Augment the student's explanation as needed. Ask the students wearing jeans, but not blue jeans (or jeans and a t-shirt) to stand up. Remark that the set is smaller than the jeans only set. Everyone may sit down. Example: jeans NOT blue jeans

Explain that nesting is used in complex searches; parentheses separate the phrases. Example: (jeans NOT t-shirt) NOT blue jeans

NOTE: If the students are largely elderly or disabled you may choose to ask them raise their hands, or do something else, instead of standing. My first preference is asking them to stand because it keeps them awake and attentive.

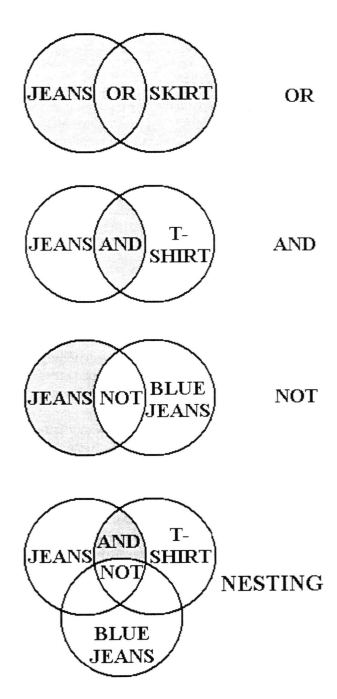

OR

AND

NOT

NESTING

Hands-on Activity

Write a search topic on the board or on an overhead. Ask students which terms in the topic they would use in a search. Underline them. Guide the class through a brainstorming session to find synonyms for the search terms. Simultaneously write the synonyms in columns on the board. Ask the class to name the operator that belongs between the "students" and "cheat" columns and also between the items in the "students" column. Add them to the diagram. Write out a Boolean logic search with some of the new terms.

Example Topic: "What happens to students who cheat in college?"
 Terms: students   cheat   college
 Search: (students OR classmates) AND (cheat OR plagiarize) AND (university OR college)

Demonstrate a few searches from the above example in tools the students are familiar with or will soon be instructed in. (Examples: OPAC and a popular online database). Mention during each search that typically a set of around 100 results is a good working size to start with, because too many results will take too long to wade through and too few will probably not give an accurate picture of the material available. Point out the tool's help buttons for tool specific guidance, because few search tools are exactly the same.

Walk through at least one example with the students following along. Mention again that typically a set of around 100 results is a good working size to start. Allow time for more examples if many students are experiencing problems. (These examples are for an online periodical index.)

Examples: madonna AND music
        cats OR felines OR lions OR tigers
        drivers AND (licence OR license)

Examples: economics
        economics AND europe
        economics OR finances
        economics NOT green
        (economics OR finances) NOT (green OR environmental)

Students may now do independent searching on a topic of choice or related to another assignment. For this assignment, students will fill out the Search Diagram worksheet. Based on the search diagram, students will perform four (4) searches using at least three (3) Boolean operators each. Four successful searches must be diagrammed on the bottom of the page, including the tool searched, and the number of hits. Students working in pairs may not turn in the same work.

Note: The number of successful searches may be increased to match another required assignment.

204

Evaluation

Students will be graded based on their ability to successfully perform four searches. Students must redo the assignment if they turn in the same assignment as their partner. Points will be taken off for failed searches, incomplete searches and duplicate searches.

Supplementary Materials

The materials in this section have been placed on the accompanying disk so they can easily be copied and/or modified to fit the needs of individual libraries and instructors.

- Search Diagram
- Boolean Logic Examples
- Alternate Boolean Logic Examples

Notes:

Empowering Students: Encouraging Peer to Peer Learning

JANE M. VEROSTEK

Assistant Librarian
SUNY COLLEGE OF ENVIRONMENTAL SCIENCE & FORESTRY
jmveros@esf.edu

Introduction

This activity is within the context of a 5-week, 1-credit Information Literacy class at the SUNY College of Environmental Science & Forestry. The activity involves students learning about library online public access catalogs (OPACs), completing a searching activity, and having the students teach the class where answers to the searching activity are reviewed.

Students teach and learn from each other on many levels. Having students teach each other within a formal class models this behavior and further encourages peer-to-peer instruction. Following is a description of the unit and activity involved, the purpose of the activity, and the implementation of the activity.

Circumstances of the Instruction

Below is an overview of the unit/activity discussed.
- **Unit**: Library Online Public Access Catalog Searching.
- **Activity**: Library Online Public Access Catalog Searching Activity.
  Students search for specific items (i.e., search for a thesis on trees by the author Smith, search for a topic of their choice, etc.) via all of the search options available in the local online public access catalog.
- **Student Level**: Beginner to advanced (freshman to graduate students). All levels of students learn something new from this unit and activity.
- **Class Size**: Optimal Number of Students is 20–25.
- **Class Length**: 55 minutes.

Objectives of the Instruction

The main objectives of this unit and activity are as follows:
- Review the meaning of a library's online public access catalog (OPAC).
- Describe library specific local OPAC search strategies.
- Allow students hands-on time to work through the "Library Online Public Access Catalog Searching Activity."
- Demonstrate that there can be several ways to find the same information in an OPAC.
- Review the "Library Online Public Access Catalog Searching Activity."

Components of the Instruction

For this unit on library online public access catalog searching, there are three classes.

Class 1:
Class meets in lecture room for a lecture on library online public access catalogs (OPACs) and a demonstration of different search strategies in the local OPAC.

Class 2:
Class meets in a computer lab to allow students hands-on time to work through the "Library Online Public Access Catalog Searching Activity." (See Supplementary Materials) Instructor assistance is available during this hands-on time.

Class 3:
Class meets in lecture room and the "Library Online Public Access Catalog Searching Activity" is reviewed. The twist is that the students "teach" this entire class. The preparation, presentation, and activity for this class follow below.

Preparation

Create YELLOW slips of paper for each specific activity question (i.e., search for a thesis on trees by the author Smith) and WHITE slips of paper that say "YOUR TOPIC."
Put all the slips in a box.

Presentation

- As students arrive for class they each choose one slip of paper out of the box. Students may want to know why they are choosing slips of paper from a box—tell them it is a surprise and they need to wait until everyone arrives.
- After class begins, the students are told that they will be "teaching" class.
- Ask everyone with a yellow slip of paper to raise their hand. Students with yellow slips are told that they will be demonstrating to the class how they would answer the specific question they have on their slip of paper.
- Students with a white slip of paper are told that they will show the class how they will research their particular topic.
- Initially the students will think they will be answering the questions from their chairs and may be a bit surprised when they are asked to come to the front of the room and to demonstrate their answers on the laptop/projector.

Hands-on Activity

- Questions and answers are demonstrated in the order they appear on the activity.
- As students come to the front of the room, they are introduced to the class.
- Each student walks through their answers on the laptop/projector and talks the class through their steps.
- After the students demonstrate how they answered a question the rest of the class should volunteer their answers and/or offer suggestions.

Evaluation

At the end of class 3 in this unit, the class had successfully accomplished the unit's objectives. During the initial class lecture on the unit, students learned about library online public access catalogs and also about the different search strategies available in the local catalog. In the computer lab, students had the opportunity to try different local catalog searches by working through the "Library Online Public Access Catalog Searching Activity."

During the last class of the unit where the students "taught" class:
- The activity was reviewed.
- There was great class participation.
- Students that demonstrated their answers got some great public speaking experience.
- Students saw first hand that searches for the same information can be done differently.
- Students got to know each other.
- EVERYONE had fun!

Sources:

List, Carla. (1998). *An Introduction to Information Research*. Dubuque, IA: Kendall/Hunt Publishing Company.

Supplementary Materials

The materials in this section have been placed on the accompanying disk so they can easily be copied and/or modified to fit the needs of individual libraries and instructors.

- Library Online Public Access Catalog Searching Activity
- Library Online Public Access Catalog Searching Unit Online

Notes:

210

Section 5—Internet Content and Evaluation

Internet Past, Present, and Future

Internet Directories and Search Engines

Course Research Assignments and Web Site Evaluation

List of "Best Web Sites" and Web Site Evaluation

Web Page Design and Web Site Evaluation

Finding U.S. Government Information on the Internet

Internet Past, Present, and Future

COLLEEN BELL

Library Instruction Coordinator
UNIVERSITY OF OREGON
cbell@darkwing.uoregon.edu

Circumstances of the Instruction

This assignment has been used as part of an online upper-division/graduate level course entitled "Internet Information and Culture," in which students explore the Internet in a number of contexts: informational, social, cultural, political, and economic. Because the most rapid period of growth in Internet use has occurred since the mid-1990s, following the development of the graphical web browser, few Internet users understand how the technological and social developments over the past four decades have shaped what the Internet has become in the past decade. This missing link to the past has had a profound impact on the recent history of the Internet and will continue to shape our concept of cyberspace and the ways in which we use it.

In this assignment, students explore readings and web sites about the past and present of the Internet (both the social and technical histories), then apply what they learn to try to divine its future. The activity involves individual reflection, as well as a group project, web site and presentation in class. The project works well with medium-sized classes of 30–35 students, but can be modified to accommodate larger or smaller groups by changing the size of the groups. If you do not have a computer and projector available or if students lack knowledge of web site construction, you can have them prepare posters instead of web sites.

Objectives of the Instruction

Students will:
- understand the history of the Internet and its impact on its present incarnation,
- recognize the innovators and innovations that have shaped the present-day Internet,
- apply knowledge of the past and present of the Internet by formulating predictions for its future, and
- gain experience working in a collaborative environment.

Components of the Instruction

Preparation

Prepare a list of resources about the history of the Internet, such as the one in the sample Group Project handout (see Supplementary Materials) and make a copy for each student in the class. Divide the class into small groups of up to 5 students.

Assignment

Working in small groups of no more than 5, students prepare a web site that identifies the 5 most important Internet innovators, the 5 most important technological innovations in the history of the Internet, and the 5 most important social or cultural (i.e., non-technological) innovations in the history of the Internet. Students also use their knowledge of the past and present history of the Internet to develop predictions for the future of the Internet in 10, 50, and 100 years. On their web sites, groups must justify their choices and link their predictions to the current or past incarnation of the Internet. In other words, creative predictions are encouraged but these predictions must be grounded in reality. The web sites will be presented in class.

As an alternative to providing predictions for the future of the Internet, groups may be asked to provide their dreams, hopes, expectations, and nightmares for the future of the Internet. In doing so, groups are encouraged to use art, images, quotations, web sites, and other forms of symbolism to express these dreams, hopes, expectations, and fears. One set of results from this assignment, taken from the Spring 1999 version of the online course mentioned earlier, are available at—
http://darkwing.uoregon.edu/~cbell/contours99/forum/week10.html.

Evaluation

Groups are evaluated on the content of their web site and the class presentation. Peer evaluation, where members of the group evaluate each other based on a set of established criteria, provides a positive form of peer pressure, encouraging each member of the group to contribute equally. Students should be coached on the peer evaluation process and provided with the evaluation criteria before they begin working on the project (see Supplementary Materials for a sample peer evaluation form). The peer evaluation score is combined with the group score, and should constitute no more than 50% of the entire grade for the assignment. A brief but good article on using peer evaluation is by M. Sweet and listed in the Sources.

Sources:

The resources below are companions to some of the web resources mentioned in the group project.

Hafner, K., & Lyon, M. (1996). *Where wizards stay up late: The origins of the Internet.* New York : Simon & Schuster.

Segaller, S. (1999). *Nerds 2.0.1: A brief history of the Internet.* New York: TV Books.

Segaller, S., Cringely, R. X., & Gau, J. (1998). *Nerds 2.0.1: A brief history of the Internet.* Alexandria, VA: PBS Video.

Sweet, M. (1999, Winter). Petting the shark: Using peer evaluations. *Lizard: Laser Insights, Zany Alternatives, Riveting Dialogue 47,* 1–2. Available on the web—
http://darkwing.uoregon.edu/~tep/lizard/pdf/liz_48.pdf

Supplementary Materials

The materials in this section have been placed on the accompanying disk so they can easily be copied and/or modified to fit the needs of individual libraries and instructors.

- Group Project Worksheet
- Peer Evaluation Form (Sample)

Notes:

216

Internet Directories and Search Engines

Amy W. Boykin

Asst. Reference Librarian
Christopher Newport University
awboykin@cnu.edu

Circumstances of the Instruction

At Christopher Newport University, Library Science 220 is a one-credit course that introduces students to the Internet and e-mail and demonstrates effective research techniques that they may use. Several librarians have taught this six-week course at various times; this assignment was originally devised in 1997. It has since been revised and updated several times to reflect student interests and the changing Internet.

About halfway through the course, students are introduced to the myriad ways there are to search the Internet, and especially emphasized are the directories and search engines that are available. The 100-minute session is divided in half by a 10-minute break. The first half of the class is a lecture/demonstration combination with some hands-on time for the students. After break, the rest of the class is dedicated to the assignment described in this lesson plan. The instructor is able to walk around the class during this time, answering questions and making sure that everyone is on the right track. The students usually finish the assignment in class and hand it in, but it is not due until the following class period.

This assignment is appropriate for any size class as long as there are hands-on opportunities. The assignment can also be used effectively with small groups of students—two or three students working together—with the assignment parts equally divided between group members.

Objectives of the Instruction

The students will:
- discover the differences, pros and cons, in using Internet search engines and Internet search directories,
- compare and contrast results after Internet searches, and
- recommend a search tool based on the current topic and previous instruction and experience.

Components of Instruction

Preparation

The assignment is made up of three parts with a survey-type question at the end. The instructor may create, modify, and/or print out the appropriate number of assignment sheets. (I use colored paper for the assignment to distinguish it from the handouts.)

If using an electronic classroom or lab, the instructor should check the lab before the session to see which computers are working. If there is a teacher/instructor station to project examples on a screen/board, verify that the equipment is working and make sure there is sufficient room for the expected class or group size.

Because this is usually taught in the third class meeting, students have already chosen a topic for their final project and they will use this topic to complete the assignment. For a one-shot session, plan to have a list of topics available to hand out, or assign/hand out individual topics as the students come into the classroom.

If this assignment is being used in a series of sessions, the instructor can help students prepare by asking them to read or view Ross Tyner's web page *Sink or Swim: Internet Search Tools & Techniques*—http://www.ouc.bc.ca/libr/connect96/search.htm.

Presentation

Before class, ask the students to look at Ross Tyner's web page (the URL is above). With this background in mind, begin the first half of the session with questions such as "Why is it difficult to search the Internet?" and "How do you find what you are looking for on the Internet?" After mentioning the similarities between search engines and directories, talk about the differences. The focus of the discussion can then shift to search engines and why there are so many of them, as well as what makes them different from each other. Finally, ask the students about multi-threaded, meta or multiple search engines, such as *Dogpile*, *Mamma*, and *Metacrawler*, and how they work. After spending a few minutes discussing limiting types of searches (search for people, for images and graphics, for company information, or for software), use the instructor's computer set-up to demonstrate some various strategies to use, such as "+" and "-" signs, quote marks around phrases, and Boolean operators. The Boolean operators are illustrated in Ross Tyner's web page.

Just before the break, the class spends 10 minutes working to create a "My List" of search engines and directories. The students are given a handout with four URLs that take them to a list of lists. They visit up to three of the four web sites to compile a personal list of potential search tools.

After the break, hand out the assignment (available in the Supplementary Materials section) and go over each step, explaining how it relates to the session purposes of exploring various ways of searching, and realizing the benefits and restrictions of each tool. As the students work along, it is beneficial for the instructor to walk around the classroom to be available for any questions.

Evaluation

The success of this assignment hinges on the students' willingness to persevere to the end. It may seem unnecessary to search the same topic in three different places but the differences in the result sets may convince them that the effort was worth it. Because this is part of a series of class sessions, I am able to ask questions the next time we meet. For a one-shot presentation, it would be helpful to gather the students back together with 5–10 minutes left in the session. This is when the instructor can ask individuals which search tool was most effective for the chosen/assigned topic. For a multiple session course, the instructor is able to compile the answers to the last question and see how many "yes" and "no" answers there are, and then ask during the next session why the students answered as they did. This helps all of the students realize that there is no right answer, and that some tools are more helpful than others in certain situations.

For grading this assignment, the instructor may allow a total of 25 points for the assignment and take off a point or two where the questions are not answered fully. As a variation, the entire assignment may be worth 100 points and each question with its parts worth 30 points. The final survey-type question may be counted as 10 points to make the total equal to 100.

Sources:

Sink or Swim: Internet Search Tools & Techniques
http://www.ouc.bc.ca/libr/connect96/search.htm

Virtual Chase: Pick a Search Engine
http://www.virtualchase.com/howto/engine.html

Supplementary Materials

The materials in this section have been placed on the accompanying disk so they can easily be copied and/or modified to fit the needs of individual libraries and instructors.

- Lists of Search Engines and Directories
- Assignment: Search Engines & Directories

Notes:

Course Research Assignments and Web Site Evaluation

CHRISTOPHER COX

Reference/Instruction Librarian
WORCESTER POLYTECHNIC INSTITUTE
ccox@wpi.edu

Circumstances of the Instruction

Faculty often request that librarians teaching course-related instruction sessions spend some time talking with students about the fallibility of web sites as academic resources. Faculty members, specifically ones unfamiliar with what information is available on the web, often falsely believe that there is nothing of scholarly value to be found there. Students, in turn, often feel that everything published on the web is of the same scholarly value as any resource to be found in the library. Because of the importance of web site evaluation to these faculty members, I often request a separate hour for web site evaluation in addition to the hour for this topic I usually do on library resources in order to set the record straight. The following exercise would also be an excellent addition to any Internet resource evaluation unit taught in a for-credit information literacy course.

I have used the exercise below in physics, history, English, and social science classes of varying levels. I have even presented it to faculty and staff members of the Worcester Consortium of Colleges with equal success. In the exercise, students are divided into groups of two or three, depending of the class size. Because each group must have their own computer, the size of the classroom or lab may determine the optimal class size for this exercise. A class of 30 students is the largest in which I have used this exercise.

The students are directed to a web page containing the text of their assignment or some bogus assignment the instructor and I have fashioned (or that you may fashion), followed by a list of five web sites on the assignment's topic. Each group is asked to rank the web sites from 1 to 5, with 1 being the best, 5 being worst. They are asked to base their rankings on each web site's usefulness in completing the assignment. When the groups have finished, the rankings assigned by the groups are discussed and the reasoning behind their decisions explored. Evaluation criteria are listed on the board based on this discussion.

The students are provided with copies of the "Evaluating Web Resources Checklist" (see Supplementary Materials) and, after a short presentation of the criteria included in it, the groups are assigned one site each to evaluate with the checklist and to determine whether, based on that evaluation, they feel their initial ranking of the site was correct. The entire exercise takes about an hour.

A conglomerate of other web site criteria lists exist; my intent in creating the set of criteria was to develop a list of yes or no questions that students could answer to determine the quality of a web site. The checklist asks students to determine the reliability and credibility of the author; to determine the site's scope, coverage, and currency; to determine the accuracy of the information included and assess bias; and note the site's overall usability. The more yes responses assigned to a site under scrutiny, the more reliable the web site should be considered.

Objectives of the Instruction

- To demonstrate to students that all web sites are not of equal quality.
- To encourage thinking about what makes a web site relevant to a specific assignment.
- To encourage thinking about what makes a web site a useful resource in scholarly research.
- To help them develop criteria for evaluation of web sites.
- To introduce them to the criteria used by others in the evaluation of web sites.

Components of the Instruction

Preparation

Finding Web Sites

This is probably the most time-consuming part of the preparation. After determining the topic, use search engines such as *AltaVista* and *HotBot* as well as a multi-search engine such as *Metacrawler* to find web sites that demonstrate the various evaluation criteria listed on the "Evaluating Web Resources Checklist."

Shakespeare Sites for Presentation
http://www.wpi.edu/+library/Training/webeval.html
Examine this site where the assignment was for students to find a biography of Shakespeare. Here are five of them, ranked, and the reasons for the rankings.

The William Shakespeare Home Page
http://www.geocities.com/Athens/Acropolis/7696/
This site has little value to the completion of the assignment. The site's URL or web address gives no indication of the type of information that might be found on the site (Greek history, maybe?). The site is part of Geocities, *Yahoo*'s personal web site area, usually a bad sign when it comes to finding academically valuable sites. There is no author or authority information listed, even though there is a *Hotmail* e-mail address and a guest book for comments. The colors are horrid, there is no date of creation, and none of the links work. Ranking = 5

A Biography of William Shakespeare: A Man of Varied Respect
http://wwwwms.bham.wednet.edu/biograph/shakes.htm
Despite the decent format and presentation of this site and the addition of web links to other Shakespearean resources, the questionable research, sketches and spelling errors make this site of

no use to any competent researcher. Not bad for a twelve-year-old, however. The site was created by a student of Whatcom Middle School in Bellingham, WA. Ranking = 4

The Life and Times of William Shakespeare
http://www.stratford.co.uk/hislife/home.html
This site includes sections on Shakespeare's life as child, playwright actor and family man. The URL even includes the name of Shakespeare's birthplace "Stratford." But who is the author and where did they get the information? It turns out the site is sponsored by the VIS Communication's Group Stratford Shakespeare Club. In their own words, the web site "is part of a larger sales and marketing initiative being developed for Stratford-upon-Avon and its surrounding area." Might this result in bias? Ranking = 3

The Seven Ages of Shakespeare's Life
http://castle.uvic.ca/shakespeare/Library/SLTnoframes/life/lifesubj.html
Although menu titles might strike one as odd (they are taken from a Shakespearean soliloquy), this site includes quite a bit of detailed information. There are hot-linked explanations provided of the various stages of Shakespeare's life, and even links to additional References and Further Reading. The information is not complete, however, the site having been set up as an advertisement for a forthcoming CD-ROM edition of Shakespeare's Works. How could the BBC Education Web Guide have given this site its seal of approval? Ranking = 2

Shakespeare Resource Center
http://www.bardweb.net/man.html
A well-documented site with very detailed information, this is the best of the lot in addressing the assignment. Ranking = 1

Lists of other examples I have used in various classes are included at the end of this lesson plan. I usually choose no more than five sites, thus giving the groups ample opportunity to view all of them in the allotted time.

Creating the Web Site

If the class is associated with a course, create a web site of library resources for it. For this exercise, add the text of the assignment, the instructions for the exercise, and the list of web sites to the class' course site. This way the students can go back and refer to the list of sites whenever they like. For an information literacy course, add the above information to your course site.

Ranking the Web Sites

Rank the sites prior to the class to make sure you have included a good selection of sites representative of the various evaluation criteria, as well as to ensure that you present them randomly on the web page.

Checklisting the Web Sites

You may wish to apply the "Evaluating Web Resources Checklist" to each site you have chosen prior to the class to avoid any problems.

Handouts

Photocopy the "Evaluating Web Resources Checklist" and include a link to an electronic version of it from the course web site.

Technology

Make arrangements to have a projector and screen in the room so everyone can see and scrutinize each web site together. You should also check the computers you are using or perhaps even book a larger room to accommodate your class.

Presentation

Ranking the web sites

Have the students congregate around the computers in groups of two or three. Direct them to the course web site including the sites they will evaluate. Read the assignment and the instructions to the exercise aloud. Explain that they are to rank the web sites from 1 to 5, 1 being the best and 5 being the worst. Tell the groups to be prepared to defend the reasoning behind their decisions. (20 minutes)

Discussion

Each of the web sites is displayed in front of the class and the groups are asked how they ranked each site. Students defend their rankings and offer reasons that eerily resemble evaluation criteria. List these on the blackboard under the heading: "What Makes a Scholarly Web Site." (20 minutes)

Evaluating Web Resources Checklist

Distribute the "Evaluating Web Resources Checklist." Explain that the criteria for the checklist are taken from various other checklists used by other librarians. Note that it includes much of the same criteria they used in the class to rank the sites. Go over the criteria listed on the checklist (Authority, Scope, Currency, Purpose), filling in anything not mentioned in the discussion. Then, assign each group one of the sites and ask them to use the checklist to evaluate the site. (15 minutes)

Wrap up the session by explaining that, for their original rankings to hold up, they should have more yes responses for the site they ranked first, and more no responses for the site they ranked last. Finally, urge them to use the checklist to help them evaluate web sites as they conduct web research for their project or paper. (5 minutes)

Assignments

If this assignment were given in an for-credit information literacy course or if a course professor offers you the opportunity to follow-up on your presentation, you may want to ask your students to return to the next class with the URL of one web site which they feel would be of value to their research, accompanied by a completed copy of the "Evaluating Web Resources Checklist" for that site.

Evaluation

This exercise allows students to discover the evaluation criteria themselves, gets them actively involved in the evaluation process, and keeps them engaged, as well as offers them a tool which they can use to evaluate other web sites. They key is finding interesting and sometimes humorous examples of bad sites that illustrate what's out there. Laughter and realization tend to go hand in hand. Also, many students often ask for blank copies of the "Evaluating Web Resources Checklist" to use in their own research, a sure sign that they found the exercise beneficial.

Sources:

Evaluating Web Resources Web Site
http://www.wpi.edu/+library/Training/webeval.html
Includes links to "Best Web Sites" lists, example sites to demonstrate and use for evaluation, and links to other web sites that offer tips on web site evaluation.

Examples of courses at WPI that have included this exercise:

HI 1332: Introduction to the History of Technology
http://www.wpi.edu/+library/Training/Courses/HI1332/sokala00.html

MG 3400: Production System Design
http://www.wpi.edu/+library/Training/Courses/MG3400/gerstc01.html

PH 3301: Electromagnetic Theory
http://www.wpi.edu/+library/Training/Courses/PH3301/swartza00.html

SS 1301: U. S. Government
http://www.wpi.edu/+library/Training/Courses/SS1301/ballerb99.html

Supplementary Material

Access the Internet for this resource; it is not included on the accompanying disk.

- Evaluating Web Resources Checklist
  http://www.wpi.edu/+library/Training/evalchecklist.pdf

Notes:

226

Lists of "Best Web Sites" and Web Site Evaluation

CHRISTOPHER COX

Reference/Instruction Librarian
WORCESTER POLYTECHNIC INSTITUTE
ccox@wpi.edu

Circumstances of the Instruction

According to a study completed by Inktomi and the NEC Research Institute, the World Wide Web contains at least 1 billion unique web pages.[i] In an effort to help us separate the wheat from the chaff, each year major magazines publish "Best Web Sites" lists. *Forbes, Yahoo Internet Life!, PC Magazine, PC World, Popular Science*, and *U.S. News & World Report* are just some of the examples. I often look at these lists and think: How on earth did that site get included? And where's the one I use every day?

Unfortunately, many of the readers of these magazines simply take the determinations of these agencies for law, never stopping to ask why the organization included them, or what evaluation criteria the editors used to evaluate the sites which are included. It is interesting to note that most magazines offer no obvious evaluation criteria to explain why certain sites were chosen for inclusion over others. My concerns about how and what sites were included in these lists led to the following exercise.

This exercise need not be associated with a specific course assignment. It need not even be associated with a specific course. It has worked in general library instruction sessions on web site evaluation and would be a welcome addition to any for-credit information literacy course unit on this topic. Students at any level can benefit from this instruction, although it would be of greater interest to students who have not previously thought about web site evaluation. In the exercise, students are divided into groups of two or three, depending of the class size. Because each group must have their own computer, the size of the classroom or lab may determine the optimal class size for this exercise.

Ask the groups to look at each of the sites listed in a category chosen from one of the "Best Web Sites" lists. After examining the sites, a discussion is conducted of why they think the magazine chose to include the sites they did, whether they agree with the magazine's choices, and if they know of any other sites they think would have been better choices for that category. Evaluation criteria are listed on the board based on this discussion. The students are then provided with copies of the "Evaluating Web Resources Checklist" (see Supplementary Materials) and, after a short discussion of the criteria included in it, the groups are assigned one site each to evaluate with the checklist to determine if the site's inclusion by the magazine is supported by its score. The entire exercise takes about an hour.

---

[i] For more information on this study, see http://www.inktomi.com/webmap/.

A conglomerate of other web site criteria lists exist; my intent in creating this set of criteria was to develop a list of yes or no questions that students could answer to determine the quality of a web site. The checklist asks students to determine the reliability and credibility of the author; to determine the site's scope, coverage, and currency; to determine the accuracy of the information included and assess bias; and note the site's overall usability. The more yes responses assigned to a site under scrutiny, the more reliable the web site should be.

Objectives of the Instruction

- Teach students to critique other's evaluation techniques.
- To help students develop criteria for evaluation of web sites.
- To introduce students to the criteria used by others in the evaluation of web sites.

Components of the Instruction

Preparation

Finding Lists of Best Web Sites

The web is replete with "Best Web Sites" lists. Yahoo! lists them under the category: *Computers and Internet > Internet > World Wide Web > Searching the Web > Indices to Web Documents > Best of the Web*. Because of the size of the Web and its unedited and communal nature, anyone or any organization can publish a list of sites they use and like best. Most of the popular magazines that publish "Best Web Sites" articles offer web companions to them that include the same or an expanded list of sites with hyperlinks. Links to the lists I often use are included at my *Evaluating Web Resources* web site—http://www.wpi.edu/+library/Training/webeval.html.

Evaluating the List Sites

The next step is to take a look at the categories on each of the lists you have found, decide which list you like and then choose a category based on the course you will be teaching to or some other factor. If no course-related topic exists or if you are not teaching this exercise for a course or are using it in an information literacy course, pick the most interesting and debatable category.

Evaluating the Evaluators

Most of the "Best Web Sites" lists offer no information about how the web sites were selected or evaluated. I usually try to contact the editors or writers of the articles ahead of time to find out what evaluation criteria they used. Most do not respond, but the responses I do receive usually provide good fuel for discussion.

Selecting Sites from the Lists

Some of the list categories may include too many sites for your students to judge effectively in the time you may have. Stick with five or less, choosing them from a category if it is too large.

Creating the Web Site

If the class is associated with a course in an academic discipline or an information literacy course, create a web site of library resources for it. For this exercise, add a link to the web version of the "Best Web Sites" list you have chosen or include links to the sites in the category you have chosen if the list appears only in print. This way the students can go back and refer to the list of sites whenever they like. Avoid photocopying a printed list or to ask the students to type in the URLs; they waste an awful lot of time doing this.

Checklisting the Web Sites

You may or may not choose to apply the checklist to each site in the category you have chosen.

Handouts

Photocopy the "Evaluating Web Resources Checklist" and include a link to an electronic version of it from the course web site.

Technology

Make arrangements to have a projector and screen in the room so everyone can see and scrutinize each web site together. You should also check the computers you're using or perhaps even book a larger room to accommodate your class.

Presentation

Evaluating the Editor's Choices

As the students arrive, ask them to congregate around the computers in groups of two or three. Ask them if they are familiar with those annual "Best Web Sites" lists that are in all the magazines. Bring a few in and pass them around. Ideally you will get some nods of recognition.

Tell the class they are going to evaluate the sites chosen in a category from one of those lists. For this example, I will use the All-Sport category from *U. S. News & World Report's Best of the Web* list—http://www.usnews.com/usnews/issue/001204/nycu/allsport.htm. The students are told to think of themselves as magazine editors (or as acquisition librarians, perhaps). Their job is to ask themselves: "Do I agree with the sites the editors chose? What sites would I have included if I were the editor(s)?"

Direct the groups to the course web site that includes a link to *U. S. News & World Report's Best of the Web* list. Bring them to the All-Sport category and ask them to look at each of the web sites included and decide whether they agree with each choice. Ask them to also come up with the name of at least one site they may often use in that category which they think is equal to or better than the sites chosen by the list's editors. (20 minutes)

Discussion

First, ask the students to go back to the list's main page—
http://www.usnews.com/usnews/nycu/tech/tebest.htm—and see if they can find anywhere on the web site where it mentions what criteria were used to evaluate the sites included in the list (In this case, the answer is, there is none).[ii] Display each of the web sites in the category and ask the class what they thought of each site and whether they felt it worthy of inclusion. What criteria did they think the editors of the magazine used to choose the web sites they included? These criteria are listed on the board under the heading: "What *U. S. News and World Report* Thinks Makes a Good Web Site."

Have your students suggest other sites in the same category that they feel should have been included (*ESPN.com* anyone?). Have them come up to the front of the class and show the others their site. (20 minutes).

Evaluating Web Resources Checklist

Distribute copies of the "Evaluating Web Resources Checklist." Explain that the criteria for the checklist are taken from various other checklists used by other librarians. Note that it includes some of the same criteria they believe the editors used to choose the sites from the lists. Go over the criteria listed on the checklist (Authority, Scope, Currency, Purpose), filling in anything not mentioned in the discussion. Finally, assign each group one of the sites from the All-Sport category and ask them to use the checklist to evaluate the site. (15 minutes)

Wrap up the session by explaining that sites included in U.S. News' list should have earned more yes responses than no responses. If they did not, perhaps they are not of high enough quality to have been included. Urge them to use the checklist to help them as they look at other web sites or conduct web research for their project or paper. (5 minutes)

Evaluation

This exercise, at the very least, usually gets students talking. It empowers them to criticize and not take for rote the "Best Web Sites" lists they are continually bombarded with. It arms them with a powerful tool that they can use to evaluate other web sites.

This exercise, however, is not foolproof. Here are a few warnings. Be careful of the type of list you choose. Watch out for those lists that lack clear and consistently applied criteria for the sites they have chosen beyond that of being "cool" or simply "my favorite."

[ii] I e-mailed *U.S News and World Report* and asked them what criteria they used to evaluate the web sites they included in their "Best of the Web" List. According to Tim Smart of U. S. News, the sites were amassed "largely on the suggestion of our many staffers who are quite familiar with the various web sites in their area of interest." In terms of evaluation criteria, Tim responds, "We did not use any specific criteria, but we wanted sites that were easily accessible, worked well in terms of loading and being bug free, and also that seemed new and incorporated the latest technology (such as Flash animation). " As I mentioned before, responses such as these cannot help but spur spirited class discussion (Personal e-mail from Tim Smart of *U. S. News and World Report* <tsmart@usnews.com>, Tuesday, December 5, 2000).

While I must admit I like it better when students are actively engaged in the session, you may have to rein them in when it comes to suggesting other web sites. Things can get rowdy. Make sure you keep the exercise on track and the discussion under control. Some of the web companions to these magazine's "Best Web Sites" lists, including *U. S News and World Report*, allow you to vote for or submit your favorite web sites. I usually urge the students who do not get the chance to show their sites to the class to submit them to the magazine editors.

I have also run into trouble when it comes to scoring some of the sites on these lists. The checklist relies heavily on web site content, something that many "Best Web Sites" lists rank secondary to criteria such as "design, navigation, speed and customization," which all fall under "Usability" on the checklist.[iii] I usually point out the fallacy of worrying more about loading time than information when evaluating web sites.[iv]

Variations

This exercise can also be completed using lists of web award winners (The Webbys for example), librarian-evaluated "Best Web Sites" lists such as those included in publications like *Choice*, *Library Journal*, or RUSA's "Best Free Reference Web Sites" published annually in *Reference & User Services Quarterly*, and evaluated subject directories. Evaluated subject directories employ specific criteria to evaluate which sites are included in the engine. Sites such as *Librarian's Index to the Internet*—http://www.lii.org, *INFOMINE*—http://infomine.ucr.edu/, and *Argus Clearinghouse*—http://www.clearinghouse.net/—all would work well. For others, see the "Evaluated Subject Directory" under "Recommended Search Tools" on my *Advanced Web Searching* site—http://www.wpi.edu/+library/Training/SearchEngines.

"Best Web Sites" Lists

"Best of the Web". *Forbes*. September 11, 2000. Entire issue.
http://www.forbesbest.com/

"Best of the Web." *U. S. News and World Report*. Vol. 129, No. 22 (December 4, 2000). 50.
http://www.usnews.com/usnews/nycu/tech/tebest.htm

---

iii *Forbes.com*, in listing the evaluation criteria for its "Best of the Web" list (http://www.forbesbest.com/) lists content first, followed by "design, navigation, speed and customization."

iv My college's own Eleanor Loiacono has designed a system called WebQual which scores sites based on a dozen qualities determined by users. The main criteria measured are informational fit to task, interactivity, trust, response time and design issues. Richard T. Watson, director of the University of Georgia's Center for Information Systems, "fully expect(s) that WebQual will become a widely used standard in academe and industry." We will have to wait and see. The resemblance to both Forbes and U.S. News' criteria makes me wary. ("Rating a Web Site: WPI Professor Devises System to Judge Quality," WPI press release, October 16, 2000 [http://www.wpi.edu/News/Releases/20001/webrating.html]).

Butner, Richard. "50 Most Incredibly Useful Sites." *Yahoo! Internet Life*. Vol. 6, No. 7 (July 2000). 116.
http://www.zdnet.com/yil/content/mag/0007/useful_main.html

Grimes, Brad and the Editors of *PC World*. "Best of the Web". *PC World*. Vol. 18, No. 8 (August 2000). 100.
http://www.pcworld.com/reviews/article.asp?aid=17178

Kirschner, Suzanne Kantra, editor. "50 Best of the Web". *Popular Science*. October 2000. 43.
http://www.popsci.com/features/bow00/

Wilmott, Don. "The Top 100 Web Sites and the Technologies That Make Them Work". *PC Magazine*. Vol. 19, No. 3 (February 8, 2000). 144.
http://www.zdnet.com/pcmag/stories/reviews/0,6755,2394453,00.html

Sources:

Evaluating Web Resources Web Site
http://www.wpi.edu/+library/Training/webeval.html
This site includes links to "Best Web Sites" lists, example sites to demonstrate and use for evaluation, and links to other web sites that offer tips on web site evaluation.

Supplementary Material

Access the Internet for this resource; it is not included on the accompanying disk.

- Evaluating Web Resources Checklist
  http://www.wpi.edu/+library/Training/evalchecklist.pdf

Web Page Design and Web Site Evaluation

CHRISTOPHER COX

Reference/Instruction Librarian
WORCESTER POLYTECHNIC INSTITUTE
ccox@wpi.edu

Circumstances of the Instruction

I am often called upon to teach classes for other departments within the Information Technology division of which the library is a member. As a result, I now teach HTML for the WPI Web Development Office. In my Basic Web Design course, I exemplify the difference between good and bad web design by having the students evaluate two personal home pages. This exercise has also come in handy in some of the general web site evaluation sessions I offer, since a web site that is easily navigable, has thoughtful and appealing graphics, and an obvious or familiar structure is often one which scores high on any evaluation and one that we want to return to again and again. This exercise does not usually last more than 15–20 minutes, but it does serve as a beginning to discussion of how design impacts the evaluation of web resources.

Class participants are divided into groups of two of three. They are given a piece of paper or directed to a web page with links to the two web sites I have chosen for evaluation. I ask them to look at both sites and decide which one they think offers a better design to explore the site's content. This is followed by discussion and my own comments on the sites as they are projected on a screen in the front of the room. Elements of good web design are noted on the board. After discussion, at least in the Basic Web Design class, I make a presentation on web site design principles and how they impact the creation of a web site. Topics can include organization and how to storyboard a new web site, hierarchical versus linear web page organization, the benefits of topic and subtopic menus, the use of graphics and proper link usage, HTML etiquette, etc.

This exercise can be done with any level of student, as well as with faculty and staff. The optimal number of participants may depend on whether the participants work in groups at their own computers or if they simply evaluate sites projected in front of the class. If they work at computers, the optimum number would be about 25–30 students. This exercise should work with classes of any size. In very small classes, you could always forego the group idea and let the students work on the sites individually.

This exercise would work as part of a for-credit information literacy course unit or in a general session on web resource evaluation. Other aspects of web site evaluation such as authority, accuracy, and bias may also make good separate exercises where time is at a premium. Just be sure to emphasize that applying one criterion alone will not guarantee the quality of a web site.

Objectives of the Instruction

The students will:
- learn the elements of good web site design and construction and
- evaluate web sites based on design.

Components of the Instruction

Preparation

Choose Web Sites to Evaluate

This can be tricky. The exercise can work with any two web sites that aim to accomplish the same task, i.e., two news sites like *ABCNews.com* and *CNN.com*; two shopping sites like *Amazon.com* and *Sears.com*, etc. Simply make sure that the web sites chosen perform similar tasks and that they occupy the same web site category: personal, commercial, organizational, etc. Be sure to choose one good example and one bad example, so that there can be adequate means for comparison and discussion.

Webpagesthatsuck.com can be an excellent resource for sites with, shall we say, inadequate design. As mentioned above, I have had success with faculty web sites in the past. The two names and URLs of the sites I use, along with an analysis of each, is listed below. Both were created specifically for the class to illustrate good and bad design techniques. I thought it best to avoid using actual faculty members' web sites.

I added the HTML criterion because I urge my students not to experiment with HTML editors like Microsoft FrontPage until they have a good grasp of the code and what the editors actually do.

Jared Thatcher's Home Page	Allan Anderson's Home Page
http://www.wpi.edu/+library/Training/Web/T/	http://www.wpi.edu/+library/Training/Web/A/
Busy tiled image background	Solid color background
Includes contact information (phone number, e-mail address)	Includes contact information (e-mail address)
More of a home page only, not really a web site	A completely designed, thoroughly thought out web site
Organized menu of links	Organized menu of links
Broken image links	Good use of images; homepage image a little large
Need to scroll to view complete page – could miss some	Entire page fits on screen (1024 x 768 pixels)
Links to "Education and Experience" and "Research Projects" broken	No broken links
Background and link colors continue through some pages of site, not others (Senior Seminar)	Background and link colors continue through entire site

Back links used on some pages, not others	Menu and picture at top of each page for easy navigation
Colors of background, links, text do not work together	Colors of background, links, text work well together
No last updated date (1998?)	No last updated date (1997?)
Simple look, all plain text, not many graphics	Slicker, more professional look
HTML editor used: Microsoft Word	HTML editor used: Netscape Gold

Take Notes on the Web Sites

Do your homework ahead of time. Go to class with detailed notes on each site, including a list of examples of good and bad design for each. Make sure that the sites are functioning so that you can have visual examples when discussing topics and criteria relating to their evaluation.

Creating the Web Site or Handout

I have previously used a print handout listing the URLs for both sites, but will probably add the links to the sites to my *Creating Web Pages Using HTML* web site— http://www.wpi.edu/+library/Training/Web. It takes much longer if the students have to type in the URLs for themselves.

Tweaking the technology

Make arrangements to have a projector and screen in the room so everyone can see and scrutinize each web site together. You should also check the PCs you are using or perhaps even book a larger room to accommodate your class.

Presentation

Evaluating the Design of the Web Sites

When the participants arrive ask them to form groups of two or three in front of a computer. Distribute a handout with the names and URLs of the two sites you have chosen. The participants are asked to look at both web sites and decide which one of the two offers a better design to explore the site's content. They are told to be prepared to give reasons for their decisions. (10 minutes)

Discussion

Look at both web sites as a class. Participants argue for which site they feel is best and discuss what they like and dislike about the design of each. List the sites on the board and list good and bad traits for each, somewhat like the table included above. (5 minutes)

This discussion can be used as a springboard to discussion of web site design techniques. For example, both of the web sites I use are examples of hierarchical design, where there is a list of links and the site is navigated in any order the web surfer chooses, offering greater flexibility. A linear site would be one set up like a Microsoft PowerPoint presentation, where the web surfer must navigate the pages of the site in the exact order the web site creator has dictated.

Assignments

Ask the students to take a look at the web sites they use most often and write a short essay about why the site's design initially appealed to them and why it continues to draw them back. You could also have them each bring in the URL of a site whose design they admire and the URL of a site they dislike and present the two in front of the class. This would certainly be of benefit to them, since the sites they admire would no doubt make good templates for the design of their own personal web sites.

Evaluation

This exercise works well in the HTML class, serving to actively engage the participants in thinking and evaluating the web design. Here are a few warnings. When choosing web sites, be careful not to choose sites from your own university. Criticism of another faculty or staff member's web site, whether they attend the class or not, travels fast and could lead to undo controversy and bloodshed. I recommend using the ones I have created or create your own.

Even if you use this exercise in an HTML class, make sure you emphasize that looking at a web site's design is only one aspect of web resource evaluation. Looking at web design is often little different than deciding whether the content of a site is scholarly or not.

Sources:

Creating Web Pages With HTML
http://www.wpi.edu/+library/Training/Web
This site includes handouts and exercises used in all three of my "Creating Web Pages With HTML" sessions.

Evaluating Web Resources Web Site
http://www.wpi.edu/+library/Training/webeval.html
This site includes links to "Best Web Sites" lists, example sites to demonstrate and use for evaluation, and links to other web sites that offer tips on web site evaluation.

Klein, Leo Robert. "Web Design and Sin." *Library Journal netConnect*. Summer 2000.
http://www.libraryjournal.com/klein.asp
An interesting article that basically translates as web beauty is in the eye of the beholder.

WebPagesThatSuck.com
http://webpagesthatsuck.com
Make sure your web site is never selected as the "Daily Sucker." Join Vincent Flanders as he offers tips on how to create well-designed web pages, and to avoid "mystery meat navigation."

Supplementary Material

Access the Internet for this resource; it is not included on the accompanying disk.

- Evaluating Web Resources Checklist
  http://www.wpi.edu/+library/Training/evalchecklist.pdf

Finding U.S. Government Information on the Internet

CAROL A. SINGER

Assistant Professor, Reference Librarian
BOWLING GREEN STATE UNIVERSITY
singerc@bgnet.bgsu.edu

COLEEN PARMER

Associate Professor, Head of Government Documents
BOWLING GREEN STATE UNIVERSITY
parmer@bgnet.bgsu.edu

Circumstances of the Instruction

In 1996, the U.S. Government Printing Office (GPO) issued a *Study to Identify Measures Necessary for a Successful Transition to a More Electronic FDLP*.[1] A key assumption of the transition plan was that nearly all of the information provided to libraries through the Federal Depository Library Program (FDLP) would be electronic by the end of fiscal year 1998. Since the release of this report, access to government information has steadily migrated into the World Wide Web environment. Currently users find themselves struggling amidst a vast, bewildering array of electronic reports, agency web sites, and search engines. No single search engine can provide access to all U.S. government information on the Internet. Instead, users must employ several search tools if they are to locate all the relevant information on their topic.

This class presents three search strategies for finding United States government information on the Internet. It could be presented to any level of college or university student but is aimed at upper level undergraduates or graduate students. The class will be most effective as a hands-on session, but could be given as a demonstration. The optimal number of students would be about 20, assuming enough workstations are available in the classroom. The unit could last one or two hours, depending on the amount of time given students to work on their own. We have assumed this is part of a larger course and that the students will have already learned how to construct a search strategy and how to use Boolean operators and search engine math.

Objectives of the Instruction

After completing this unit, the students will:
- know that U.S. government information is issued in many formats;
- know that there is no one site that lists all U.S. government information on the Internet;
- identify one bibliographic index that covers U.S. government information on the Internet and know how to use it;
- identify one Internet search engine that covers U.S. government information on the Internet and know how to use it;
- identify one site that lists U.S. government agency web sites and know how to use it to find web sites; and

- understand the main advantages and disadvantages of each type of finding aid.

Components of the Instruction

Before the class is taught, the instructor should check to see that the sites listed in the outline of the unit are still valid, and identify current URLs if they have moved or replace them with better sites if necessary. The instructor should check all examples to ensure that they still work and to update search results. The instructor should make photocopies of the exercises and the assessment instrument.

The instructor will hand out the exercises and the assessment instrument. A detailed script for the presentation is given below. An outline of the presentation will be found in the Supplementary Materials. The students can follow along as the instructor shows the examples. The practice exercises and/or the hands-on exercises may be done during class or may be given as an assignment to be completed before the next class. The assessment could be completed at the end of the class, if desired.

Presentation Script

Introduction

Government information may be defined as any information produced by or for a governmental body. The governmental body could be a national, state, or local governmental organization.

The United States government releases information in a variety of formats, including paper, microfiche, maps, multimedia productions, CD-ROMs, and online resources.

Some types of information produced by the government might be legislative, legal, regulatory, statistical, or reports needed for the administration of departmental or agency programs. For this presentation, we'll look at how to find information generated by the administration of departmental or agency programs.

Remember to always look at the help screens to find more information about how to use each of the databases and search engines presented in this session.

Search Types
Searching a Bibliographic Index With Links To Full-Text Resources
There are several advantages to using a bibliographic index. First, you can search by issuing agency, title, and subject or keyword. The subject headings are assigned from a controlled vocabulary and the records are composed by people trained to do this. The *Catalog of U.S. Government Publications* is created and maintained by the U.S. Government Printing Office (GPO) and is free. Coverage begins in 1994 and it indexes only U.S. documents. The *Catalog* includes all formats of publication—paper, microfiche, maps, CD-ROMs, and online resources— and you can easily identify libraries holding tangible material you want to borrow. Like other

bibliographic indexes, the *Catalog* is a good tool to search if you already know the title of a document.

Begin with a keyword search of titles about juvenile delinquents in boot camp programs. Type **"boot camps"** in the Keyword Search box and be sure to include quotation marks (" ") around the phrase. The system will find only records that contain those two terms together. Browse through your results screen. Notice that many of the records do not have URLs. Remember, the *Catalog* includes titles that are not online. Find a record that has a link and click on "Full Record." The record contains an array of bibliographic elements including title, agency, format, URL, and subject headings. Use your browser to return to the results screen. If you were to click on the URL you would be connected to the issuing agency's web site and an online full-text copy of the publication. But instead of doing that, return to the search screen and do another keyword search of the term **terrorism**.

Enter **terrorism** as a keyword and look at the results. Note that we found 40 (forty) records, and we would find more if we increased the maximum records display. There are so many results that it is difficult to identify online titles. Let's go back to the search screen and enter a search in the Keyword Search (Online Title) box. Type **terrorism AND http**. Be sure to capitalize AND. Look at the results. Notice that we get fewer results and that they all have URLs. The search pulled up only titles containing both the term **"terrorism"** and **"http"** from web addresses in the record. Combining terms with the operator "and" limits search results to records that contain all the terms you enter.

The *Catalog* is the best search tool to begin with if you know the title of a document. Return to the search screen once more and try to find a specific document. Enter **"facts on working women"** (don't forget the quotation marks) in the Title Search box. Our search returns several titles including the one we wanted, *Facts on working women: hot jobs for the 21st century*.

Finding and Searching Agency Web Sites

Government agencies are mounting more publications on their web sites every day and many have developed sophisticated search engines. If you know the issuing agency, it is better to search that agency's web site first. Some topics naturally lend themselves to such an approach. For instance, if you wanted to locate tax forms, you would search the Internal Revenue Service site, and likewise you would search the Education Department for topics about education or the Labor Department for topics about employment.

The *Catalog of US Government Publications* includes several Related Finding Aids. Click on the **Agency Websites** button. This link connects you to a search engine, *Federal Agency Internet Sites*, developed by Louisiana State University Libraries. You can search an index or browse a list of agencies. Select the link, "Search the List of Federal Agency Internet Sites." Let's see if we can find an agency that issues reports about our first topic, **"boot camps."** Since this topic concerns juvenile justice it is likely that the Justice Department has issued some relevant publications. Type **Justice** in the search box. Our search results include links to the Justice Department and a number of bureaus under the department. Note that one of the agencies is the **Office of Juvenile Justice and Delinquency Prevention**. Click on that link and search **"boot** camps" on the agency search engine. Like the *Catalog*, you must enter quotation marks around the terms to search for a phrase. Leave the Query Type default set as Concept. A Concept search will look for the words and phrases you typed as well as related concepts. To see more information about how to use this search engine, click on the "help text" link. Documents matching your query are displayed in order of relevance, with those judged most relevant listed first. This search demonstrates the power of agency searching; we found significantly more results on the OJJDP site than we did searching the *Catalog*.

Use your browser to return to the *Federal Agency Internet Sites* search engine and try to find an agency that issues information about global warming. The Environmental Protection Agency studies all sorts of environmental issues including global warming. Enter **environmental protection** into the search box and connect to the EPA site. Click on the search button and type the word or phrase you wish to find: **global warming**. You do not need quotation marks to search phrases in this search engine. The Search Tips for this search engine are displayed just below the search box. The EPA has created a whole web site on the topic of global warming. Click on the *EPA Global Warming Site*. EPA says, about this page "With the Global Warming Site, we strive to present accurate information on the very broad issue of climate change and global warming in a way that is accessible and meaningful to all parts of society – communities, individuals, business, public officials and governments."

It is clear that agency sites are wonderful resources and that their search engines can help you locate vast amounts of relevant, authoritative, and current information. But you don't always know which agency to search, or you have a topic that many agencies cover, or you want to find more than just federal government information.

Internet Search Engines That Search for Government Information

The major advantage of using an Internet search engine is that it retrieves only information on the Internet, instead of identifying books, reports, CD-ROMs, or other formats. Only a small portion of government information on the Internet is listed in bibliographic indexes, and sometimes you cannot identify all of the agencies or departments that might produce information on your topic. Internet search engines also allow you to search for government resources other than documents, such as service sites or databases.

Some general search engines, like *AltaVista*, allow you to limit your search to only those within the domain **.gov**. However, you can also use *Google Uncle Sam* to limit your search to only government sites. *Google Uncle Sam* indexes all government sites that include **.gov** or **.mil** in the URL. It is most efficient for finding U.S. government information, but includes some sites from state or local governments. However, many state and local government sites don't include **.gov** in the URL, so *Google Uncle Sam* won't identify those sites.

The simplest way to perform a *Google Uncle Sam* search is to enter your search terms in the search box and hit the enter key (or click on the *Google* Search button). *Google* will automatically retrieve only sites that include all of your terms and will combine the terms using the Boolean AND. Type **trade china** in the search box to retrieve sites that include both terms. Scroll down the page to show the variety of entries retrieved by this search. Each record includes

240

the page title, phrases that describe the page, the URL, the size of the page text, and a link to a cached copy of the page. If you fail to retrieve the page using the link, you can click on the cached link to see a copy of the page at the time *Google* indexed it.

In addition to the automatic AND, *Google* allows you to use OR in the search and to enclose phrases within quotation marks. To find information on global warming in Ohio or Michigan, type **"global warming" (ohio OR michigan)**. Do not forget to capitalize the OR.

To find more information about how to search the *Google Uncle Sam* search engine, click on the Search Tips link at the top of the main page.

Evaluation

Have students complete the Assessment Tool (see Supplementary Materials) following the lecture/demonstration and hands-on practice. This instrument should provide insight into whether students successfully met the proposed objectives of this session.

Sources:

Catalog of U.S. Government Publications
http://www.access.gpo.gov/su-docs/locators/cgpindex.html

Google Uncle Sam
http://www.google.com/unclesam/

Additional Readings for the Instructor:

Farrell, Maggie. "Search Engines for Federal Government Information." *Dttp; A Quarterly Journal of Government Information Practice and Perspective* (Fall, 1999): 6–7.

Hernon, Peter, John Shuler, and Robert E. Dugan. *U.S. Government on the Web: Getting the Information You Need.* Englewood, Colorado: Libraries Unlimited, 1999.

Notess, Greg R. *Government Information on the Internet.* 3rd edition. Lanham, Md.: Bernan Press, 2000.

Robinson, Judith Schiek. *Tapping the Government Grapevine: the User-Friendly Guide to U.S. Government Information Sources.* 3rd edition. Phoenix, Arizona: Oryx Press, 1998.

Supplementary Materials

The materials in this section have been placed on the accompanying disk so they can easily be copied and/or modified to fit the needs of individual libraries and instructors.

- Outline of the Presentation
- Practice Exercises
- Out of Class Assignment
- Assessment Tool

Notes:

1. Study to Identify Measures Necessary for Successful Transition to a More Electronic Federal Depository Library Program: As Required by Legislative Branch Appropriations Act, 1996, Public Law 104–53; Report to the Congress. Washington, DC, U.S. Government Printing Office, [1996].

Section 6—Social, Ethical, and Legal Issues Related to Information Literacy

Hey, That's No Fair! Copyright and Fair Use Case Studies

From Ethics to Copyright Law: Protecting Intellectual Property in the 21st Century

Digital Divide

Androids, Cyborgs, and Robots: A Glimpse Into Technoculture's Future

City Council Lab

Virtually Homeless

You Be the Judge: Internet Filters and Censorship

Hey, That's No Fair! Copyright and Fair Use Case Studies

SUSAN E. BECK

Head, Humanities & Social Sciences Services Department
NEW MEXICO STATE UNIVERSITY
susabeck@lib.nmsu.edu

Circumstances of the Instruction

The concepts of both copyright and fair use are frequently misunderstood in their daily application. This is especially true nowadays with the emergence of the Internet—an information source thought by many to be copyright-free. The Internet's accompanying tools such as Napster, MP3.com, and FTP have made copying and transferring information almost effortless. Not only is the information, regardless of format, easily copied with the click of a mouse but also the copy itself is a perfect replica of the original. However, in trying to make sense of how copyright is applied to new technologies such as the Internet, students first need an understanding of what copyright is all about: its scope, purpose, and its history. Students need to be aware of two basic rights involving intellectual property. First, they should understand the rights of the copyright holders who govern whether and how their intellectual property shall be copied. By the same token, students should also know about the rights of the individual to copy that same intellectual property for one's education or recreational use. More often than not, though, these two concepts oppose one another. Thus, in learning the complexities of current applications of basic copyright law and fair use, students are better equipped to deal with future copyright challenges.

This activity is designed for an upper level undergraduate information literacy course with an enrollment of 24 students or less. It could just as well be modified for a lower level undergraduate course. The activity can be done in a regular classroom; it does not require computer access. Students will require Internet access, however, to do the background readings in preparation for the class session.

The entire lesson can be accomplished in a 70-minute class session but it could be divided into two 50-minute sessions. If following the two 50-minute session model, the lecture and group activity would comprise the first 50-minute session and the second session would cover the whole class discussion and summary.

Objectives of the Instruction

Students will:
- understand the concepts of copyright and fair use;
- demonstrate an awareness of the applications of both these concepts through analyzing a federal court case involving copyright infringement;
- understand and apply the four-factor test for fair use to an assigned federal court case; and
- evaluate the court case using the four-factor test and knowledge of copyright infringement.

Components of the Instruction

Preparation

Students must study three web sites in preparation for the class session on copyright.

- 10 Big Myths About Copyright Explained
  http://www.templetons.com/brad/copymyths.html
- When Copying Is OK (Nolo's *Legal Encyclopedia*)
  http://www.nolo.com/encyclopedia/articles/pct/nn75.html
- Fair Use Test
  http://www.benedict.com/basic/fairuse/fairtest.htm#Top

The instructor needs to:
1. Prepare an introductory lecture on the history, purpose and scope of copyright.
2. Find several federal court cases that involve some aspect of copyright infringement and a claim of fair use. The following have proven successful with this class activity:
   a. Princeton University Press v. Michigan Document Services, Inc.
      99 F.3d 1381
   b. American Geophysical Union v. Texaco, Inc.
      60 F.3d 913
   c. Feist Publications, Inc. v. Rural Telephone Services
      499 US 340
   These cases also concern copyright infringement
   d. Basic Books, Inc. v. Kinko's Graphics Corp.
      758 F.Supp. 1522
   e. Campbell v. Acuff-Rose
      510 US 569
   f. Harper & Row v. Nation Enterprises
      471 US 539
   g. Los Angeles News Services v. Tullo
      973 F.2d 791
   h. National Rifle Association of America v. Handgun Control Federation
      15 F.3d 599
3. Prepare a summary of each of the selected cases, being sure to note both the plaintiff's and the defendant's arguments. It is important to change the names of both parties. It is a good idea to omit or change any other identifying characteristics of the case as well. (See Supplementary Materials)
4. Create a worksheet for groups to use for their case analysis, decision, and summation.

Presentation (10-15 minutes)

The class begins with a short lecture on copyright, its definition, purpose, and history. The instructor also reviews the web readings on fair use. Next, the instructor prompts the students to supply the four factors courts apply in determining fair use and writes these on the board so students can refer to them during their group work.

Activity (25-30 minutes)

The instructor divides the class into several groups of three or four students each and distributes a federal court case summary to each group along with the worksheet, **Hey, That's No Fair! Or Is It? You Be the Supreme Court.** The instructor explains that each group will be analyzing an actual federal court case and deciding whether copyright was violated or note. The instructor urges the groups to apply the four-factor test of fair use and encourages groups to try to reach a consensus. Either way, the group and its possible dissenters need to summarize their court case and be able to justify their decision to the rest of the class. While groups work on their case analysis, the instructor circulates among groups, answering questions, assisting with understanding the case, and prompting them to consider alternate viewpoints.

Discussion (20-25 minutes)

One by one each group presents their case, first summarizing the main points of the case and then noting both the defendant's and the plaintiff's arguments. The groups give their summation, explaining why they ruled in favor of either the plaintiff or the defendant. When they give their summation, groups need to cite which factors of the fair use test they did or did not apply. If not all members of the group agree, those that dissent must present and explain their rationale. In cases where more than one group examines the same case, both groups present.

After all groups have presented, the instructor summarizes the federal courts decision and reveals the name and citation of each case.

Evaluation

Because this is an active learning exercise, it is quickly apparent whether students have grasped the basic concepts or not. This is also the case when groups present their findings. During the final whole class discussion, the instructor has another opportunity to determine whether they understood the basic principles. If the instructor determines that the majority of students have not figured out the main points of the lesson, then a short quiz can be given in the following class session.

Supplementary Materials

The materials in this section have been placed on the accompanying disk so they can easily be copied and/or modified to fit the needs of individual libraries and instructors.

- Lecture Notes on Copyright & Fair Use
- Case Study #1: Publishers vs. Copyshop
- Case Study #2: Publisher vs. Telephone Company
- Case Study #3: Scientific Publisher vs. Multinational Research Company
- Worksheet for Hey, That's No Fair! Or Is It? You Be the Supreme Court

Notes:

248

From Ethics to Copyright Law: Protecting Intellectual Property in the 21st Century

COLLEEN BELL

Library Instruction Coordinator
UNIVERSITY OF OREGON
cbell@darkwing.uoregon.edu

Circumstances of the Instruction

Parts of this lesson were conceived as part of a course for freshmen students exploring the use and misuse of information. Others were conceived in preparation for an upper-division undergraduate course on information research and the information environment. Many students have grown up with computers, the web and Napster, and learn to "copy and paste" at a relatively early age. Yet few students are taught to fully appreciate intellectual property issues that affect their use of the information they find in electronic and other forms. To many of them, copyright seems like an antiquated law that has no place in an environment where information is easy to access and use. This lesson uses scenarios to which students can relate to discuss plagiarism, documentation, and copyright issues. This lesson takes two 50-minute class periods to complete.

Objectives of the Instruction

- Make students aware of intellectual property issues, especially plagiarism, documentation, and copyright.
- Have students test their assumptions against existing policies, practices, and laws regarding information ethics and intellectual property rights, with particular attention to copyright.

Components of the Instruction

Preparation

Prepare a transparency of your institution's policy on student academic integrity. Make a copy for each student. If your institution does not have one, you can borrow one from another institution, such as the University of Oregon—http://darkwing.uoregon.edu/~conduct/sai.htm.

Prepare a handout on documenting sources, or use one of the many available on the web. An example of one, entitled *How to Cite References (Using Style Manuals)* can be found on the web at— http://libweb.uoregon.edu/instruct/pubs/08-style.pdf.

Prepare 3–4 transparencies that present scenarios such as the ones described below, along with follow-up questions. Each transparency should describe one scenario and include the follow-up questions. The first two scenarios have nothing to do with information but provide situations that force students to examine their ethical and legal assumptions about property. The next two scenarios use information as the central theme but still require students to check their ethical and legal assumptions about intellectual property.

Prepare a quiz on copyright that presents situations in which different parts of the copyright law would apply; a sample quiz is provided, along with the answer key. Make enough copies of the quiz for each student to have one. Then make enough additional copies on a second color of paper so you can distribute one quiz for each group of 3–4 students.

Prepare a transparency of the copyright disclaimer that the American Library Association recommends for use in libraries: "The copyright law of the United States (Title 17, United States Code) governs the making of photocopies or other reproductions of copyrighted material. Under certain conditions specified in the law, libraries and archives are authorized to furnish a photocopy or other reproduction. One of these specified conditions is that the photocopy or other reproduction is not to be "used for any purpose other than private study, scholarship, or research." If a user makes a request for, or later uses, a photocopy or reproduction for purposes in excess of "fair use," that user may be liable for copyright infringement."

Prepare a handout that describes the fair use exceptions in the copyright law. A nice example of this is the *Checklist for Fair Use* prepared by the Copyright Management Center at Indiana University— http://www.iupui.edu/~copyinfo/fuchecklist.html. The checklist provides a list of decisions about the purpose of the work, the nature of the use, the amount of the work, and the effect of the use in determining whether use of a particular piece falls under the fair use guidelines.

Presentation/Activity

Class Session One

Do not provide a lengthy introduction; just tell students what the topic of the lesson is. Have students read the first scenario: "You are shopping at The Gap. A woman you don't know places a scarf underneath her jacket and leaves the store without paying for it." Have students discuss the following: "How do you feel about this? Do you think she has done anything illegal? Why or why not? Do you think she has done anything unethical? Why or why not? Is there a term or phrase to describe what she has done?" Ideally, there will be very little disagreement on these questions.

Present the second scenario: "You have ordered a sub to go at a local sub shop and people are watching as you wait near the front counter for your name to be called. Another student walks up to the counter, places his order, then asks for a cup for water. He is given a small cup, easily distinguishable from the cups provided to those who purchase a soda. He then walks over to the soda dispenser and fills his cup with Dr. Pepper, which he drinks while standing in the corner, out of view of the front counter. He smiles and winks at his friend, then refills his cup, still out of view of the front counter." Ask students to respond to the same questions you asked earlier: "How do you feel about this? Do you think he has done anything illegal? Why or why not? Do you think he has done anything unethical? Why or why not? Is there a term or phrase to describe what he has done?" Ideally, students will disagree with each other on some of these questions – this scenario is not as clear-cut.

Present the next scenario: "You are writing a term paper, it is getting close to the deadline, and the words are not flowing. A couple of the sources you found say it so much better than you ever could, so you just copy a few key paragraphs into your paper – you tell yourself that your professor will never know the difference. All of a sudden, the words start flowing and you end up with the best paper you have ever written. You decide your paper won't work without those paragraphs, so you keep them." Ask students to respond to the following questions: "How do you feel about this? Do you think you have done anything illegal? Why or why not? Do you think you have done anything unethical? Why or why not? Is there a term or phrase to describe what you have done? What could you have done differently?" Ideally, at least one student will come up with the term "plagiarism." Hand out your institution's policy on student academic integrity, and have students take turns reading sections of it out loud. Ask students why they think the university has such a policy, and if they think it is a valid expectation. Hopefully, another student will suggest that documenting the sources you used would help you avoid plagiarism. At this point you can hand out the guide on documenting sources and briefly discuss documentation styles.

Finally, present the last scenario: "You have a web design business in addition to being a student, and are designing a Flash movie for a client. You are looking for some music to plug into your movie, and you and your client decide that Tom Waits' "Eyeball Kid" would be perfect. You finish the project, and your client loves it. He mounts it on his web site, but a month later contacts you to ask you to redo it, because he's received a letter from a law firm representing Tom Waits' recording company telling him he's breaking the law by using this music without permission." Again, ask students questions about this scenario: "How do you feel about this? Do you think you have done anything illegal? Why or why not? Do you think you have done anything unethical? Why or why not? Is there a term or phrase to describe what you have done? What could you have done differently?" By now, students will see the questions coming. If you're really lucky, a student will bring up copyright. If not, you can wrap up the class session by introducing copyright and assigning a basic reading on copyright, such as *What is Copyright Protection?*— http://www.whatiscopyright.org/.

Class Session Two

Hand out the copyright quiz and have students complete it, then turn it in. Then have students break up into small groups of 3–4 students and retake the quiz as a group; make sure they put all of their names on the group quiz. While students are taking the group quiz, grade the first quiz.

Once students have completed the group quiz, have them trade quizzes with another group, then grade the quizzes as a class, discussing each question and the particular pieces of copyright legislation that apply.

1. "You are working on a history project on the Oregon Trail, and your parents remember that there are some old journals and diaries in a trunk in the attic. You find one from a woman who came to Oregon from St. Louis in 1873. There is a piece of paper inside the journal

showing this woman's family tree, and your family is not on it. There is also a notation that she died in 1942. You decide to create a web page for your project and put the journal on the web. Can you do that without violating copyright?"

No. In the U.S., copyright applies during the lifetime of the copyright owner plus 70 years. Since the author of this work died in 1942, copyright still applies. If she had been related to you, her copyright would have passed on to her family, and you as a member of her family would have the right to use it. But that is clearly not the case.

2. "You just bought a copy of Stompin' Tom Connors' latest CD and you and your friends are listening to it. One of your friends wants to borrow it, but he only has a cassette player. Can you legally make a copy of the CD on audiocassette for your friend?"

No. Sound recordings are explicitly named in the copyright law as being protected, as are most creative works. You may make a "backup" copy for your own personal use, but you may not make a copy for someone else's use.

3. "You are on a student government committee that is creating a public awareness poster, and you want to use the Nike slogan, "Just do it!" Can you use it without violating copyright?"

Yes. Titles, names, short phrases, and slogans, familiar symbols or designs, mere variations of typographic ornamentation, lettering, or coloring, and mere listings of ingredients or contents are not protected by copyright. There may be another form of intellectual property protection involved, such as a trademark, but it is not a copyright violation.

4. "You are being given an award for community service, and are called upon to give a speech. You didn't even know you had been nominated, and you haven't prepared anything. You give a speech off the top of your head, and it is incredibly thoughtful, insightful, and "together." One of your peers sitting in the audience copies down a large portion of your speech without your knowledge and uses several lines from your speech two weeks later in a speech of her own. Did she violate copyright?"

No. A work must be fixed in a tangible form in order to be protected by copyright. If your speech had been prepared in advance and written out, it would be protected, but because it was extemporaneous, it is not copyrightable. Your peer may have created an ethical dilemma for herself, but she was perfectly within her legal rights where copyright is concerned. Note that if the speech was recorded as part of the ceremony, she may have violated someone else's copyright.

5. "You are surfing the web one day and come across this really cool picture that would be perfect for your web site. There is no copyright notice on the web site, so you save a copy of the picture and put it up on your web site. A couple of weeks later you get an email message from someone claiming you violated their copyright by doing this. Did you?"

Yes. It is not necessary to place a copyright notice on your web site (or any publication) in order to have copyright protection. All creative and intellectual works are protected by copyright as soon as they are fixed in tangible format.

6. "You write an article that gets accepted for publication in one of the student publications on your campus. Before you publish your article, you sign a piece of paper transferring copyright to the publisher. Is it OK for you to put a copy of the article on your web site?"

No. If you have transferred the copyright to someone else, you do not retain any rights to it, unless the copyright owner gives permission or you specifically retained the right to use it in this manner when you transferred the copyright.

7. "You are taking an Exercise and Movement Science class, and you have to develop a web page describing Body Mass Index (BMI). You find a table in a magazine that calculates BMI's for various weight and height measurements, and decide to recreate it on your web site. Can you do this without violating copyright?"

Yes. Information that is common property and that contains no original authorship, including standard calendars, height and weight charts, tape measures and rulers, and lists or tables taken from public documents or other common sources, are not protected. If the information is presented in a unique or creative way, such as a table that uses symbols to represent quantities, the presentation is copyrightable, but the data is not.

Hand back the first quiz, and give students an opportunity to compare their responses to the group quiz they graded. If you choose to record the scores, collect all of the quizzes, and add the group score to the individual score, to create a score out of 14 (you do not want the group quiz score to impact negatively the individual score, or vice versa, which you would do by averaging the two scores).

Display transparency showing the ALA-recommended statement on copyright. Ask students to translate the notice into plain English. Ask students if they can define what constitutes "fair use."

Display the *Checklist for Fair Use* transparency, and work through it with students. Use examples from the quiz students took earlier to test against the fair use checklist.

If there is still time left, you might discuss a recent copyright issue, such as the Napster case, and discuss the problem, the issues involved, and the outcome.

Evaluation

Students' performance on the copyright quiz will demonstrate their understanding of copyright law, and their ability to distinguish between ethical and legal issues. Opportunities for documentation built into future assignments will demonstrate students' understanding of documentation practices.

Supplementary Materials

The materials in this section have been placed on the accompanying disk so they can easily be copied and/or modified to fit the needs of individual libraries and instructors.

- Transparency: Scenario One
- Transparency: Scenario Two
- Transparency: Scenario Three
- Transparency: Scenario Four
- Copyright Quiz
- Transparency: ALA's Recommended Copyright Disclaimer for Libraries

Digital Divide

DEBORAH BERNNARD

User Education Librarian
UNIVERSITY AT ALBANY, STATE UNIVERSITY OF NEW YORK
bernnard@albany.edu

Circumstances of the Instruction

This session is designed to introduce students to an ethical issue that is associated with our information society — the digital divide, the growing division between those who have access to information and those who do not.

College and university students are frequently unaware that the information technology widely available to them on campus is a rare privilege. Although many students are experienced users of computers, they do not realize that whole populations do not have access to computers and the Internet. They also are unaware that lack of access to information technologies can severely limit future employment options.

Lecture, class brainstorming, and small group exercises based on the reference source the *Occupational Outlook Handbook*, are all present in this session. Optimal class size would be 8–20 students, though the group exercise can be altered to accommodate for a larger class.

Objectives of the Instruction

- Students will understand the meaning of the phrase **digital divide.**
- Students will learn which populations are most unlikely to have access to information technology.
- Students will understand that expertise in information technology of all types translates into a more secure and financially rewarding future.
- Students will understand how necessary information technology is to their everyday existence.
- Students will learn how to use the *Occupational Outlook Handbook*.

Components of the Instruction

The instruction is divided into three sections:

Lecture (5–7 minutes)

Short lecture by the instructor explaining the phrase **digital divide.** Digital divide refers to the growing chasm between those in our society who have access to information technology and those who do not. Even though the cost of computer hardware and software continues to fall, the divide is not closing. Instead, those who already have access now have more access, while those who never had access still do not. In the United States, groups who fall on the wrong side of the digital divide are those who reside in rural areas, those who are African American or of Hispanic origin, the under educated, low income groups, and those who are physically disabled.

Brainstorming (10 minutes)

The instructor asks the class to generate a list of activities for which they use computers and the Internet regularly. As students call out activities, the instructor or a volunteer student writes them on the board. The list can get quite long and will usually include:

- E-mail
- Word processing
- Listening to music
- Shopping
- Calculating
- Reading news
- Research
- Checking out the weather
- Using spreadsheets
- Document delivery
- Ordering pizza
- Playing games

If the students don't mention any of the above, the instructor should add them. The list helps students understand the extent to which they rely on information technology to help them perform routine tasks and for entertainment. At this point, the instructor can mention that all of the above online activities are denied to those who do not have access to computers or the Internet.

Hands-on Exercise (20–30 minutes)

This is a hands-on exercise suitable for groups of 3 to 4 people. Each group should have access to the Internet. If you do not have Internet access, providing a copy of the *Occupational Outlook Handbook* for each group will work just as well.

Divide the students into groups. Describe the *Occupational Outlook Handbook* to the students. This is a reference source compiled by the United States Department of Labor. It provides a description of more than 250 common occupations. Included in this description are: the type of work involved, the training and/or education needed to perform this work, a forecast of the occupation's rate of growth or lack of growth and the median salary each occupation returns.

Instruct each group to access the *Occupational Outlook Handbook* online at— http://www.stats.bls.gov/ocohome.htm—or pass out one copy of the print edition to each group. Have the students use this resource to complete a worksheet that has been designed to help them make a connection between well-paid careers and a person's knowledge of computers and information technology. The careers that the students are asked to investigate are all middle-class occupations. Disparities in earnings are significant but not huge.

Once the groups have completed their worksheets, generate discussion by asking each group to explain why they were asked to do this exercise. There will be some smart answers, *because the teacher is nuts*, etc. Keep encouraging them to think about what pattern the worksheet shows and they *will* make the connection between salary and information skills. After all groups have had their say and the discussion is winding down, you may mention Bill Gates' technology skills just to drive the point home.

Evaluation

Evaluation is based on students' participation in both the brainstorming activity and the group activity. Active participation in the closing discussion will also provide feedback on the lesson. Worksheets from the group activity will be collected to determine how well students use the *Occupational Outlook Handbook*. The instructor will also gather information about the hands-on activity by facilitating the groups as they work through the assignment.

Supplementary Material

The material in this section has been placed on the accompanying disk so it can easily be copied and/or modified to fit the needs of individual libraries and instructors.

- Digital Divide Hands-on Exercise

Notes:

Androids, Cyborgs and Robots: A Glimpse into Technoculture's Future?

JEFFREY HARR

Instruction/Technical Services Librarian
ONONDAGA COMMUNITY COLLEGE
harrj@sunyocc.edu

Overview

One approach to teaching about technoculture (the fusion of technology and culture) is to examine some of its potential applications and their corresponding implications. The following problem-based learning activity is specific to artificial intelligence applications.

Humankind's imagination and the will to persevere are incredibly strong and, more often than not, will not be denied. It was not that long ago that the notion of manned space flights was considered whimsical, presumptuous and belonging more in the realm of science fiction than of science. It bears mentioning that the science fiction genre was often derided as far too implausible to warrant literary merit considerations yet, when it comes to technological prognostications, some authors have been unerringly accurate in foretelling what has come to be. Our imagination now has a conduit and a catalyst – the computer – which has made much of what was previously thought to be impossible, possible. Even in its infancy the computer's seeming capacity to simulate intelligent behavior piqued the interest of a small cadre of computer scientists.

This interest spawned a new field in computer science, artificial intelligence (AI), which is commonly defined as the ability of a machine to perform functions normally associated with human intelligence such as the ability to generalize, discern meaning, learn and reason. A symbiotic relationship between the computer revolution and AI research has existed since the advent of the first electronic computer. Contemporary AI scientists, such as Kevin Warwick, Ray Kurzweil and Hans Moravec, believe the development of intelligent computers capable of independent thought and actions sans human mediation, oversight or participation is on the not-too-distant horizon.

If a significant part of our relationship with technology has to do with how much we are remade by the things we create, current and future technological innovations merit careful scrutiny. Serious and careful consideration must be paid to where it is we are going before we get there. Therefore, educators have a moral obligation to teach students about technoculture's important topics of debate including, but not limited to, automation, artificial intelligence, biotechnology, cybernetics, Internet, nanotechnology and robotics. Enabling students to think critically about emerging 21st century technologies may equip them with an understanding of potential consequences of rapid technological advancements before they are forced to deal with the reality of those consequences.

Students also need to develop a rudimentary, varied understanding of the ethical issues that surround scientific research to participate actively in influencing decision-making processes that ultimately create and shape future realities. Embracing new technologies without question or reservation may lead us to destinations we would not willingly have chosen. Moreover, if historical precedents in scientific achievements warrant benchmark consideration, expecting the scientific community to reflect upon the consequences of the aggressive pursuit of technological discoveries and innovations is unrealistic. The specter of the atom bomb still haunts our past, clouds our present, and makes for an uncertain future. Also, a significant amount of technology-oriented research now occurs in the private sector without government oversight or regulation. Scientific inquiry, like other commodities, now has a bottom line. This is cause for considerable concern. Ethical consideration is often the first casualty in the effort to maximize profit.

Information Literacy Goal

The primary instructional goal of this unit is to help students acquire an awareness and appreciation of some of the major issues, and their corresponding ramifications that have to do with technoculture's important topics of debate.

A secondary goal is to cultivate students' critical thinking skills by requiring students to use a form of reasoning, projective investigation, to present plausible answers, scenarios, etc., to a series of speculative questions that may evolve into important issues of debate.

Note: These goals may not be easily accomplished. It's difficult to imagine, much less predict, what the innovations and rapid changes we are seeing now will mean in ten, fifteen or twenty years. However, bear in mind that what does not work is often as interesting as what does. Students may find that there are no simple answers or prudent approaches to some of what they are learning. This is an important lesson in and of itself.

Circumstances of the Instruction

- Student learning level: collegiate (preferably first and second year students).
- Optimal number of students: 15–25. A larger class size will greatly reduce the possibility of having a meaningful discussion.
- Unit length: subject matter warrants a 3-credit course but content could be embedded into a 2-credit, quarter course.

Objectives of the Instruction

- Introduce students to scientific research areas that may produce future technological breakthroughs.
- Develop students' awareness and appreciation of technoculture's complicated ethical issues.
- Develop students' awareness and appreciation for the manner in which technology changes our lives.
- Develop students' awareness and appreciation of the possibilities for creativity technology enables.

- Introduce students to the some of the emerging folkways and mores of technoculture.
- Develop students' ability to speculate on the role machines will play in the not-too-distant future.

Components of the Instruction

Film review and discussion on *The Measure of A Man*, episode 35 in the *Star Trek: The Next Generation* series.

Introduction

AI scientists are concentrating current research efforts in developing the self-replicating capability of machines. For example, computer scientists at Brandeis University have achieved, albeit on a small scale, autonomy of design and construction in robotics. Moreover, it is predicted that computers will have some kind on sentience within the next 50 years or perhaps, as Ray Kurzweil, author of *The Age of Spiritual Machines: When Computers Exceed Human Intelligence*, suggests, much sooner.

The poet William Carlos William once observed that a new world is only a new mind. At some point the machines will be equipped with a new mind that goes well beyond a mere simulation of the function of a human brain. Unlike earlier technological revolutions, this event will most likely occur within the next generation. If Moore's Law remains as accurate as it has been to date, by 2030 computers will be approximately a million times more powerful than their 2000 counterparts. By 2029, according to Kurzweil, they will have an approximate computing capacity of 1,000 human brains. Hypothetically, they will begin to make their own decisions. How will humans regard and interact with intelligent, thinking machines that are capable of self-creation and self-determination?

Preparation

Develop discussion guide for *The Measure of a Man* to help students take note of what is transpiring and what to pay particular attention to.

Students should view the program prior to the discussion. Have them view it on their own as opposed to showing film to the entire class (though it should be on hand to illustrate salient points). This approach provides the opportunity for students to view it as many times as they deem necessary so they can offer meaningful contributions to the discussion.

The Measure of a Man synopsis
Stardate 42523.7 ... while on a tour of the Enterprise, Captain Bruce Maddox announces that he has orders to disassemble Lt. Commander Data for a scientific study that will hopefully lead to successful replication of the android. During a meeting with Enterprise senior officers, Maddox is asked to provide specific details of the procedure. Based on Maddox's vague replies Captain Picard determines that he cannot allow Data to submit to an ill-conceived experiment. Maddox has anticipated a response such as this and is prepared. He hands Picard transfer orders for Data that reassigns him to Starbase 173 under Maddox's command.

Picard appeals to J.A.G. (Judge Advocate General) officer, Phillipa Louvois, and asks her to countermand the transfer. She refuses but advises Picard that Data does have another option. He can resign his Starfleet commission. Left with no other option, Data resigns from Starfleet. His decision to resign is challenged by Maddox who argues that Data, like any other Starfleet-owned machine, is nothing more than a piece of Starfleet property. A sophisticated machine, no doubt, but nonetheless still a machine and machines do not have rights afforded to other life forms within the Federation of Planets.

Both Picard and Maddox meet and plead their case with Louvois who, citing a twenty-first century precedent, rules in Maddox's favor. Picard vows to challenge the ruling and demands a hearing ...

Activity: film discussion. Suggested questions to facilitate and promote discussion (answers provided):

Why does Maddox want to disassemble Data?
Answer: to study Data in order to build thousands more like him.

Why are Data and others concerned about Maddox's experiment?
Answer: they believe his research lacks the specifics necessary to support an experiment of this magnitude.

Are Data's concerns valid?
Discussion: This is an important question and an opportunity to encourage students' critical thinking by asking them to comment on the rush for scientific achievement. Maddox clearly indicates his research is incomplete but he wants to move forward with his experiment confident that he will find the answers that heretofore have eluded him during the course of his experiment.

Why does Maddox challenge Data's resignation?
Answer: Maddox asserts that Data is Starfleet property and has no rights.

Discussion: When androids, such as Data, give every indication of being human (ability to think, reason, remember and have feelings comparable to humans) should they have rights?

Why does Louvois, initially rule in Maddox's favor?
Answer: she bases her ruling that Data is Starfleet property on the "Acts of Cumberland," passed in the early 21st century.

Discussion: A piece of legislation enacted some four hundred years in the past, in a very different time, is the precedent on which Louvois bases her decision. Could the Declaration of Independence also serve as a precedent?

What is Riker's case for the prosecution?
Answer: he employs what could be construed as courtroom theatrics (e.g., having Data display his unnatural strength, removing Data's arm and switching him off – "Pinocchio is broken. Its

strings are broken") to illustrate the prosecution's contention that Data is simply a machine – the creation of man.

Why is Picard inspired by his discussion with Guinan?
Answer: She implies that the Starfleet's desire to create and own a race of disposable androids is tantamount to slavery.
According to Maddox, what are the attributes that make an individual human?
Answer: intelligence ("the ability to learn and understand and to cope with new situations,") self-awareness ("conscious of your existence and actions and awareness of yourself and your own ego,") and consciousness.

Why does Picard's defense transcend the debate over whether or not Data is merely a machine?
Answer: Picard argues that, in a sense, all beings are created but that does not necessarily make them the property of their creator. He further asserts that ruling for the prosecution would forever condemn this new species to servitude and slavery. In his closing argument Picard challenges Louvois to consider the essence of the hearing stating, "now the decision you reach here today will determine how we will regard this creation of our genius. It will reveal the kind of people we are … it will reach far beyond this courtroom and this one android. It could significantly redefine the boundaries of personal liberty and freedom, expanding them for some, savagely curtailing them for others. Are you prepared to condemn him and all who come after him to servitude and slavery?"

What is the outcome of the hearing?
Answer: Louvois, in a ruling that she hopes will "speak to the future," determines that while Data may be a machine, he is owned by no one and has the right to make his own decisions regarding his life.

What role does Maddox play?
Answer: Maddox is the character that undergoes a significant transformation. He initially sees Data only as a machine, "an extraordinary piece of engineering but it [Data] is a machine. No different than a box on wheels." (He continually refers to Data as "it" until the final scene.) During the course of the hearing Picard asks him to define what it is that makes a person human.

Picard takes Maddox's criterion and illustrates how Data meets each one. Maddox is clearly shaken by this challenge to his preconceptions about Data. At the end of the hearing Data, now free to make his own decisions, approaches Maddox and offers to take part in the experiment once the scientist has successfully completed his research. Genuinely touched, Maddox observes, "he's [Data] remarkable." This prompts Louvois' comment, "it's the first time you didn't refer to him as *it*."

What is it that makes us human? Is there a distinctive characteristic that defines us as human? Is it our capacity to care that provides the ineffable human essence? Does Data have the capacity to care?
Answer: Consider what the hologram of Tasha Yar symbolizes. Data still suffers from the loss of his best friend (she was killed in an earlier episode) for whom he cared deeply. He uses her gift during times of inner turmoil – a conscious, albeit bittersweet, evocation of pleasant memories.

Activity—Projective Investigation

Discussion topics

- Should a species be created simply to amuse or serve humans?
- How will the introduction of what is tantamount to a new species change who we are and how we live?
- How will humans interact with this species?
- How will humans react to self-determination efforts by this new species?
- Intelligence produces, among other things, the instinct for survival. What happens if the species begins to act upon the instinct for survival?
- Will human and artificial life merge?
  Note: Gray, Kurzweil and others contend this has already occurred. See the *Cyborg Handbook* annotation.
- Are humans prepared for the prospect of artificial life?

Other key questions to consider

- Should scientists continue in their efforts to develop machines that might possibly make humans an endangered species? Is it ethical for scientists to continue these efforts, knowing that such a possibility exists?
- Will our attempts to create artificial life – lead to untended consequences that far outstrip intended applications?

Evaluation

Students need to be informed that attendance/participation is a significant grade component.

Attendance and meaningful participation in the classroom discussion. Meaningful participation in classroom discussion is an integral part of the learning process because students' experiences are unique and sharing them significantly contributes to the learning process. Instructor may decide to use e-mail group discussion as another discussion vehicle. Students are required to write a one-page response/interpretation to any of the projective investigation questions.

Ancillary Assignment

Have student subscribe to Cyberculture, a mailing list maintained by the Resource Center for Cyberculture Studies—http://www.otal.umd.edu/~rccs/— or any other relevant mailing list.

Have students write a 1–2 page paper that reports on (not an inclusive list):
- List activity
- List owner credentials
- Whether or not subscription was worthwhile, i.e., did they learn something about subject?
- Whether or not there were any well-known list subscribers or individuals with subject specific expertise
- Whether or not they posted a message to the list and if so, why? Have them include a copy of the message with their paper
- Whether or not they would continue their subscription. If yes, why? If not, why?

Students should unsubscribe after completing this assignment.

Suggested Readings:

Asimov, Isaac. *I Robot*. New York: Doubleday, 1950.

Asimov introduces his ethical rules for robot behavior, the Three Laws of Robotics that state:

1. A robot may not injure a human being, or, through inaction, allow a human being to come to harm.
2. A robot must obey the orders given it by human beings except where such orders would conflict with the First Law.
3. A robot must protect its own existence as long as such protection does not conflict with the First or Second Law.

Note: These rules may very well end up serving as a 21st century precedent governing robot behavior.

Bradbury, Ray. *The Martian Chronicles*. New York: Avon Books, 1997.

Part of what makes this a classic is Bradbury's insight as to why, at least officially, we have not discovered life on other planets. He suggests that we keep seeking ourselves in space and this perception prevents us from recognizing other possible forms of life. This is what Picard so eloquently and precisely asserts – Data is a new species and yet he is not recognized as such.

Dick, Philip K. *Do Androids Dream of Electric Sheep?* New York: Ballantine Books, 1996.

A science fiction masterpiece that provides a glimpse of what might happen if we turn a blind eye to the rush for scientific achievement. First published in 1968, it features a remarkable treatise on the potential relationship between humans and androids. Inspired the movie, *Blade Runner*.

Note: you might consider having students watch *Blade Runner* in tandem with this episode of *Star Trek: The Next Generation*. It may help students in their effort to answer the question, what is it that makes someone human?

Dyson, George. *Darwin among the Machines: The Evolution of Global Intelligence*. Reading, Massachusetts: Addison-Wesley, 1997.

Taking his cue from Samuel Butler's, *Erewhon*, (Butler's opines machines will surpass and then dominate their human creators), Dyson offers an insightful perspective on the past, present and future of artificial intelligence. Included is this warning, "in the game of life and evolution, there are three players at the table: human beings, nature, and machines. I am firmly on the side of nature. But nature, I suspect, is on the side of machines."

Gray, Chris Hables, ed. *The Cyborg Handbook*. New York: Routledge, 1995.

An initial look at cyborg society and the range of cyborg technologies. Contributors suggest that the cyborg society already exists (e.g., artificial limbs and organs, microchip implants, genetic engineering research, etc.) and because of this the humans merging with robots will one day become commonplace and, perhaps, a preferred way of life.

Kurzweil, Ray. *The Age of Spiritual Machines: When Computers Exceed Human Intelligence.*
New York: Viking, 1999.
>   Kurzweil predicts that as we become more machinelike and machines become more like
>   humans eventually they will become one. This eventuality, he contends, will occur in the 21st
>   century and it will be a mutually agreeable arrangement.

Moravec, Hans P. *Robot: Mere Machine to Transcendent Mind.* New York: Oxford University
Press, 1999.
>   A leader in robotic research, Moravec predicts that robots will become Earth's dominant
>   species in the 21st century. His book also serves to remind us that even the most improbable,
>   far-fetched science fiction predictions concerning the future often prove closer to the mark
>   than believed possible.

Shelley, Mary. *Frankenstein.* New York: Viking, 1998.
>   Any discussion of this subject should begin with this novel. It is at once profound,
>   frightening, bold, innovative, creative, emotional, stark; in other words, full of the wonder
>   that is humankind.

Warwick, Kevin. *March of the Machines: Why the New Race of Robots Will Rule the World.*
London: Century, 1997.
>   Warwick, a professor in the Department of Cybernetics at the University of Reading, also
>   predicts machines will replace humans as the dominant life form on earth. He warns that
>   once the first powerful machine, with intelligence similar to that of a human is switched on,
>   we may not be able to switch it off.

City Council Lab

ANGELYNN KING

Bibliographic Instruction & Collection Development Librarian
UNIVERSITY OF REDLANDS
liaking@uor.edu

Circumstances of the Instruction

Students tend to arrive in college with strongly held and fairly polarized opinions about the solutions to societal problems, and the issue of information access is no exception. But part of information literacy is being aware that there may be *more* than two sides to a story. Real-world decisions at work, at home, and in the community are rarely as easy as they might seem in the classroom.

This exercise was employed as part of a 4-credit freshman seminar entitled "Information, Knowledge and Power in the Electronic Age." All freshmen at the University of Redlands are required to take a freshman seminar in their first semester; classes are capped at 16 students, and the instructor also serves as the students' advisor until they declare a major. These inter-disciplinary seminars allow the students and instructors to explore ideas in a more open-ended way than they might be able to do in departmental offerings; in addition, most of these courses are designed to fulfill area requirements in the liberal arts core curriculum. This particular course was approved for both Writing Across the Curriculum and Computing Across the Curriculum.

With four groups of four students each, the city council lab takes approximately 45–50 minutes. The elapsed time will vary according to the number and size of the working teams.

Objectives of the Instruction

- Engage the students in collaborative problem-solving.
- Illustrate the difficulty, if not the impossibility, of satisfying all constituencies in public policy formulation.
- Point up some of the many conflicting viewpoints on the subject of public access to information.

Components of the Instruction

Ask the students to divide themselves into four groups of four and pretend they are the city council of a small town similar to Redlands. Their task is to formulate a policy for Internet filtering of the public terminals in the city library. In doing so, they are expected to satisfy a number of constituencies, including parents, teachers, free-speech advocates, the local business community, and others – all while remaining popular enough to be reelected.

The class discussion that follows the exercise might take a more international perspective, discussing the differences between, and the similarities of, "freedom fighting" and insurgency.

Who decides whom gets online – both as producer and consumer – and how do they decide? In many places, before you can get online, you have to be able to get out of the area in which you may be sequestered and into the area where the technology is kept. Who are the gatekeepers in **your** community?

Evaluation

The four city councils in our class came up with four completely different solutions, using a variety of tactics from raising taxes to hire more library staff to requiring underage patrons to present validated parental permission cards before using networked computers. Each group's elected representative put its proposal on the board, and then we all voted for the best policy. Here it should be noted that there were in fact very few defectors – after putting this much effort into developing their policies, the students appeared to be quite attached to them. This is not, however, an unrealistic view of politics in general.

Supplementary Material

The material in this section has been placed on the accompanying disk so it can easily be copied and/or modified to fit the needs of individual libraries and instructors.

- Classroom Assignment: Filtering Proposal

Virtually Homeless

ANGELYNN KING

Bibliographic Instruction & Collection Development Librarian
UNIVERSITY OF REDLANDS
liaking@uor.edu

Circumstances of the Instruction

While overall access to information technology itself is growing, wide social disparities persist. Last year's Department of Commerce report on the "digital divide" shows that Internet users in the United States are overwhelmingly–and increasingly–white, urban, educated and affluent. But our students tend to believe what they read in the microchip-happy, technophilic press–that the Internet is a universal communication medium, a kind of "global commons"–and that sooner or later "everyone will be connected."

If we accept that part of our mission as educators is to prepare students to become well-informed, responsible and rational members of a democratic society, then we cannot overlook the omissions inherent in this view. In addition to teaching information literacy, we need to build an awareness of issues of information equity into our instruction. We need to make the data speak to their condition, so that they do not leave college and join the burgeoning information economy completely unaware that there are large segments of the country's–and indeed the world's–population that are technologically "off the map."

This exercise was employed as part of a 4-credit freshman seminar entitled "Information, Knowledge and Power in the Electronic Age." All freshmen at the University of Redlands are required to take a freshman seminar in their first semester; classes are capped at 16 students, and the instructor also serves as the students' advisor until they declare a major. These inter-disciplinary seminars allow the students and instructors to explore ideas in a more open-ended way than they might be able to do in departmental offerings; in addition, most of these courses are designed to fulfill area requirements in the liberal arts core curriculum. This particular course was approved for both Writing Across the Curriculum and Computing Across the Curriculum.

Objectives of the Instruction

- Using a familiar application of computer technology (an interactive, online game), put students in a situation in which they must approach a problem from the standpoint of the information-poor.
- Illustrate the use of the Internet in marketing concepts, and not just products.

Components of the Instruction

In this exercise, the students log onto a game called Hobson's Choice: The Game You Just Can't Leave on the home page of *Real Change: Seattle's Homeless Newspaper*— http://www.realchangenews.org/hobson_intro.html. The initial screen of Hobson's Choice presents the following scenario:

> You were hospitalized and couldn't work for 3 weeks. You have no savings or insurance. Your landlord says "Pay up or get out!"

Several options are presented, from seeking to borrow money from friends and family to attempting to negotiate with people in positions of authority. But as you progress through the game, you find that many options have to be repeated numerous times, and most do not work. Family and strangers are equally unsympathetic to your plight. At some junctures, you find you have no option but to wait.

The students are not allowed to leave the classroom until they have obtained permanent housing. The limited options, ceaseless repetition, and constant disappointment are an integral part of the game. As the introductory screen points out, the dictionary defines a Hobson's Choice as a choice between taking what is offered or nothing at all. Many of the students reach their frustration tolerance fairly quickly and want to quit. It should not be surprising that in real life, facing real frustrations in real time, many real people stop trying as well.

Evaluation

In a later discussion, I asked the students to reflect back on what it was like when they were virtually homeless. What options did they have for finding out about day labor, food banks, emergency medical care, public assistance – all, of course, without any money? If information was available online, where was there access in the neighborhood in which they were likely to find themselves? If they were lucky enough to find themselves working, would anything be open after working hours? At the very least, the discussion engendered an unprecedented respect among this group for the public library.

The culminating project for this class was a research paper on the advantages and disadvantages of information technology. Several of the students mentioned a lack of access on the part of the poor and homeless, indicating that the subject of the lab was still on their minds several months later.

Sources:

Hobson's Choice: The Game You Just Can't Leave
http://www.realchangenews.org/hobson_intro.html

You Be the Judge: Internet Filters and Censorship

Nancy B. Turner

Electronic Resources Coordinator
New Mexico State University
nturner@lib.nmsu.edu

Circumstances of the Instruction

Censorship and intellectual freedom are essential topics for discussion in a comprehensive information literacy course. These important issues provide for heated debate in communities where Internet access is freely provided by the public library. The use of filters that prevent access to particular Internet sites, or that monitor searching behavior, has brought the censorship issue into the limelight of regular media coverage. In those reports, the ideas of intellectual freedom and First Amendment rights are vividly played out.

The censorship and Internet filters activity utilizes current news and draws upon students' abilities to evaluate and synthesize information presented in the media in a balanced way. The exercise provides great fuel for a lively discussion of censorship that is current and relevant for students.

This activity can be structured in different ways, depending on the class level and time frame. The overall time requirement is 45–60 minutes, including 30 minutes for in-class participation. At least six students are required for a lively discussion, although a larger class of up to 24 students is ideal. Students should possess basic skills in searching an electronic index/article database. The censorship activity can be successfully used within any class for which censorship, First Amendment rights and intellectual freedom are topics to be covered: sociology, political science and literature as well as courses devoted to information literacy.

Objectives of the Instruction

Upon completion of this activity, students will be able to:

- analyze a current issue of censorship and intellectual freedom from multiple points of view;
- articulate these issues verbally and in writing; and
- relate the concept of censorship and intellectual freedom to a controversy in the news, such as the use of filters for Internet access in public libraries.

Components of the Instruction

Presentation (10-15 minutes)

It is necessary for students to have some grounding in the general concepts of censorship and intellectual freedom. Students should be assigned a general reading to provide this background. Using a lecture or class discussion, the instructor should review the concepts and provide a historical perspective. Suggested readings and web sites are provided in the Further Readings section.

Hands-on Activity (20-25 minutes)

Student participants will need to use a computer workstation with access to an electronic database. *ProQuest, Lexis-Nexis Academic Universe*, or another full-text article database is necessary. Students are directed to search for current news stories on the issue of public libraries and Internet filters. Since the activity requires reading online, the activity works best if students search individually. Fruitful search terms are those that yield news on current debates in communities on filters in public libraries that provide access to the Internet.

Suggested search terms:
public libraries
filters
censorship
Internet access

Since the hands-on activity entails the synthesis of information and is not a test of search strategy, the instructor will save instructional time by preparing a worksheet that details a search strategy (see Supplementary Materials).

Instruct students to read news articles, taking note of arguments for and against filters. These notes should be recorded on a worksheet. Based on their reading and notes, students discuss the issue in class, pro and con.

Variations

If students do not have access to a computer or an article database, the instructor can provide copies of news articles to the students, making sure that the information is rich enough to fuel two sides of the issue. An alternative controversy in the news that relates to censorship and intellectual freedom is the use of explicit or violent language within song lyrics.

Class Discussion (15-20 minutes)

After completing the activity, students are divided into small groups of 4–5 students. Each group will collaborate to produce a list of arguments for filters and against, using material gathered. The instructor moderates a discussion with the class, calling on each group to flesh out considerations on both sides of the Internet filter debate. The discussion should be moderated to ensure that it is balanced, participation is equitable and opinions are expressed in a civil manner!

Evaluation

The success of this exercise is demonstrated by the enthusiastic discussion of the issues. Students should be expected to articulate both sides of the argument. If a worksheet is used, that can be collected for evaluation and grading by the instructor.

Suggested Readings:

Abilock, Debbie. Internet Censorship Issues and School Libraries
http://www.nueva.pvt.k12.ca.us/~debbie/library/policies/censor96.html

Bonfire of Liberties. A visually-interesting online exhibit on censorship through the ages from the Texas Humanities Resource Center.
http://www.humanities-interactive.org/exhibit1.html

Hinckley, Steven. The First Amendment in Cyberspace: Background and Historical Perspectives. A useful general reading provided by the Library of Congress Network Advisory Committee.
http://lcweb.loc.gov/nac/nac30/hinck1.html

Intellectual Freedom Office, American Library Association. Many links to information on the ALA's perspective on Intellectual Freedom, including a useful handout in PDF format, *Intellectual Freedom and Censorship Q&A.*
http://www.ala.org/alaorg/oif/

Minow, Mary. Filters and the Public Library: A Legal and Policy Analysis. Comprehensive, thoughtful, and well-researched article by a lawyer and librarian.
http://www.firstmonday.dk/issues/issue2_12/minow/

Understand Software that Blocks Internet Sites. From the *Internet Advocate*: A Web-based Resource Guide for Librarians and Educators Interested in Providing Youth Access to the Net.
http://www.monroe.lib.in.us/~lchampel/netadv4.html

Supplementary Material

The material in this section has been placed on the accompanying disk so it can easily be copied and/or modified to fit the needs of individual libraries and instructors.

- Censorship Worksheet

DATE DUE